Presents

Naomi King's

O.P.P.

Published by THE X PRESS,16-22 MARTELLO STREET, LONDON E8 3PE. TEL: 081 985 0797

c) Copyright. Naomi King 1993.

Printed by Cox and Wyman Ltd,Reading, Berks.

This story is dedicated to my sisters in spirit. You deserve better.

To Amisha, I can only take you part of the journey....Be a confident black woman and at ease with yourself. Be your own best friend.

ONE

It was an unusually warm autumn day, but this was no picnic in the park. The large crowd gathered around the freshly dug grave, were all dressed in black. Half a dozen black limousines waited, bumper to bumper in a line.

Those who knew him well couldn't quite believe he was dead. He was so full of life and only twenty-seven. Winston's early death reminded them of their own mortality. Time was slowly ticking away for each one of them.

"Me know seh it nuh Winston inna de box," Fitzroy whispered to Rosie, his baby mother, as he took his turn to shovel earth into the grave. "I'm just doing this for Andrea. To make she feel bettah."

Fitzroy had known Winston longer than most of the other mourners. They had attended school together since the juniors. They had even spent a spell together at a youth detention centre in their early days. There was just no way that could be Winston in the coffin.

Fitzroy knew his friend as the great escapologist. He had more tricks up his sleeve than Harry Houdini. Winston liked to 'tek chance,' but always managed to get out of the stickiest situation, whether with the law or anyone else. Out on the street, they called him the Teflon Don. He was invincible.

Fitzroy smiled to himself, reminded of the time when a seventeen-year-old Winston had convinced a magistrate's court, that the half a pound of prime sensimilla the police found on him was for his own personal use. It was a month's supply, Winston had claimed. And when you divided it by thirty days, it didn't seem that much. A quarter of an ounce a day, that's all. He got off with a £50 fine!

He could get away with anything. Like the time an old girlfriend caught him on the job. Actually on the job! Winston just carried on denying that she had seen what she'd seen, until the girl was blue in the face, and finally gave up. Winston's three rules in a relationship, were deny, deny and deny!

Fitzroy chuckled to himself as he thought about it. A wicked chuckle. His time was ticking away more rapidly than the others'. He knew this. He had only a matter of time to find that big, elusive skank. Like a true hustler, he made a mental note to get to the bottom of the mystery. If Winston was in hiding somewhere with a bag full of contraband money, Fitzroy wanted to know. Fitzroy never allowed friendship to get in the way of a good skank.

"Mind yourself!" Rosie's elbow nudged him into the here and now. "Remember where we are!"

Fitzroy straightened up and mimicked the placid demeanour of the other mourners. He wasn't in the habit of taking orders from any woman, but Rosie was his main squeeze. His number one baby mother. Circumstances forced her to have his best interests at heart. And she was right. This wasn't the time and the place for reminiscing on his bredrin's comical escapades.

No, he concluded. It definitely wasn't Winston. He didn't know how it had happened, but somebody else must have been driving that car. And for whatever reason, Winston was keeping a low profile. Maybe because of the bull man. Or maybe because of the money he had mentioned.

A short distance from the grave, a solitary feminine figure had peeled away from the family and friends paying their last respects. Her carefully stooped gait gave the impression of a woman burdened by grief in moderation. But look into a woman's eyes and you will see her heart. Merlene's eyes revealed her anguish. Fortunately, nobody had bothered to look deeply into the eyes of this tall and elegant woman. Why should they? As far as everyone else was concerned Andrea, not Merlene, was the chief widow here.

Merlene walked slowly to a bench and sat down. Her feet were killing her.

"Damn new shoes....is who tell me fe buy dem," she muttered to herself. Reposed, she lost herself in deep thought.

She sat down wearily, easing her feet out of the shoes and leaning back, eyes closed, as the breeze soothed her aching toes. She sighed the sigh of a thousand hardships. If only the pain deep within her could be so easily relieved. She could no longer contain the eye-water which threatened to disgrace her earlier. The tears had been held back so long, her head throbbed. She choked, covering her mouth hastily to stifle the moans which slowly erupted in the belly of her soul. As much as she wanted to bawl out with grief, the outward signs of her pain had to be tempered. It would be a complete giveaway. Everybody would want to know why she was grieving so much, for a man who was her best friend's boyfriend.

"Merlene," the voice spoke softly. "Girl, y'alright?"

Merlene looked up, surprised to see she was not alone. Beverly's voice had interrupted her private grief. She struggled to speak, but the words were not forthcoming, so she turned painfully away from her friend. She could normally tell Beverly anything. But not this. Not the relationship with Winston. How would Beverly react, to discover that Miss Prim and Proper had engaged in such an illegitimate relationship? Merlene held out her hand to her sister-in-spirit, who gave it a gentle squeeze.

"I know how you feel," Beverly chirped. "Funerals aren't exactly my idea of a good time either!"

Merlene wasn't in the mood for good cheer but Beverly wasn't to know. Who feels it ,knows it. Deep in her soul, Merlene felt the loss of her lover. Beverly knew nothing about it.

"Just give me a moment on my own," Merlene said, placing her hand on her stomach. "I've got really bad period pains. That and this whole thing with Winston, it's all a bit too much, y'know."

"Yes I understand. Just take your time, Merle. But the cars are driving off in a few minutes." Beverly hurried away to offer Andrea more solace.

Fists clenched, Merlene sighed deeply. Thoughts raced in her head, fever burned in her soul. What was she to do?

"Please God, stop the pain!" she cried out softly to herself.

After all the plans, the dreams....To be cheated in this way! Who would have believed it?

"I don't bloody deserve this!" The words were no more than a sob. "Bring him back....I need him....I ache for him. Bring him back!" The tears began to flow again.

"Winston, is how you do this to me, man? You always said that you would take me with you....wherever you were going. Winston you lied. You had runnins to do, but in her car? Why didn't you take your own car? Does it even matter? You're not with me now. All I have is memories....memories of your sweet kiss....your caress....your smell...."

Merlene's sorrow was for Winston, but the despair which caused her tears was out of greater considerations than the permanent loss of a lover. Sure, she missed Winston already. But like most people, by the time of the funeral, the grief for the dearly departed had become somewhat tempered. By now, she had accepted the fact that Winston was gone and there wasn't a damn thing she could do about it. That her dreams and aspirations had been dashed so suddenly was more difficult to accept, however. All that remained of her future plans, were ashes to ashes and dust to dust.

Merlene cast an envious eye at her best friends Andrea and Beverly, standing soberly by the grave. They were five years younger. Their faces looked fresh and their bodies fit. They still had a chance to make it in life. Despite the occasion, they managed to look sexy dressed in black. Andrea with the determined expression of a merry widow, ready to find a new man the moment the last shovelful of earth had been tipped on her departed lover's grave. And Beverly. Poor, innocent Beverly was one of those girls who just wanted to have fun. Merlene seriously wondered whether Beverly could appreciate the gravity of the occasion. The funeral was a 'potential husband situation' and as her friend knew, Beverly occupied her waking hours in pursuit of a bonafide lover.

At thirty-years-old, Merlene was feeling the anguish of a woman who now realised she would never drive through Paris in a sports car with the cool breeze blowing in her hair. She was too old to fantasise like young women do. Winston was her last chance, to fly away on a magic carpet and experience the freedom of life outside south London. It was a game of high stakes which she had played and lost.

"I'm falling....falling....," she sobbed softly. "I'm falling, but there's no one to catch me....no one to turn to. What am I going to do....?"

The seemingly endless procession of private cars followed the limousines back to Andrea's council flat. From the cemetery in Nunhead, the motorcade crawled to its destination in Brixton's 'Poet's Corner', grinding the midday traffic into a go-slow. Passing through Dulwich Village, it attracted the focal attentions of a Japanese tourist with a camera. A long-pensioned elderly black couple, stopped at the kerb to salute the procession. The wife couldn't resist observing that this was, "the only time a crowd of yout' nah play no reggae."

"But wait," her aged husband remarked, "half of dem don't even wear 'at! What a disgrace, Betty. Young people really do not have any shame."

Winston was a popular man. A bit too popular if you ask me, Andrea thought, from the back of the lead limousine. There were too many 'widows' at Winston's funeral. Too many women she had never seen before. Everywhere she turned there was some woman avoiding her eyes or grinning behind a veil. She had begun to feel pissed off at her dearly departed.

"Some gyaal nevah have no shame," she remarked aloud.

"What do you mean?" Merlene asked nervously.

"Didn't you see them at the graveside? Whispering loud enough for everyone to hear, about how close dem was to Winston and so on?" Andrea kissed her teeth. "Dem gyaal too

8

renk. Dem pretty, but dem character dirty. Can you imagine? Even at a funeral! No respeck! Talking as if I'm deaf or sump'n."

"Yeah, I know what you mean," Beverly added. "I heard a few of them talking like they were married to him."

"....They think they can just rope in to my yard afterwards and come eat my food and drink my drink!" Andrea kissed her teeth again.

"Do you want us to make sure they don't come inside?" Merlene offered.

"Nah," Andrea declined. "Let them come. I want everyone to see them for what they are - leggo beast!"

The loss of a husband can make the most devoted wife cynical. All sorts of whores come out of the woodwork for a burial. Like they can't live with themselves unless they pay their last respects. They can live with themselves when they steal another woman's man, but they can't live with themselves if they don't pay their last respects. Even if it means introducing suspicion in the minds of the woman left behind.

Andrea had only herself to blame. She had suspected Winston of playing away from home many times, but hadn't done anything believing it would all stop, once her seven years of bad luck was completed. Today, the very day she buried Winston, was the day her seven years of bad luck finished. Can fate really be so cruel, she wondered.

She had never been able to prove anything. He had stayed out too many nights and had come home smelling of cheap perfume too many times. But Winston had denied everything outright. He claimed he didn't know anything about the mysterious midnight telephone calls when the line would go dead if Andrea answered. Whenever Winston answered however, he would close the bedroom door to make it difficult for her to overhear his whispered words in the hallway.

Suspicion was no good to her. She needed to catch him red-handed. Confronting him with nothing more than circumstantial evidence, would cause a 'blam-blam.' The very thought of an accusation was enough to spark Winston's short fuse.

It's impossible to keep a man on a leash. Throughout their seven-year relationship, Winston sowed his wild oats regardless. She didn't know it for sure, but she *knew* it.

One thing Andrea was sure of, had she died, no men would have shown up at her funeral, telling everybody what a good lay she was. She made sure, that the men she met didn't even have her phone number, much less her address. The more she thought about it, the more angry she became. Winston must have been having it away with a whole posse of women. As far as she was concerned, that was slack. there was no other word for it but slackness.

Sinking into the limousine's deep leather seats, she comforted herself with the thought that she had her closest friends Beverly and Merlene supporting her at this emotional time. She needed her sisterhood at a time like this, she knew she could rely on them.

He had been watching her silently from the other side of the room for some time. There was no mistaking the message in the disarming, dimpled smile and the warm inviting eyes. As she felt her bosom harden, Andrea readjusted her blouse and then blushed, realising that Donovan was still observing her closely. It had been seven hard years of taking whatever bad luck life dished up for her. Now that her seven year term was over, she intended to enjoy the fruits of life. If Donovan makes a move, she told herself, I might just take a bite.

"Everyt'ing will be alright Andrea. Trust me." Fitzroy's voice was like the Messenger of Doom, waking her from her private daydreams.

"Let me tell you somet'ing," he whispered. "I know for a fact dat Winston nevah dead!"

Andrea was tempted to fling her glass of red wine in his face. She was tired of the gathering, tired of everything.

About thirty of the guests had crammed into her tiny living room for the funeral reception. Beverly and Merlene were helping out making sure that the guests all had enough to eat and drink. It was an ordeal that the next of kin were expected to go through. Why was it, Andrea wondered, that your friends and family always throw a great party for you when you're dead, when you're the one person who can't attend? Winston would have loved the plate of rice and soft boiled banana.

Andrea wished everybody would simply disappear - particularly Fitzroy. She needed time to pick up the pieces of a life without Winston.

She knew the youth from time. He was Winston's closest male friend. She didn't much like him, because she knew that he was criminal minded. He was always talking about "the old days", the criminal days, with Winston. They would sit and talk to the early hours, smoking weed and playing cards, while Fitzroy animated the conversation with memories of daring, illegal escapades from their younger days. But whereas Winston had changed his ways, she knew that Fitzroy was still a baby gangster and a hustler. Not to be trusted one bit. He had even tried it on with her one time, when her man was away on business. She had tried to ban Fitzroy from the flat, without success. Winston wouldn't hear of it. Fitzroy was his best friend and that was that. Well, Fitzroy was somebody else's problem now. With his spar dead, he would have no reason to drop by Andrea's modest council flat uninvited.

"Winston tell me seh, he was going to pull a skank," Fitzroy continued at low volume, looking over his shoulders suspiciously for prying ears. "He said that he might have to disappear for a while. Y'know. Me sure dat dis t'ing is a set up. Dat can't be Winston in the coffin, Andrea. Me ah tell you! Dat cyaan be him!"

Andrea cast Fitzroy a dismissive look, sizing him up scornfully. Unlike the big 'supes,' who paraded up and down Atlantic Road in their shiny flash motors, Fitzroy had not seen the fruits of his life in crime. He had no future, no prospects and he never had any money. He was condemned to a life of signing on the dole, in between spells at Her Majesty's pleasure up on Brixton Hill. Jail was an occupational hazard for this small time crack seller. Fitzroy liked to play big shot, but he was really small time. Idiot bwoy, big-shot with toy gun, Andrea thought, dream your dreams while you draw your dole money.

"What are you talking about Fitzroy!" the exasperated 'widow' cried out.

More than anything, she pitied him, because he hadn't grown up. He hadn't understood that his contemporaries had all left the fantasy 'wild west' life of youth behind them. Everybody else was getting on with life, buying homes, starting families, while Fitzroy believed he was still part of a bad bwoy posse of outlaws, tearing up Brixton with a 'matic. The brightest hope in Fitzroy's life was another spell on Brixton Hill. At least there, he could learn a trade. He had been virtually illiterate when he first got sent down for a jail term. But he had learned to read while serving a stretch. Fitzroy was living proof that jail is the poor people's private school.

"He's not dead! Winston's not dead. He's alive!" the would-be Dillinger protested. "He buried the money, man. He's just waiting to tek it! A whole heap of money!"

Frustrated by Andrea's casual manner, Fitzroy had blurted out the words a little too loudly. A deafening silence fell over the packed living room at the mention of money, with each guest craning his neck to be within earshot.

"Yes, alright...." Andrea smiled apologetically to the guests who, resumed their natter, the situation now under control. "You find me proof of the money, and I'll believe you," she assured Fitzroy, while taking the opportunity to start up a conversation with someone she hardly knew. She looked around the room casually, hoping to catch Donovan's attention, but he was nowhere to be seen. Andrea grunted. Once again, Fitzroy had come between her and a man. Fitzroy was a born hustler, she thought to herself. He would even try to pull a skank at a funeral.

Fitzroy's outburst had struck a chord in Merlene's soul. All day long, she had managed keep her own personal grief a secret, while displaying outwards the moderate sorrow she was expected to show in deference to her friend's loss. She was fearful of giving herself away every time Andrea spoke to her. She had never believed she could lie in her best friend's face, but here she was, doing a perfect job of it. Merlene spoke with forked tongue but her eyes told the truth. People were too busy trying to score themselves, to read the truth in her eyes.

Merlene had been so absorbed with her own game of deception, she had clean forgotten about the money. How did Fitzroy know about it? Winston must have told him. The bastard! How could he tell anyone, when he knew where it came from? She was the one who was going to go to prison if anyone found out. If he told Fitzroy about the money, who's to know what he told Andrea! How could she be sure of how much, or how little Andrea knew? And what was she to do about the missing money? Where was it? Now that all her dreams had been shattered, she had neither the will nor the inspiration to pull the skank on her own. Most importantly, she didn't have the bottle to do it without Winston. Her eyes couldn't hide the terror of being caught with her hand in the till.

The skank was simple but original, the product of a fertile imagination and reading too many Victor Headley novels. Merlene had hit upon it during the course of a lazy afternoon at her job in the accounts office of the council. For her, the idea of the skank was sufficiently exciting. Winston's reaction however was far more serious. He constantly raved about the idea.

"Me love the beauty of it," he had said. "Me love the beauty and the simplicity....It's the perfect skank."

Winston persuaded Merlene to put the idea into practice. A few weeks earlier, the first instalments of grant money had come through for the twenty fictitious students that Merlene had inserted unto the council's student grant list. £34,000 in all. Winston had called her the night before his death and assured her that he had cashed all the money, through various phony bank accounts that he had going, and that he would transfer all the money into her name in the next few days. The ulcer in her stomach burned like crazy every time she thought about £34,000 in cash out there somewhere, just waiting to be picked up.

Merlene didn't get a wink of sleep that night. By morning, she looked haggard. Good job she had taken the day off work.

She planned to pay Fitzroy a little visit. His outburst had sounded ridiculous, but she was hoping that he might know something which could shed some light on the missing money. She was clutching at straws, but then again, she had run out of ideas. She had to discover the fate of the money and quick. Perhaps there was something in what Fitzroy had said about Winston burying the money. But what if the secret of the money was buried with Winston? Time was running out.

Before she stole the money, Merlene had never seen £34,000 in one lump sum. She believed, that in life, everybody gets one chance to taste the crock of gold at the end of the rainbow. It doesn't matter if it's luck, chance, robbery, murder....whatever! This was the first time in her life that the possibility of being able to walk away with £34,000 in her pocket (legally or otherwise), had been presented to her. She either had to take the money or leave it.

She didn't have the guts to do it straight away, though. She needed someone to reassure her. That someone was Winston, her part-time sump'n.

"Is a lucky t'ing that you know the runnins," Winston said. "Get the money and leave the job. By the time the money's found missing, they might not even be able to connect you with the disappearance. Either way, by the time they find out, we'll be relaxing on our island in the sun!"

"But do you think it's worth it? To give up everything I've built up, working for the council," Merlene asked him, still not convinced.

"How you mean, man? No budda worry 'bout dat. Where's your job going to take you? In life, you must tek chance to live it up a while. Now listen me good an' listen me well. If you nah ready, step aside. I can deal with the cheques myself, with no comeback to you."

Winston was so eager for the skank, he even promised he would leave Andrea and run off to the Caribbean with Merlene if they pulled it off. With the money, they could set themselves up nicely on one of the islands for the rest of their lives.

"We've got to try a t'ing Merle....You nah see we situation? We could set up nice together. Back-ah-yard. Just buy a lickle piece of land by the sea, y'know. But we nah have no money?

What better chance are we going to get in life?"

That Merlene really did want to spend the rest of her life with Winston was beyond question. He was the best thing that ever happened to her. She also knew she wasn't going to get much further in her job. She was a bookkeeper. She couldn't get further promotion, unless she took some more exams. She was a 30-year-old single parent. Where was she going to find the time to go to evening classes? Anyway, she could take all the exams in the world and still not get anywhere. Talent is luck. The important thing in life is courage.

Now, with no Winston and no money, her dream of running off to the Caribbean was unrealistic. If she could get hold of the money however, she still stood a chance of setting herself up in Jamaica. Back home, her son Marlon would get a chance to grow up healthy and strong and conscious of his roots. £34,000 would certainly smooth his way in life in the Caribbean, whereas it wasn't much to sniff at in London. Like most people whose families left the island for economic reasons in the fifties and sixties, she dreamed of roping back in there. But to do that successfully, you had to return home with money to start some production.

She had no intention of returning the money. That kind of thing is out of date. Merlene may have been Miss Prim and Proper to all her friends, but never judge a book by looking at the cover.

As far as she was concerned, she was entitled to the money. She was the one who had risked everything in pulling the skank. There was still the possibility that she could be found out, that's why she didn't want to continue the skank. But what's done is done, and there was £34,000 already out there with her name on it. All she had to do was find it.

The weather had turned chilly for the time of year, but Merlene refused to allow the biting wind to interfere with her resolve. She had determined that the only way to dance her sorrows away, was by taking positive steps to recovering the money.

It was the first time she had been on the estate since she left school. In those days it was a really nice, clean, newly-built estate. Now, the yellow-bricked blocks stretching from Brixton to Stockwell were considered the roughest in the area. Merlene was visibly shocked to see the extent to which the familiar walkways and lawns had fallen into dilapidation. The Stockwell Green Estate had seen better days.

She was looking for number one -hundred- and -twenty-nine. 125, 96, 127, 128, 134.... The numbers didn't follow any

14

order.

"You know where Fitzroy lives?" she asked the two youngsters leaning casually over a balcony.

The youngsters turned around. They were dressed in the familiar ragga style that was popular with South London youngsters of every race and creed. Merlene recognised the familiar bullet-holed baggy jeans, the baseball hats and ragga shoes. Those were the type of clothes Marlon was always begging her to buy for him, she thought absentmindedly. She also noticed the spliff that was being passed casually between them. The two boys weren't much older than Marlon and they had already started smoking spliff! Goodness, she thought, what's the world coming to.

The boys grinned at each other. They liked to smoke spliff to show that they were hard. They could see that Merlene thought they were hard. It boosted their confidence. The taller, skinnier of the two spoke first.

"If me ah go do sump'n fe you, wha' you ah go do fe me?" he asked in a Jamaican accent learned in a secondary school in Camberwell.

"Look I haven't got time for playing games," Merlene retorted exasperated. "Do you know where Fitzroy lives or not?"

"Well, that depends...."

"Oh shut up!" Merlene interrupted, turning around to continue her search.

"Okay, okay okay....hold on!" the tall boy shouted, reverting to his natural South London cockney. "Fitzroy's is the last flat along. The one with the big gate in front of it."

Merlene continued walking, stopping only when she got to the the end of the long balcony, in front of a wrought-iron security gate, recently fitted over the council flat door. The life Fitzroy lived, he needed at all times to keep a distance between his runnins and the local police. They had tried to break down the door several times, but without success.

"Fitzroy....! Fitzroy...! It's me, Merlene," she shouted through the door.

The door opened slowly. As it opened, the sharp, acrid smell from a red-hot pipe of crack cocaine rushed out, smacking Merlene squarely in the nostrils.

"Come in Merle," a smiling Fitzroy beckoned.

The flat was a pig sty. Fitzroy the crackhead, used the floor as a sink, a wardrobe, a waste bin - whatever!

"I can't stay long," Merlene said hurriedly, "but as I said on the phone I need to find out some things....I'm desperate."

"Why *you* need to know about Winston so badly?" Fitzroy

asked suspiciously.

"Because we had some runnins..."

"Yeah it's like me say," Fitzroy interrupted her, "he's not really dead. He came and saw me before the crash and explained the whole thing. The whole plan. He was involved in some lickle jugglings, seen?! A council t'ing for students, y'know....to get a whole heap of money. £50,000....I think. He was checking some part-time gal, y'know, who worked at the council. Some high-class sump'n. Winston wasn't in a position to treat her the way that she wanted. So they worked sump'n out, y'know. He told me he might disappear, fly back-ah-yard with the 'ooman, an' lie low."

Merlene blushed modestly. There was no point in correcting the inacuracies in Fitzroy's story. She was annoyed and embarrassed that Winston had told his friend so much. But right now it was more important to get the information she needed. She had to come clean.

"Look Fitz, it was Winston that died. Definitely. I saw him myself. There's nothing that anyone can do about it. But right now, there's something more important than that. Fitzroy....I have to find that money. You see, I'm that other woman. I helped Winston pull the skank...."

Merlene studied Fitzroy's reaction to the news and decided that she had to lie to impress on him the urgency of recovering the money. She was sure that if she told him that she intended to find the money and do a runner with it, he would have wanted a share. She didn't trust Fitzroy, but then again, what other leads did she have? "....And now that he's gone, I have to put the money back. I need to know where that money is. Did he say anything about where he hid the money?"

"Bwoy....!" Fitzroy was clearly bemused. "So is you 'im talk 'bout?"

"Yes, yes, yes!" Merlene repeated. "The important thing, is that I get hold of the money as fast as I can and return it. I've only got a few months before the whole thing could be found out. I'm desperate!"

"Put back the money? Cho! You're crazy, man! Put back £50,000! You mus' be crazy! We have to find the money, and split it. You and I. Fifty-fifty. That's what we ha' fe do."

Merlene looked at him blankly. That it was only a question of £34,000 was neither here nor there. She realised she had made a mistake confiding in a known hustler. A villain through and through - one of those youths whose main role in life is to skylark on street corners and screw up his face, acting like a big top ranks.

"Fitzroy, I'm not doing any sentence for what I don't know. The money has to be returned," she insisted, nervously following his wild eyes as they spun around in their sockets propelled by cocaine.

"Easy daughter," he reassured her. "You an' me baby, we could be a team, t'raas-claat! Like Bonnie an' Clyde....you bound to get some sweetness!"

Merlene stared at the youth incredulously. He had the nerve to chat her up? This youth who used to love kicks on the corner, all day and all night long? This youth now immersed in crack smoke, puffing furiously at his pipe? Merlene considered herself a superior social class to Fitzroy and she was determined to let him know.

"You must be joking, Fitzroy! Me and you? You think I would waste my time with a one such as you?!" Merlene taunted.

"Tek a look at yourself," Fitzroy replied cold and calculated. "....You a huff an' a puff an' gwaan like you the champion. But remember - how it go? Thou shalt not steal, thou shalt not kill nor *commit adultery*. Ah no me seh so! A de bible seh so!"

Merlene couldn't believe what she was hearing. Arguing with Fitzroy was distasteful. She had her standards and he didn't come anywhere near them.

"You can live your life while I'll go on with mine," she said. "I can see I've wasted my time here. I'll wish you good luck and goodbye."

She brushed past him and headed out of the flat. Fitzroy called after her.

"An' how will you find the money without me?! You coulda search Inglann but you couldn't search Miami....or Toronto....or New York. The money could be in all dem places. You need me 'ooman!"

Merlene continued down the dark walkway without turning back. Fitzroy was right. She didn't have a clue as to where to look. But, she hoped she would never have to stoop so low as to ask for his help.

Winter, summer, spring or autumn, gal pickney run dance hall. The dancehall gyaal dem have an incredible effect on most men. They can make particularly tight men lose their hearts, their minds and their wallets, buying up the bar. Concrete Jungle in Vauxhall was a venue which always allowed women free entrance before midnight and on this mild evening in early October, the ravers were out in force.

Jamaican women look good. Every man knows that. And where Jamaican women go, men will soon follow. Tonight, the promoter and his idren were standing at the entrance singing "tra-la-la-la-la-la-la-lee", because the dancehall was cork and the liquor sell off. Dancehall full and security maximum. Everything in the dance was sweet.

The deejays were deejaying their gun lyrics when Fitzroy entered. The music relaxed him, as he took a swig from his can of Kestrel Export in the darkened, sweaty, smoky venue.

Fitzroy usually went dance to look a woman. But tonight, he went carrying some protection. He had got word on the 'frontline' wire, that Errol Holt suspected him of ripping him off on a racket. Nothing moved in Brixton without the say so of the Holt brothers, Barrington and Errol. Barrington was cool, a real professional, but Errol, the youngest and wildest, was a feared bad bwoy. Fitzroy had to find him first and sort out the misunderstanding. He carried protection, just in case.

"You might not remember me, but you once danced into my life," the voice whispered in his ear.

Startled, Fitzroy turned to come face to face with a sexy, red-skinned girl with a wig, a micro-miniskirt and one of those suggestive smiles men say they can't resist. He recognised her as a young girl he had tried unsuccessfully to get off with two months previously - same place, same time. One of those girls who knew that the body she had would cause confusion; anytime she passed by, men were bound to feel attraction. Fitzroy examined her top to toe, licking his lips. Mmmm, maybe some other time. He wouldn't feel comfortable tonight until he had sorted out his business with Errol. He felt confident that he'd be able to deal with her later. Since he'd come a man, he'd got to understand that you can get any woman, if you have the ambition.

"Girl child, nah bother run me down, right now," Fitzroy spoke slowly and in a low, sincere voice. "You have 'nuff man....As one gone, you get a million an' one."

The girl looked at him, practically saying 'I wanna ride you!' She wasn't used to being turned down. She went close up behind him, and slipped her arm around his waist, reaching out to lightly pat his groin. She had the face of an angel, but the heart of a Jezebel.

"Baby I can hold you where it feels good tonight," she purred so closely that he could feel her warm breath caressing his earlobe. "I have the time, but do you have the stamina?"

Fitzroy stiffened. It was tempting. The girl was lovable. He had always believed that a woman is supposed to get all the love that she wants. But not tonight. He couldn't resist showing her that she wasn't irresistible. That would pay her back for turning him down the last time.

" 'Ooman nah worry yourself...," he said with a smirk, hidden from the girl behind him. "....cause everything criss and clean...."

He felt her release the groping hand hurriedly, and a moment later heard a large crash and commotion from behind. He spun around quickly, about to reach in his pocket for the protection.

The sight before him left even Fitzroy with a feeling of distaste. The girl lay sprawled out on the floor, the table she had been thrown across, on top of her. The glasses of beer on the table, had emptied their contents over her blouse and micro-miniskirt, giving the leering idlers, a free wet t-shirt exhibition. A huge, angry man was standing over her.

"You bitch!" the man screamed, "I turn my back for one minute and you're rubbing up against a nex' man!"

Fitzroy watched how the man was carrying on. Pointlessly working up a storm. After the storm, there must be a calm, he thought to himself. He hoped he would never embarrass himself like this over a woman.

"Just' cool off, man. Don't juggle with the gyaal life, boss. Are you listening me?"

He didn't want to get mix up, by pushing his mouth in something he didn't know. At the same time, he didn't want to see the girl get battered further. It wasn't like he was Rambo, either. He simply felt he had to defend the gal pickney.

The angry boyfriend looked up. "Who the hell are you?" he spat venomously. "And whose army have you got wit' you? Otherwise, you buck up on me, you're bound to fall!"

Fitzroy took the threat seriously, the man was built like a big stone wall. But then again, the man didn't know about Fitzroy's protection.

"Look boss, t'rough say I have no argument, what goes on between man an' 'ooman is your business, seen?! I understand that if your 'ooman steps out of line you must manners it. But leave it in your yard. Don't tek care of it inside a club. I'm giving you due respeck, because I man want you to come in here without anyone su-su 'pon you!"

The boyfriend rolled up his sleeves. He knew that he could take on the skinnier man and flatten him with ease. "Well, we'll see who's gonna bodyguard *you*, mister bodyguard?"

He lunged at Fitzroy. The smaller man was quicker however, and niftily stepped to one side, sending the boyfriend crashing uncontrollably into the bar behind him. By the time the man had taken a minute to compose himself, he found himself staring into the barrel of a 'matic, which Fitzroy had drawn out with the speed of a bullet.

"I can be as good as the best of them, and as bad as the worst so don't tes' me," Fitzroy hissed slowly. "Me ah no bad bwoy, but you ha' fe mind how you ah talk...."

The simplest thing is just 'blam! blam! blam!!' The moment a man gets a gun in his hand, he is transported back to the days of Jesse James or Al Capone. Accustomed to this rude boy business, the ravers had scattered, every man looking a place to hide his head. If Fitzroy hadn't been acting out a scene from *Dirty Harry*, he may have seen one of the burly bouncers from Pitbull Security, the baddest security firm in South London, creeping up on the left flank, with a baseball bat in his hand. The bat came crashing down on the gunman's wrist. He yelled with pain as his grip released the pistol, sending it clattering to the ground. The gun was picked up by another of Pitbull's bouncers. In a flash, the bouncer had Fitzroy pinned to a wall, the baseball bat at his throat. Fitz struggled in vain, realising now, that he was in serious trouble. But pinned to the wall, the baseball bat at his throat, is how he remained until the police came to collect Fitzroy and gun.

The sound system had been switched off, the venue lights switched on. The restless crowd had no choice but to hang around, while the twenty or so officers had finished questioning each and everyone of them in turn. Everyone had their own version of what had taken place.

"Yes, the yout' badder than a bull in a pen. Him flash certain lyrics and dem start fight...Me bawl, 'we come here fe dance and have 'nuff fun, don't shoot your breddah down!'"

"An' then the boyfriend seh, 'cause you don't see me about, you check seh me sarf...! Your biggest mistake is taking me for a pushover....Don't try an' push me over, just because I don't run up my mouth. An' I don't brag and show off. An' the gunman seh, 'you big today, but little tomorrow.'"

"What a way the earth ah running man! Ah when it ah go done? I wonder when dem put down the gun? Ah weh dem get it from, eh? Me warn the deejay, stop boosting them gunman friend. But dem nevah stop until the place get hot. Me warn all the rude boys, 'put down your guns and come....' It's time fe tell the politicians, stop giving the youth dem guns!'"

Old time people used to say, you talk too much, you will pay for what you don't eat.

TWO

From corner to corner, you can hear the yout' chatting the Brixton talk. Brixton talk is not no American talk. It's not no Canadian talk, not even Jamaican talk. It's poor people talk, street talk, rude boy talk. Contemporary Afro-Saxons favour a lingua that is a language of their own - a cross between Jamaican patois and Yankee talk, blended with their local street talk. Brixton talk is coming on like it's a Yankee yardman's cockney.

"So where d'you want to go raving tonight? I wouldn't mind checkin' out Kilimanjaro."

"Nah man! I'm going up town. I'm reaching Moonlighting if it kills me. If it's like the last week, the place will be fire. Remember the last time, when the whole dance mash up?"

"How y'mean? Of course I do. All five, six hours an' nobody nah sit down. The whole place mash up."

"Yeah man, that was safe!"

"Safe? It was *seff!?*"

The two women laughed as they recalled a good night out.

"An' you remember that nasty Christian bwoy who was tryin' to check you?"

"Oh don't....Don't! I'm not having it."

"Ahahahaha! Yes, what was his name again? Lancelot?! Ahahah! Yes, him dance a lot, but me nevah see him lance a lot!"

"No, that's just out of order, Angie. You know I don't like to be reminded of that. That's out of order!! But that is not my biggest problem, because me can love any man. You nah see't?"

Andrea smiled at the two younger women. She didn't much like them. As far as she was concerned, they were sneaky like a snake outta grass, but Angie and Dawn were regular customers. They had to be. Looking sexy was their full-time occupation. They spent their mornings in the gym to stay trim and they spent their afternoons up West, buying expensive clothes, make-up and perfume. They would literally starve themselves to squeeze into a size 8. But no matter how good they looked in their leggings, they didn't look their best until they returned to Brixton in the late afternoon to get their hair done.

Ebony Hair salon was a shabby little premises in the half of the Brixton Arcade on the North side of Atlantic Road. Wedged between a Nigerian grocery store selling red-hot chillies and gari on the one side, and Neville's Record Shack, constantly blasting the latest dancehall releases on the other side, it was inconspicuous enough not to attract any passing trade. But Andrea's reputation for doing wonders with a pair of scissors and a clump of weave-on hair was legendary. With a decent lick of paint, the place would be packed constantly. But Sister Anthea was happy with the little money her business brought in. She was set in her ways, too old to be motivated by wealth.

Andrea loved and respected Sister Anthea, but she was thinking of setting up her own place. There was no future for her at Ebony, not on £200 a week. Winston had only been buried two days but already the bills had started coming through her letter box - including one for the next repayment on her car, which Winston had obligingly written off in his fatal crash. Sister Anthea wasn't interested in attracting more customers and Andrea couldn't live on the money she was earning.

"Girl child, I beg you....nah budda burn up me head with that stuff," Angie warned as Andrea applied the relaxer on her hair. Andrea simply smiled. They were her last two customers of the day. Customers always thought they knew best. Angie wanted the type of short, relaxed cut that was so popular amongst black American actresses. Andrea couldn't work miracles. If Angie wanted that style, she had to be prepared for a bit of scalp heat.

"Anyways," Angie continued, turning to Dawn, "tonight I'm going to take it easy....so easy don't you know. Unless Barrington reaches, in which case I'll have to lively up myself."

"Barrington?" Dawn queried. "Barrington? What about Linvall? I thought you were checking Linvall now?"

"Yes me mash it up already, so it's no problem," Angie replied sarcastically. "I tried it once now. I don't want to repeat it. Him is not advanced."

"I know what you mean. He doesn't know the first thing about making a woman feel nice. Y'know. I remember when I was checking him, he would always say, 'you are my number, you are my number one', and call it foreplay. Can you imagine? And he's tight with his money."

"Woman," Angie eyed her friend menacingly. "Me still wonder how he got my phone number! Anyways, he called me up and started talking about how we could be a team. About how he needed a woman to wash his clothes proper an' cook his dinner proper."

"He never, did he?"

"What d'you mean he never, when I'm telling you that's the kind of foolishness the man ah deal with? No, man. I'm saving myself for Barrington. You nah see how the boy sweet so?

22

Dresses stush and drives a wicked Mercedes."

"So you're moving with Barrington now," Andrea asked in passing as she treated her customer's hair.

"What's it got to do with you?" Angie snapped.

"I'm just asking that's all....You know how he earns his money don't you? Also don't you think he's rather old for you? He's old enough to be your father."

Angie flashed Andrea a cold, dismissive look.

"I said what's it got to do with you?"

Andrea got the message and continued with Angie's hair.

"You see what I mean, Dawn," Angie continued. "Bush don't have ears, but someone may be in it, hearing you....Me nah too listen to what people say, y'know. 'Cause plenty people are just hypocrites, spreading rumours!"

Andrea simply frowned. She realised she was the object of Angie's derision, but it didn't faze her.

Angie and Dawn were only nineteen, but they had taken over the scene. Everywhere they went, men's dripping tongues were bound to follow. They practically threw themselves over any man willing to flash a £20 note in front of them.

For every new generation that passes, another one is waiting in the wings waiting to take over. Every day, some yout' somewhere, hangs up his raving hat and passes it on to the next yout'. Every day, some yout' says goodbye to the old hangouts 'pon street corner and gets married. Even before the service is over, there's a next yout' standing on his spot hustling same way. When Andrea and her posse gave up their claim to Brixton a few years earlier, Angie and Dawn inherited the mantle and now spent their time fighting to maintain their position as the most eligible gyaals in South London.

"I nah deal with no kind of hearsay," Angie continued. "Strictly rumours them spreading. Ah me know Barrington, y'know..."

The tangy smell of hair relaxer greeted Merlene as she entered the salon a couple of hours later, the serene hum of a hair-dryer offering a welcome break from the hustle and bustle of a Saturday afternoon in the market.

"Hi Merle," Andrea greeted her friend enthusiastically. "How are things? What's news?"

"Nothing much," came Merlene's sedate reply. "How are you?"

"Well....you know....Ain't got no shoes upon my feet but still I'm dancing. I hope you haven't come to get your hair done. I want to get away early tonight."

"Don't worry yourself. I only dropped in to see how you

were doing....I was shopping in the market anyway and passing by."

"That's safe. Take a seat, I'll be done in a few minutes."

"Don't rush my hair you know," Angie said quickly. "Mind yourself, y'know. I've got to look my best tonight. I don't want no rush job."

"Relax," Andrea assured her. "I've finished the styling. You're nearly done."

Angie turned to Dawn and continued her conversation.

"Niceness is what I appreciate, y'know? Anyways as I was saying, Barrington loves me bad. Bad-bad! I didn't believe it at first, but now I've seen it with my own eyes, and actions speak louder than words...."

The hair done, Andrea left Angie admiring herself in the mirror and went across to Merlene.

"I'm sorry about that," Merlene said, nodding towards Angie and Dawn as they inspected the reflection of Andrea's handiwork. "Those girls are just feisty!"

"Don't worry about them, they're harmless," Andrea assured.

"Slack more like. They want to mind who they disrespect."

"Ah mek dem gwaan. I give thanks and praises for all the girls them. Without them I'd be out of a job. Angie and Dawn aren't too bad, they're just like we were six or seven years ago."

"I don't remember letting my tits hang out of my blouse when I went out," said Merlene with exaggerated modesty.

"Yeah, we stopped just short of that," Andrea reminisced with equally exaggerated regret.

"No, those girls...those girls are just like....I mean, we at least kept our clothes on until we got under the sheets! Those girls may as well be streaking."

Pleased with the job well done, Angie settled the bill.

"He says he loves me, but the only thing that I'm worried about," whispered Angie as she and Dawn walked out the door, "is that he's a bit funny. He wants me to come with him to an orgy....No, it's not what you think. All I have to do is watch...."

Exhausted, Andrea turned to Merlene with a sigh of relief.

"I'm burned out!"

"You're getting old," Merlene teased, jabbing her younger friend's pert behind.

"It's alright for you, I'm working twenty-four sevens, what with one thing and another. And look how your hair so twist up, Merle. Honestly, I'm rushed off my feet, but I still manage to keep my hair nice." Andrea pulled out a comb and began straightening Merlene's hair out. "If you don't take care of it Merle, it will start breaking up."

"Yeah, I know, I know," Merlene answered with a smile on her face. She remembered how Andrea was always poking in her friends' hair whenever she got a chance. But Merlene didn't have time for her hair to be styled. She turned serious.

"Are you sure everything's okay about Winston and the funeral and all that?"

"Oh yes, yes....," Andrea waved the question away with a hand. "Winston's dead, but life goes on. It's difficult grieving for someone you didn't even know."

"What do you mean?" Merlene asked agitated.

"I'm finding out something new about Winston every day. Things I should have known by rights...."

Merlene had begun to sweat as she shifted uneasily in her seat. "Like what?" she asked, waiting to exhale.

"I got a letter from a woman who claims she was his baby mother...."

"You nevah!" Merlene cried out with relief.

"Yeah man! Oh that was years ago, before Winston and me, y'know. The kid's eight years old now. It was his birthday yesterday. When she didn't get the yearly cheque for the kid's birthday, she called up to cuss Winston out. Can you believe that? And she was living just around the corner until recently. The las' place she lived was Brixton 'frontline', before the government pull it down."

Merlene shared a feeling of genuine empathy with Andrea.

"I'm really sorry to hear that, Andrea."

"I'm not," Andrea stated boldly. "It doesn't bother me at all."

Despite her friends resolute words, Merlene could see that it hurt Andrea. She feared how Andrea would act if she discovered....No, no. That was unthinkable.

"She said that she thinks that Winston had another baby mother as well. But she's not sure where the woman lives."

The news upset Merlene. She just couldn't believe that Winston could have had two kids out there somewhere, without mentioning a word about it. By not saying anything, it was as if he had deceived her. Why had he not mentioned it?

Andrea felt precisely the same way and asked herself the exact same questions. But neither of them knew what the other was thinking, and for a moment, neither of them cared. They were each engulfed in their individual deception.

"Why did she call you?" Merlene asked eventually, underwhelmed by a feeling of guilt before her girlfriend's own feelings of grief.

"Can you believe it, she asked if Winston left any money."

Merlene's eyes lit up. The real reason for dropping by to see

Andrea, was to find out if Andrea knew anything about the missing money. She hadn't known how to bring up the subject without arising suspicion.

"A man dies and suddenly his next of kin come out from under their rocks and start asking for money!"

"It's truly a shame," Merlene agreed. "So did he...? Did Winston leave any money....?"

"Money?! Joke you ah joke, Merlene. When las' you hear about a man leaving money? Enh? When las' you hear that!"

Merlene could see that Andrea was agitated, but she was compelled to pursue the issue.

"I just thought, maybe. You know, Winston was always doing so many things, he seemed to have his finger in so many pies...."

"Pies? You can say that again. Pies, with bodies shaped like a coca-cola bottle without the top."

"I just thought he might have a bit of money lying around...? So he didn't have anything?"

"You know something I don't know?" Andrea asked unsuspiciously. "Winston never left' a will nor no insurance. He left me bills to pay, but no money to pay them with."

Merlene sighed. "I'm sorry to hear that," she said.

"Oh forget it. Forget it! Look, honestly Merle, the sooner I get that man out of my system the better. I can't believe he deceived me like that. When we first started seeing each other, I asked him straight whether he had any kids or not. Me vex bout dat. He lied to me. Why did he do that?"

Merlene put her arm reassuringly around her friend. She didn't have the answer to the question, as much as she desired to know herself.

Wrapped in her girl friend's warm embrace, Andrea couldn't resist the urge to break down in tears. Winston had let her down badly. Call it delayed reaction, but she was finally feeling it.

"Why isn't it possible to find a good man?" Andrea blurted out tearfully. "Just an ordinary guy who's honest. Someone who won't tell me no lie. Someone who'll tell me the truth. Someone who'll simply say, 'me love you an' you love me', without any bullshit. Someone who comes straight without faking it. How come there aren't any men out there like that, Merle?"

"There are, Andrea. Really there are."

Merlene's words did little to comfort the distressed woman.

"No, when it comes down to the test there aren't. Winston never stopped telling me how much he loved me. And the first thing I find out when he's dead and buried is that he had a couple of kids out there. What kind of love is that, Merle?!"

"Easy now, Andrea. You don't know for certain that they are

his kids."

Andrea flashed Merlene a quizzical look. Was she hearing, right? She had always respected Merlene for being older and wiser, but what she was talking right now was pure naivety.

"Of course I know!" she blasted. "Winston's guilty, oh yes, he's guilty. I should have used my woman's intuition long ago. All the signs were there, but I didn't see them. Now, I'm putting all the little pieces together, and it all makes sense. I've been a woman too long to ignore the signs staring me in the face. I haven't got the proof Merle, but deep in my heart, I know he deceived me."

"Let me take you home," Merlene offered eventually. Put on your clothes, girl, and we'll go to a party."

"Thanks Merle, but I've really got to be on my own tonight."

"Are you sure?"

"Yes. Really. I'll be alright, Merle."

Merlene was reluctant to go. She hung around until Andrea had locked up and then insisted on accompanying her friend half way up Railton Road. Across the road, outside the little group of shops that constituted the 'frontline', Andrea waved her friend home.

"I'll be alright. You go on off home," she commanded. It's a good thing the good Lord is around to pick us up whenever we go down, she thought to herself.

Merlene took her leave, ignoring the catcalls from the group of five or six men across the road.

Andrea continued her way down Railton Road, pushing her way past the kerb dealers trafficking their goods to passing motorists. No matter what anyone said, she adored Brixton. She romanticised it all out of proportion. No matter the season, this was still a community that existed in black and white and pulsated to the great tunes of ragga reggae. She thrived on the hustle and bustle of the crowds and the vibes. Winston had always dreamt about returning to Jamaica to set up home permanently. Even though she enjoyed her annual trips to the land of wood and water, she knew that she could never leave Brixton permanently.

To her, Brixton meant beautiful women, beautiful men and street smart guys who seemed to know all the angles. To others, Brixton was a city destroyed by drugs, crime, loud music. Andrea was as tough and romantic as the city she loved. Brixton was her town and it always would be.

Andrea was awakened early Monday morning by the shrill

ring of the telephone. Shaking herself into full consciousness, she picked up the receiver to hear a firm, authoritative voice on the other end of the line.

"Miss Dunbar?"

"Er....yeah....who's this?" Andrea couldn't believe that anyone had called her so early

"It's Notting Hill police station, Miss Dunbar. You are registered as the owner of the black Volkswagen Golf which was involved in an accident on The Westway recently?"

"Yeah, yeah. That's right? Is there something wrong?"

"No, nothing wrong Miss Dunbar....just that we've finished examining the vehicle. We'd like you to come down and sign for the contents of the car and arrange for it to be removed from our premises. As you know, it's a total write-off."

Andrea winced. She didn't like talking to policemen at the best of times, least of all when they had the upper hand. What did he expect her to do with a total write-off?

"Can't this wait?" she asked irritably.

"Well, not really madam. If we have it removed, you'll be sent a bill. And you'll still have to come down and sign for the contents...."

"Alright, alright! I'll be down later today."

"Just let the desk sergeant know when you arrive, and oh....bring some identification."

Andrea slammed the phone down to avoid thanking the cop. What a cheek! Your boyfriend dies in a car crash, and they expect you to clear up the mess. What else can you expect from bull? She had wanted to spend the day taking in the recent events and contemplating the future without Winston.

Even though Andrea had been Winston's main squeeze for the past seven years, he had always refused to get married. He just wasn't interested in the 'm' word, yet they practically lived together as man and wife.

"I don't need a piece of paper telling me that you're my queen," Winston had explained repeatedly, "I know that already. We don't need that. We're Africans y'know. All we have to do, is jump over the broom and it done."

"It done" and "it finish," were Winston's ways of terminating any discussion. End of argument, as far as he was concerned. Andrea had often wondered about Winston's passionate aversion to wedding bells. He was afraid, no, terrified of walking down the aisle. Few black men walk down the aisle willingly. Andrea knew that. She had guested at more than one shotgun wedding. But she couldn't understand why Winston enjoyed living as man and wife, while baulking so firmly at the thought of going legal. They were engaged the year before. He didn't mind that, for as far as Winston was concerned, the engagement could last twenty years, just as long as they didn't have to walk down the aisle at the end of it. Most women would immediately jump to the conclusion that if a man shies away from marriage too strongly, he must have a part-time t'ing going on. Andrea wasn't convinced it was that simple. She was prepared to put up with the odd fling here and there. Winston spent Friday nights clubbing with the boys. They were bound to stumble on a few of those slack women, who go to dances looking another woman's man. On Friday nights, Winston wouldn't come home until morning, when he would crumple up on the bed, reeking of booze, spliff and perfume. He had to be sleeping around. He probably suspected that her weekend trips to her sister in Birmingham, were not completely innocent. But he couldn't say a thing. Not unless he was prepared to explain the Friday night perfume. He was the one who, at the very beginning of their relationship, had insisted that no questions should be asked. As long as the other party didn't know, it didn't hurt. Suspicion is merely irritating, but confirmed knowledge is downright painful.

Winston was a smooth operator. He could sweeten up a girl nice. He had sweet-talked Andrea so often. Even if she saw him walking down the road with his arms around another woman, she wouldn't make a big t'ing out of it.

"No matter who you see me with, you are still my number one," he had assured her several times. "My main squeeze. No matter what the situation, we'll talk about it indoors. So I beg you, don't bother washing our dirty linen in public."

Andrea didn't simply fall head over heels for the sweet talk. She knew her worth, and was totally confident about herself. Andrea was as good as an eligible bachelor when Winston appeared on the scene. He was getting a good deal and he knew it.

If only Winston hadn't got so under her skin, she sighed, as she thought about how much she had really loved him.

She was still thinking about Winston's reluctance to get married when the taxi dropped her outside Notting Hill police station. A sense of guilt riddled her every thought. She ought to be playing the part of the grieving widow, rather than the suspicious girlfriend. It would do no good thinking about what could have been, or should have been, or may have been; when the truth is that nothing would come of that thinking. Winston was dead. That was the main thing. She'd rebuild her life, starting with the removal of her Golf. She had called a breaker's yard before she left home. Andrea winced, as she caught a glimpse of a tow-truck in the police station yard, hoisting up the burned-out remains of what was her motorised pride and joy.

"Yes....what can I do for you, Miss?"

The voice from that morning's telephone call greeted her from behind the desk.

"You called me this morning....Andrea Dunbar....I've come to collect my Golf."

"Oh that's you, is it?" The policeman grinned, turning and looking out the window behind him to admire the wreck. "Ooooh," he grunted, as if having to look at the wreck was too painful a sight. "Right mess the deceased made of your motor. Knew him well did you....?"

"Yeah! What's that to you?" Andrea answered sharply. Ever since the unfortunate incident when she had boxed a feisty customer at the hairdresser's salon she worked at as a trainee, police stations had made her feel uneasy.

The officer looked at her, and smiled.

"Well Miss....Miss....Miss...." the officer trailed his finger down the record book.

"Dunbar!" Andrea interjected.

"Ah, yes," the officer exclaimed, simultaneously arriving at the name in his book. "Andrea Winsome Dunbar, is that right? Of Shakespeare Road, SE24?"

"Yes, that's right," Andrea replied hurriedly. "Where do I sign?"

"Hold on just one moment!" There was a hint of triumph in the policeman's voice.

A scowl appeared on Andrea's face. She kissed her teeth and sighed in disbelief, as the officer walked over to a man in plain clothes, standing in an office doorway.

He returned.

"Well Miss Dunbar, if you don't mind....We'd like to ask you a few more questions about the vehicle....This way please."

Andrea stared directly at the officer. She was still angry, but her scowl was now tempered with a touch of humility. If the cops were bent on wasting her time, there was no point in arguing.

She followed the officer to a tiny office in the building's inner sanctum, where she took a seat opposite the plain clothes detective.

"So Miss Dunbar...!" He jumped up suddenly, producing a briefcase from under his desk. He slammed the briefcase onto the table and popped the lock.

Andrea couldn't believe her eyes. It was Winston's case. There was no doubt about it. She recognised the jet black snake-skinned briefcase she had bought him for his birthday the previous year, with the initials W.P. inscribed in gold leaf on the side. But the inside of the case was lined with more money than she had ever seen. Fivers, tenners, twenty pound notes.

"Can you explain this money we found in your boyfriend's car?"

"What....? Er....I suppose it's money that Winston had with him for a business deal. He was a music promoter....He promoted concerts. He often carried large sums of money, to pay artists and that sort of thing."

"What! That's a lot of money to be carrying about!" The officer's tone suggested that he didn't believe a word of it. "Five thousand pounds! Supposing he got mugged...?"

"Well, that's the way he did business. What can I say?"

Andrea realised how incredible the story sounded, but no other explanation came to mind and right now, she had to buy time with some story or other. Otherwise she would never see that money.

"Have you got any proof?" the detective asked sarcastically.

"How do you expect me to have that? He did his business his way, and didn't take too kindly to people knowing what he was up to."

The detective knew she was lying, but there wasn't much he could do, except use some delaying tactics.

"Well, Miss Dunbar. All we can do for the moment is hold on to this money, until my officers have made checks and I am satisfied the cash doesn't correspond to any money reported missing recently. Meanwhile, if you come up with any information, please call the station immediately. You can ask for me, I'm Detective Constable MacInnes."

He wrote his name and number hurriedly on a sheet of paper, handing it to Andrea while he held the door open for her exit.

Outside, a heavy downpour had been sent down from the heavens to dampen the day. Excepting the briefcase, the police had signed Winston's possessions over to Andrea. Looking at the downpour, she pulled her dead boyfriend's Burberry raincoat over her shoulders and raced down the road to Holland Park underground station, passing the remains of her once-gleaming new Golf, now dangling unceremoniously behind the tow-truck, waiting to be taken to its last resting place. She took a last look at it before crossing the road to the tube station.

Along with most of her fellow passengers in the rush hour

tube traffic, she was soaked to the skin. But that didn't bother her. The image of the suitcase full of money flashed repeatedly through her mind. Thousands and thousands of pounds! What was Winston doing with all that money? Even though Winston, like most men, kept his wallet close to his chest, she was convinced he had his eye on a criss secondhand Mercedes 190 that a financially-strapped friend was selling for seven grand cash. She had overheard him speaking on the phone, saying he only needed a couple of grand more. That was about a month ago. If he had come into a lot of money suddenly, he would have been driving the dream Benz and not her Golf on that tragic night. She held Winston's raincoat tight, and pushed her hands deep into the side pockets. Almost indifferently, she pulled out a postcard from one of the pockets, and read it casually.

Darling Winston,
Looking forward to spending the rest of my life with you, on our beach in the Caribbean.
Your future wife.

Andrea didn't recognise the handwriting or the words. She turned the card over and over, looking for clues. It had been sent to an address she didn't recognise. It had a West End postmark dated in September, shortly before Winston's death. None of it made any sense. Who had sent it? Could Winston possibly have been contemplating running off with another woman? And what about the money? How did it all fit together?

Suspicion and an air of mystery dominated her thoughts as she waited on the southbound platform of the Victoria Line at Oxford Circus. Winston had died leaving a trail of mystery and suspense for her to solve. A muffled message was repeated over the station's speaker system.

"Owing to a security alert, Victoria Line trains will only be operating between Walthamstow Central and Kings Cross...."

"Blast!" Andrea thought. And headed towards the up escalators. Outside, the rain had stopped. It didn't take her long to spot a black taxi depositing its passengers outside Hamley's.

"Brixton!" she shouted as she climbed in. "Shakespeare Road." The driver grunted and drove off sullenly.

As the cab rolled around the lower Regent Street curve towards Piccadilly Circus Andrea, exhausted, laid her head back on the seat. Taking a moment to think, she took off the raincoat, and went through its pockets systematically. She recognised his house keys. More interestingly, she found his cheque book in an inside pocket tucked discreetly into the lining of the coat. And there it was, the entry on the last stub! The money in the suitcase! Drawn in cash! There was no other explanation. He must have drawn out the money for the Benz! The police were so hopeless that they had missed the evidence. Andrea paused to read the card again. *Looking forward to spending the rest of my life with you, on our beach in the Caribbean.* It didn't make any sense. She rustled quickly through the plastic bag filled with Winston's effects, almost shrieking with alarm as she pulled out the dead man's passport. There could only be one reason for Winston to have his passport on him at the time of the crash. Yet he hadn't mentioned a word about travelling overseas.

Old time people used to say, 'when you pass away, even nanny goat know your secret!' Andrea sat down on the thick piled carpet of her living room, immersed in boxes filled with Winston's belongings. Fire burned in her eyes as she went through everything meticulously. Everything. She wanted revenge. Winston deceived her, but how could she get her revenge? Was he not beyond her now? She inspected his suits for unfamiliar strands of hair. She went through his record collection, reading the inscriptions for tell-tale signs. It no longer mattered that she didn't replace the albums in order. Winston couldn't lose his temper now. It was her temper which had to be controlled. Seven years of their relationship lay strewn across the thick pile carpet, but she didn't give a damn. You could smell badness on her breath. She wanted revenge. But how could she exact revenge from a dead man?

She thumbed her way hungrily, through the pile of unopened letters addressed to her late lover. A phone bill reminder. A car tax reminder. An indecipherable letter from someone called Junior. She then turned her attentions to the few books which graced the shelves, turning them upside down, in case any incriminating slip of paper should fall out from between the pages. Then it was the turn of Winston's entire wardrobe. This was her revenge! Winston's most intimate life was now in her hands to do with it what she would. That was sweet revenge.

Andrea was determined to get to the bottom of this mystery. The infidelity didn't bother her as much as the deception that went with it. Those words on the postcard.... The familiar tone of the words.... The writer sounded so confident that they would spend the rest of their lives together. Andrea couldn't believe she had been living under the same roof as this man, as if they were husband and wife, while he was living a double life. Why should he lie? If he wanted to be with another woman, he could simply walk out the door and have done. She wouldn't have put up an argument. They had a no-questions-asked-no-strings-attached relationship. Why had he gone to the bank and taken out all the money he owned in the world, money he was planning on spending on a dream car? There were so many unanswered questions.

She spent the evening going through his belongings. He owned only two books. Amongst the stack of unopened letters were some from his bank manager reminding him of his overdraft limit, a couple of recording contracts, and some letters from the Social. Winston was hardly a man of letters. Andrea went through the stack of photos in the crumpled manila envelope. Photos of Winston at school, of him looking cool, drinking with the boys and with Andrea. There were several photographs of ex-girlfriends, few of whom Andrea recognised.

No clues. What was the next step? She rolled onto the bed, lying face up. Whoever said it was right, she thought to herself, the only man you can trust is a dead man. She picked up the photograph taken at their engagement party at the Roof Gardens in Kensington. Winston smiling seductively, his arm around Andrea's waist. Those were happier times. The pair looked like a couple of star-crossed young lovers on their first date. How ironic. She felt a deep anger erupting in her belly as she stared lifelessly at Winston's leery grin. It was a stupid grin. It had always been a stupid grin. The stupid grin of a stupid man.

The bastard! She had allowed him more freedom than a woman should allow a man, and this was how he repaid her. It didn't matter who the card was from, the message was clear. Winston had been living a lie. Like a double agent, he had promised his allegiance to her and to another woman. She understood now why Winston never wanted to get married all these years. She had provided him with a place to stay and some spending money every now and then. And all the time, he had been planning to elope with some other woman. He didn't even have the bottle to tell her. What a bastard! And to think that she was so cut up about him dying.

To think that she had cried for a week. And like a good widow, she had stayed celibate in deference to Winston, even though Donovan had left several messages for her in the last few days, wanting to move in on the dead man's property. And she had been tempted too. Because like every woman, Andrea had physical needs. But she had not encouraged his advances, thinking that if Winston was up there somewhere watching her every move, he would feel she was spitting on his grave by getting off with somebody so quickly. All these things she had done out of respect for his memory, and in return, he had reached from the grave and slapped her in the face. The bastard!

Andrea ripped the photograph down the middle. With the half from which Winston's smiling face now peered on its own, she wrote: *The only true man, is a dead man,* and pinned it to the headrest of her bed. She had had her revenge on the dead man.

Ain't no use holding on to a love that's wrong. Ah nuh lie?!

"I wonder what both of them were thinking. Dem ah plan and scheme, to con me?," she muttered aloud.

She didn't want to go on thinking about Winston running off with some other woman. "Me life too short for a next woman tek part," she figured. But at the same time, her mind wouldn't let it drop. She had to find out what was going on, before she closed the chapter on Winston's double life.

Don't take Andrea for no loafter. She knew what she was doing in her relationship with Winston, and she thought she knew everything about him. But men can be devious, y'know.

You can never know wha' ah really gwaan with any man. Promise is a comfort to a fool. Looks are deceiving, child. Don't underrate no man. You have to check every lickle t'ing they do and maybe you'll find out sump'n. Open up to the cold facts staring you in the face. Get a deeper reasoning before you deduce your conclusion. The most obscure little detail could give you a big surprise. Big enough to wipe the smile off your face when you realise what your man is up to.

Never again would she trust a man. She would sleep with men, use them then cast them aside, but never again would she speak love to any man. All the diamonds and the pearls, all the money in the world, would never again buy her love.

Backwards never, forwards forever and ever. Andrea picked up the phone and dialled Notting Hill Police Station.

"Detective Constable MacInnes? Andrea Dunbar. That money came from my man's bank account. I've got the counterfoil. Okay! I'll come down and collect it tomorrow morning!"

Her seven years of bad luck had truly come to an end. She would cash in on Winston's death, she told herself, ''cause respect is overdue.' The money would help realise her dream. She would make Sister Anthea an offer for the lease of the Ebony salon. A safety net for the future. Tomorrow is promised to no one. When you think it's peace and safety, it could be sudden destruction.

Yes, she decided, revenge was sweet.

THREE

Half of Brixton knew that Max was back. You could see the guys on the corner, with their tongues dropping down to the ground when they heard the news. The reaction of their women was more like, "Why she never bother stay in Jamaica?" They knew that Max's return would up the stakes. They would have to work harder to find a man. Every man wanted their woman to look like Max. She was the measure for half of the women on the sunny side of the Thames.

Beverly got the news at the same time as the others. She recognised immediately the voice on the answering machine. "Hello Beverly. Yes, this is the Max, back from Jamaica and ready to roll. I'm calling the posse together. At Dunn's River. Tonight at eight. Try to reach!" Merlene and Andrea had received similar messages. It was just as well that Max's return had called the Four Musketeers together, because Beverly had some big news of her own to announce. It had been six months since she had seen any of the girls. Six months in which a lot had happened. She wouldn't normally dream of upstaging Max's return (she loved her soul sister too much for that). But for once, what Beverly had to say was as exciting as any new developments in Max's life.

Maxine Livingstone, was Merlene's younger sister. One of the most stunning girls South London had ever seen, she was five feet nine and carried it well. A stunner! She was also one of the posse's most lethal assets.

Since school days, Max, Andrea and Beverly had been the tightest of friends. Later, Merlene joined them to make up the foursome, even though she was five years older than the others. They were inseparable. They went out together, stayed in together and shared each other's innermost secrets. Their friendship had earned them the Four Musketeers nickname in their early raving days, when their appearance at any club or blues would turn women's heads, whilst the guys stood with their tongues hanging down to the ground. In their prime, the Four Musketeers were legal, crucial and bad like Rambo.

"Ooooohhhh Max!" Beverly screamed as she entered Dunn's River at eight-fifteen. Max jumped up, arms outstretched.

"Whoooaah Be-ver-lee!" she sang out. They paid each other

loud compliments.

"Girl, you look good...you look fresh," Beverly said, admiring Max's fit body. She was truly impressed. Max seemed to look better every time you saw her. "It look like Jamaica treat you good."

"How y'mean?" Max quipped. "In Jamaica the people dem love me, any which part me go. The men treated me real good. I was wining and dining every night. It's amazing that I never put on more than a couple of pounds."

Walking arm in arm towards the table at the back of the bar, where Andrea and Merlene were waiting, the two women continued to gossip in the mix of patois and cockney that was colloquial to everyone in south London, but which in north London is only mastered by younger Afro-Saxons.

Dunn's River was the classiest little bar in Brixton. A cross between a coffee bar and a wine bar, it had become *the* place to go to. It was a little expensive for the area, ensuring that the management didn't have to forcibly dissuade riff-raff from entering.

"Yes girl," Beverly continued, "you look stush! I can bet you knocked them out over there."

"Things have changed over there y'know. Jamaica the land of wood an' water *an'* man slaughter, is how dem call it now. Street life rough, because the yout' dem under pressure. Gun ting is a serious somet'ing over there. More time the yout' ain't joking, y'know. Especially when dem sniff dat white t'ing..." Max's gaze was downcast momentarily. However, she was not one to dwell too long on serious subjects.

"But the night life over there is firin', " she added quickly. "You won't believe what the girls look like over there and what they're wearing! They've all got big American sugar daddies and they dress to kill, in batty riders, short, short, *short*, micro-miniskirts....You wouldn't believe it! They've got it all hanging out over there."

Beverly smiled. "Max is back!" she said admiringly. "The return of the don*ess*. Original! Original! The foundation!" Max had the ability to brighten up the gloomiest day. She was really good value.

If any of the other members of the posse were jealous of Max's good looks, they never showed it. Max naturally attracted most of the men, but that didn't matter. Since schooldays, the others had used her to get whatever they wanted from men. They had encouraged her to get off with any man who came bearing gifts. At the same time, they had been right at her side when some jealous girlfriend had tried to come test her.

"Ah you dat Andrea?!"

A male voice came booming. Andrea spun her head around quickly. She didn't need to, she knew exactly who the voice belonged to. Donovan was one of her sweet boys. He approached the table, with his woman dangling tightly on his arm.

"Andrea, I called you 'nuff times already, man. I was going to come check you."

"Well, now you've seen me, what can I do for you?"

Donovan stared at her sheepishly. "Oh you nevah met my woman yet, did you?"

"No I don't believe I have," said Andrea politely, if somewhat disintrestedly. She stretched her hand out to the woman.

"The pleasure's all yours I'm sure," Fay hissed and kissed her teeth. "So....you know *my man*?"

Max was quick to sense the heat of the situation. She had seen too much of the world and had witnessed the subtle battles for supremacy, between two women, over one man so many times. She jumped to her friend's assistance by hugging the startled Donovan as tightly as she could. This gave Andrea the opportunity to game, set and match her rival, while Max gave the pleasantly surprised man, a quick feel up.

"Don't budda hug her too tight," Andrea addressed Donovan teasingly, yet seriously "Because you *know* you're a man dat don't know your own strength!" The tease was aimed at Donovan, though Andrea couldn't resist casting Fay a triumphant smile as she spoke.

"I know some women who wouldn't know what to do with that strength!" she concluded as she twisted the knife in some more.

Max released herself from Donovan's pawing grip and added purringly on behalf of her friend, "Well Andrea's certainly right, you are a man dat don't know your own strength...Hope to see you around sometime..."

Fay shot Andrea a glance that spelt murder. Donovan's woman knew, however, that there wasn't much she could do. She wasn't the sort of woman that would baulk at a public scrap with another woman. But Andrea was surrounded by her posse. Together, they could make mincemeat of Fay. Besides, Donovan had warned her about embarrassing him in public after the last time, when she was seen rolling in a fight for her man in the foyer of Elroy's, the popular night spot at Clapton Pond. No, this time a deadly look would suffice. Fay left things at that. She'd be in trouble if she tried to test Andrea.

The four girlfriends could barely refrain from bursting out with laughter as Fay and Donovan turned to leave, tails between their legs. This was the kind of biting verbal assault, they were so famous for inflicting in the old days. They had dispatched 'nuff potential threats in the same manner. Together, these sisters were tuff.

"So how long have you been dealing with Donovan?" Merlene asked mockingly.

"About three months!" Andrea's answer was swift and defensive. She would rather have dropped the subject, but her friends were intent on pursuing it.

"So the two of ouno is an *i-tem?*" Max asked.

"We *were* an item," was Andrea's cool reply. "He told me seh, him an' her done...."

"Is it serious?" Merlene enquired.

"Well, it was half-serious for me, but as you can see the man is on a leash. Chained to a man face-woman body. So me nah want him! He used to tell me how much he loved me and cared, and then all on a sudden, a next woman appears and him expect *me* to stand aside! If you run out, you mus' know you cannot come back in. From you is gone, a nex' man fe get the wedding ring. Man an' man ha' fe know, that ah we run this area!"

"They never know the use of a good thing, until they lose it," Merlene agreed solemnly. "When they've lost it. They feel it."

Andrea had become a hard woman. Starting up a hairdresser's salon in the middle of a recession wasn't easy, but she had managed, with Winston's money, to become one of the most successful hairdressers in south London. She created new styles every week, outdoing her competitors with her newly discerned, cut-throat business acumen. She built on the contacts she had to get in touch with several of the top celebrities. Soul crooner Kwame and supermodel sex kitten Pearl Jones were just two of the supes that had their locks washed and cut for free in return for their endorsement of Andrea's salon. It was a shrewd move. Once *The Voice* discovered where all the celebs went to get their roots seen to, the resulting feature brought in more customers than Andrea could handle. Every woman wanted their hair done, "just like Pearl's."

But success had brought with it a change of character. She wanted to make up for the seven lost years. All the things that she went without, all the hardships she suffered. She wanted to make amends and quickly. She was harder - not only in business, but also socially. In the six months since Andrea discovered Winston's double life she had cultivated a voracious sexual appetite, dating men who were only too willing to satisfy her needs. She would treat her men ruthlessly. She discovered what all women realise eventually - that their strongest power over men is *punanny* power. She could make men stand with their tongues dribbling, just by promising them some. She didn't really care if they belonged to some other woman or not. It wasn't her look out. She didn't tell any of the men to betray their women. That was their decision. She wasn't really out to take anybody's man, but men came on to her....and if they said they were single, then as far as she was concerned, they were single. She didn't have the time to sit, go back and cross reference or check. If the man says he's single, she accepts his word and plays by it, and that's cool by her. Andrea had become the kind of woman that men fear most, 'cause she was prepared to tek way your money, break your heart and leave you alone.

Andrea succeeded in turning some of her men into sex slaves. Those were the men she kept on longer than the usual one night stand. Donovan was such a one. He was so hooked on her, he'd jump up and down on his head if she asked him to. Andrea cast him a pitiful look as he left the bar. She knew that Donovan would now suffer the same fate as all the other ex-boyfriends, who had lied to her about their 'marital' status. She needn't waste time in confronting him, simply because that's the man's problem, not hers. He said he was single, she accepted it, and that was fine. But at the same time, she didn't have time for no *dibbi dibbi* man. She would not allow a repetition of the episode with Winston.

"Anyway, she keeps Donovan, he doesn't keep her," Andrea concluded, smiling mischievously. "So therefore, where do I fit in? An' you know seh I have expensive tastes!"

Beverly looked at her best friend confused. She couldn't understand her. Andrea had been fortunate enough to have a good man at home. But she didn't appreciate it at the time. Beverly was confident she wouldn't play away from home if she had a good man indoors.

It was barely six months since Andrea's man had died. Family and friends remarked with more than a hint of snide about Andrea's speedy adjustment to 'widowhood.' She wasn't married to Winston, but as good as. Everybody knew that their relationship was modern and everything, but nevertheless, people expected a decent period of mourning. Andrea's behaviour since the accident, was nothing short of scandalous. There had been several carryings-on. One man, after the next, each of them finding short shrift with Andrea's time, patience and tolerance.

"Andrea, when are you going to take somebody....you know,

decent?" Beverly sounded concerned, but the observation came with a sting in its tail.

Andrea turned to Beverly, breathing irony with every word, "Decent....? *Decent*....?! So this new man you have....him *decent*?"

"Yes he is!" Beverly answered sharply.

"Well if he's so decent, how come we haven't met him?" Andrea asked.

"Well, you are going to meet him...very soon," Beverly replied confidently, mysteriously and somewhat snobbishly. "In actual fact, I'm going to invite you all to the celebration of my wedding."

The three other women were momentarily stunned by Beverly's news. Maxine boxed over her drink, Merlene choked on hers, while Andrea simply sat with her mouth wide open.

"*Married*?.....You mean as...a piece of paper? Married?...As in church and pastor? Married?" a dazed Maxine asked, once she had caught her breath.

Beverly feigned surprise at her friends' reactions.

"What are you talking about? Why you so shocked? I've met somebody, me and him are a union....Therefore, we've decided to go in front of the pastor at the end of next month and get his blessing. Not everybody wants to live in sin!"

The other women weren't going to let her off the hook that easily. Andrea was first on the attack.

"Oooohhh, you're getting married?! Now that you have two children by two different man, you're going to find respectability and get married?!"

"How you can put it like that?!" Beverly retorted. "Anybody can have two children by two different man!"

"Exactly," Andrea was quick to reply. "Exactly!"

Maxine decided to step in quickly before things got out of hand.

"Putting aside all of that, the important question is...You love the man?"

"Of course I do!"

"What do you mean the important question....does she love him?" Andrea butted in. "The important question is does *he* love her? Never mind whether she loves him. Is not who you love, is who love *you!*"

Merlene had remained relatively quiet during the debate, thinking deeply, as the others wrestled with the subject. She couldn't help feeling jealous about Beverly's marriage news. Merlene and Winston had planned to get married once they got to the Caribbean. He had promised that they would. She had no reason to doubt his word. He had explained that he and Andrea had never married, because he knew deep down in his heart of hearts, that she was not the right woman. Not for him anyway. Merlene was that woman, however. They would marry and spend the rest of their lives together, on a small boat anchored in a tiny bay called Paradise. And they would start a new life, a new family. That was now never to be. Winston's car accident had put paid to that. Her possibilities had been shattered. All she was left with now was a heart that pined for a departed loved one and a £34,000 headache.

"How does he treat the kids?" Merlene asked finally.

"He's good with them," Beverly replied confidently, glad for the respite from the hostile questions. "He adores them, they adore him...."

"Well, if you love him and he loves you, then we back you. That's all there is," the older woman concluded. "We're your friends. We're happy if you're happy, and if you're happy, we'll back you to the hilt. There's no 'whys' or 'buts', we're there for you."

An impartial observer hearing Merlene's words would consider her a hypocrite. There was nothing she could do about that. What can you do when you fall in love with your best friend's man? It's easy to say you would never do it, but what do you do if it happens anyway? She had tried to deny her feelings for Winston when Andrea introduced them, early on in the couple's relationship. She had tried, but without success. Since then, every word she spoke to her friends had sounded deceitful. It didn't matter if they were talking about the most trivial matter, like the latest reggae dance craze; Merlene always felt she was being dishonest. How could she tell them what she had done? She was the eldest in the posse. The one that the others came to for advice and support. She was the moral conscience of the group. She just couldn't face the shame of telling them the truth. Had she been honest at the beginning, when her affair with Winston was little more than a fling, she might have had to endure Andrea's wrath, but it would have been a weight off her shoulders by now. The fact is, she wasn't honest then, and it was too late to come clean now. She didn't even have the bottle to tell Max, her own flesh and bones, Max regarded her elder sister with hallowed sentiments, veneration which Merlene was not prepared to see diminished.

Raising her glass to a toast, Merlene continued.

"I think we should celebrate the first marriage amongst our sisterhood. May I be the first to say, congratulations!"

Maxine and Andrea were quick to join in the toast, laughing and embracing Beverly, then each other. This was how it had always been between them. They may joke and joust in mock battle, but the bottom line was they would always rally to support each other. At least in the old days. It was five years since the posse's glory days. Five years in which each girl had grown into an individual woman.

"Listen," Merlene raised her glass once more, "I've known you from time, right....? An' the four of us, y'know we've been through some real trials and tribulations....So, I want to be the first to say I'm happy for you. I'm glad for you. I hope that this man gives you everything you want, everything you need, everything you deserve....And basically, we wish you all the luck. You deserve it after all this time. Let's hope that this is an omen for the rest of us. That we'll each find our knight in shining armour."

Andrea raised her glass adding: "Seriously, I just want to say, I agree with what Merlene says....But you just mek sure seh, you keep your eye on your man. I don't mean that funny, y'know? Know who you're dealing with. Beverly, just don't tek it the wrong way. You're dealing with life here and this is a reality nowadays. Start as you mean to go on. Don't let the man t'ink seh you is any door mat....Y'know?"

Beverly understood well what her friend was saying. Andrea more than anyone knew how little the domestic contract of marriage would mean to a restless man. She had notched up more than her fair share of other women's men, in a romantic history which read like a fearsome warning to women everywhere, never to trust your closest female confidante when your man is around. Beverly hadn't forgotten how Andrea had stolen the first boyfriend she ever had, all those years ago. But that wasn't important at the minute. Beverly was about to make the biggest decision in her life. The decision that would make her respectable.

She wanted a big wedding. "The social event of the year," she confided. "Everybody will be there. All three or four hundred at least."

"Personally I wouldn't have a large wedding," Andrea chirped. "When I get married, it's between me and my husband. I don't want to sleep with his family, and he don't want to sleep with my people dem. Anyway, it's always other people saying, 'yeah have a big wedding,' just so they can go there and work some science on you."

Some would say Beverly was acting recklessly, marrying her fiance after having known him for only a matter of months. At the same time, though she had two kids by two different men - both of whom it was revealed after her pregnancies, had fathered several children between them, all over north London. A woman with that extra baggage is always on the look out for a potential father to her kids. If she can find a worthwhile man, best she grab him quick.

Beverly had a good feeling about Thomas. She was prepared to rush into the marriage, because the man swore he would stay faithful and she wanted to believe him. She needed urgently to build a formal home for herself and her children. Her kids needed a father and for that, she needed a husband. Thomas treated her and the children well. But at the end of the day, man is dog. They only need one sniff and they're away. While they were simply dating, Beverly had been prepared to tolerate the odd infidelity, although as far as she knew, Thomas was totally faithful. She was however, not prepared to be made a laughing stock as a married woman. Thomas had pushed her to get married and he had sworn eternal faithfulness.

Beverly put an arm around Andrea, giving her a little squeeze.

"I understand....I understand. I'm not taking it the wrong way, and you're right...But I do know what I'm doing."

"Love is not to gamble and love is not to boast," Andrea continued. "If a loving dat you want, you know you don't have to marry. When you're independent, you have your own key. Nobody can tell you nut'n. Although me have my reservation about marriage, I support you same way. But remember two things. One, you mus' learn to satisfy....Right from the start. And you must always watch the woman that behind you....An' me nah tek back dem lyrics. 'Cause it's the original wickedness. Anywhere man go, gal pickney ha'fe follow! Yeah...!?"

"There's nothing much left for me to say," Maxine quipped, "other than to say, I'm looking forward to seeing this man...this Prince Charming who's going to make you Miss Respectable. Because we all know that's something you've wanted from time....After two children, you deserve this. My advice to you, is to remember that diamonds are a girls best friend. Talk don't mean a single thing....Put your glasses together again girls.

"Congratulations Beverly, we love you and you know seh we'll do anything for you. So, it's no big thing. We will be there at the wedding, cheering you on and rooting for you."

Beverly turned to Max, grateful for the nice words and the renewal of this friendship with her oldest and dearest friends.

"It's really good to see you again y'know. It's been a long time since I come out, because now I'm tied down with the kids, we don't get to go out so much."

"That's no problem," Max added quickly. She had already

worked things out in her head. Max more than any of the others had good reason to regret the demise of the posse as a social force. She had missed the old days, when they would go out together three or four times a week. That suited Max's lifestyle down to the bone. She was a good time party girl, who liked nothing better than to go out raving with her best friends. Beverly, Andrea and Max's older sister Merlene were truly her best friends. But they hadn't really raved together since back when. This was the first time the quartet had met up in the six months, since Beverly, Andrea and Merlene were brought together for Winston's funeral. The posse as such was now little more than a faded memory, from an adolescent dream. But that dream could easily be revived.

"Look, I know we've all moved our separate ways up to a point..." Max started, hatching a plan as she continued, "....An' because of work pressures and family pressures and other pressures, none of you three really has the time to meet up as regularly as we used to. But why don't we at least try and meet up once a month? We can meet up every month....In fact I t'ink seh this is what we should do! We should meet up every month, just to blow out the cobwebs and kick some dust off the heels. Y'know."

Andrea backed the suggestion immediately. She was now a free woman in several senses of the word and welcomed the revival of the old relationships with her soul sisters. Beverly and Merlene were reluctant to commit themselves to such an arrangement, citing various excuses. But it didn't take much coaxing from Max and Andrea to convince both women to acquiesce.

"It'll be just like the old days!" Andrea chirped.

The four women spent another three hours at the bar, drinking cocktails, and kicking up a storm as they steadily became tipsy.

"Big tings a gwaan for everybody else right now, but nut'n nah gwaan fe me," Merlene sulked half-seriously. "Andrea, you have your new hairdressing business, Max has got her sugar daddy and Beverly's getting married. I've got nothing like that in my life."

"Your time soon come," Andrea assured her. "Dis yah time is the black woman's time y'all! An' me nah go tek back dem chat!"

There was much gossip to be told and much fun to be had. For the first time in years, they played their own special brand of I-Spy, which they had devised as teenagers. Each in turn, would spot a guy in the bar, giving him marks out of ten in three categories: looks, style and manners. The other three girls would try to guess which of the men in the bar the marks related to. They played the game for a while, interrupted only by a momentary loss of concentration, every time new blood walked in, hungrily eyed up by the Four Musketeers.

It was past midnight when they left the bar, and the April showers were pouring down with a vengeance. Unlike men, women never stagger out of a bar. The four friends were all over the limit, but composed, not wanting to embarrass each other. Max decided to share a cab with the other women and return for her Beetle the next morning. The car, a jet-black, customised, convertible, was typical of Max. While other women were slaving hard to buy a Golf or an Escort, Max had to be different.

"That's a sweet car you've got there," Beverly complimented her.

"Yeah," Max answered. "You can buy it if you want. I'm getting ready to sell it. I want to get a Porsche next. You know, one of those really old ones from the fifties."

"Well....I do need some wheels," Beverly said, contemplating the offer. "How much are you asking for it?"

"We're sistren," Max replied. "Just let me know when you're ready and we'll reason."

Max looked fondly at the familiar sights of Brixton along the High Road, glad to be home amongst her friends. One by one the driver dropped them off at their respective homes, each woman promising to keep up the monthly night outs as they departed. They were all in high spirits, happy to have reaffirmed, the close ties that had previously bound them together.

FOUR

The reception hall was filled to the brim with wedding guests. From her seat at the top table surrounded by family and friends, Beverly looked around the hall proudly, pleased that so many well-wishers had shown up for her wedding. It was the happiest day of her life. The day she became 'respectable'. Thomas was now truly her man. Next morning her dream prince would be whisking her off to Gatwick Airport, where they would fly to a secret location. Thomas intended to surprise her. She wouldn't know where they were going until they collected their tickets at the airport. She was excited about the honeymoon, and equally so about their wedding night, which they were to spend at an expensive hotel in the West End. Thomas promised that, even though they had been living together for three months, it would be a night to remember. It would be like the first time, he vowed. A perfect, serene bride outwards, Beverly felt a tingle of anticipation in her womb as she thought about the first time she and Thomas had made love.

The bride met her groom through a telephone dating line, four months previous Before Levi (the father to her daughter Ashika) had gone AWOL, Beverly had spent her leisure time cooped up with her two kids, in her house down on the Camberwell end of Coldharbour Lane. Without realising it, she had let Levi turn her into an 'at home' person. He insisted that she stay in and look after the kids while he did his *runnins*. He very rarely took her out anywhere. Beverly literally went from being a raver one day, to being a working girl-housewife-mother the next. She didn't mind either. She was young and foolish, and thought that was what love was all about.

Thomas was a gift from Beverly's fairy godmother. Like Beverly, he was a *browning*. He was tall, handsome, and suave , with a touch of sophistication. He was however prone to being a flirt. But then she didn't know that at the time. Beverly wasn't looking to have her cake and eat it. She was looking for a man. Since Levi abandoned her, she had been through several relationships, which were all now dead stock. Thomas had arrived just as all looked lost. She would have given up on the male population entirely, if she hadn't found a decent man - preferably someone who would be good to the kids and treat her as a queen, but most importantly, a decent man.

Working nine to six at one of the top department stores on Oxford Street and then coming home to work as a mother, didn't leave much time to look for a man. Levi had tried to shatter her confidence, but failed. Beverly was confident of her ability to still go out raving and man hunting with the girls. She had good looks and an ability to pull a good-looker on the dancefloor. But because of her busy schedule, she had of late, taken the scientific route to finding a man, by meeting up with men through a telephone dating agency. A work colleague once slipped her a card advertising the services of the RSVP line and she was hooked soon after.

RSVP was the dating line most ambitious and career-minded black men and women used, not only to find romantic partners, but also to meet social and business contacts. "Every contact you'll ever need," Beverly read on the card. She decided to try it out because she needed some luck in her life and could do with the help. Later that night, she dialled the dateline number and listened to the messages. Telephone love, sounds so sweet on the line.

Thomas's message wasn't as slick as some of the others Beverly heard, but she felt his voice sounded sincere. There was something intriguing about a man who described himself as 'Good looking without the ego,' and 'looking for my soulful other half so that we can be joined together.'

Beverly took a deep breath as she cast her eye across the school hall. She wanted to laugh, cry or scream with joy. She didn't know which. This was the happiest day of her life. Thomas had come into her life at exactly the right time. He had given her that boost she so needed. She noticed her groom, now relaxed after the formal, almost sombre, church service, flirting with a couple of young women (dressed improperly in luminous green and pink dresses). Beverly didn't mind. Thomas was hers. They were now married. She felt that by marrying her, he had served notice to all other women, that he was now another woman's property. That didn't necessarily mean that he would never play away from home, but rather that all other women knew that he belonged to another woman. So they knew damn well, what they were getting themselves into. They couldn't complain afterwards if they got burned.

Dawn and Angie, the two flirty-flirty women, were friends Thomas had invited to the reception. They were old friends (meaning he had slept with them intermittently over the years).

They knew as much about his bachelor life as anyone. They weren't too concerned by his sudden conversion to marital vows. They knew he would still come by and spend the night whenever he felt like it. Had Beverly been sitting closer, she would have heard Angie urge Thomas to pay her a little visit.

"You know you're always welcome.....my door is always open to you, Thomas."

Beverly couldn't hear the words, but she saw the slimy smile of satisfaction, spread across Thomas' face when Angie whispered in his ear.

Anyone who had seen Thomas and Beverly on their first date, would have rated them as the perfect couple. After setting up the date on the phone line, Thomas had taken Beverly to Roscoe's, a trendy restaurant in downtown Brixton. Even though she went past it almost every day, Beverly had never actually been inside. It had opened up while she was doing her child-rearing at home. The restaurant, one of a group around London owned by the king of the buppies Russell Isaacs, followed the pattern of all buppie restaurants. They could rely on the odd black celebrity amongst their clientele and therefore, attracted buppie wannabes looking to brush shoulders with the likes of ex-soap star Candi Clarke and former world light-heavyweight champ, Lloyd Daley. Daley's bankrupt now, but in his heyday, boy, he could whip up a storm at Roscoe's.

Beverly couldn't help feeling important surrounded by the intellect and ambition so clearly apparent in the restaurant. Buppies were a recent phenomenon. They didn't even exist, when Beverly and her three Musketeer companions 'ruled' the streets of Brixton. "Oh, it's a nice place, isn't it?" she had remarked. "Do you come here often?"

"Yeah, it's just one of the places I pass through every now and again, y'know," Thomas lied. It was also his first time in Roscoe's. More at home in a pool hall than in an upmarket restaurant, Thomas had asked a classy friend where he should dine to impress a woman 'with high demands,' as Beverly had described herself during their first telephone conversation. He was well impressed when he set eyes on his blind date for the evening. The gyaal fit, he thought to himself.

"Baby, you better go and sort the pastor out. He's standing over the other side of the hall waiting for his tip." Beverly had decided to break up the mutual admiration club which had formed between her new husband and the ever-pouting, ever-flirting Angie and Dawn. The greedy look on Pastor Mason's face had been a perfect excuse. Thomas frowned as he turned and caught the pastor smiling in his direction.

"Yeah, you know seh Pastor Mason wants his pieces of silver," he answered sarcastically. He rustled in his pocket for some notes and swaggered over to the eager preacher. Beverly flashed Angie and Dawn that cold, knowing smile which spelled 'one-upmanship.' They returned the compliment and sauntered across the room to a group of Thomas' ragga-styled male friends, standing together in a cluster against the opposite wall. Beverly watched them closely. Some will eat with you and even drink with you, she thought, but behind your back they su-su about you. The two girls spoke to the young men, pointing derisively at the bride as they shared a joke with the guys. Beverly was intimidated, but kept her composure. Angie and Dawn were the competition. She knew that. Andrea had informed Beverly two weeks earlier, when she discovered from a reliable source that the two fresh girls had enjoyed relationships with her new husband. "An' me nevah hear yet that him finish with either!" the source had concluded.

Andrea dismissed Dawn as just a "fancy gyaal", but warned Beverly to watch out for Angie, who reputedly could win the heart of any man and was not a stranger to fighting in public over a man.

Beverly took a sip from her champagne glass, deep in thought. She tried to convince herself that she could handle any competition. She wasn't going to let some cheap whore be responsible for any misgivings she had about her husband. At the same time, she knew that no matter how much Thomas loved her, she didn't know if the man had yet been born who would turn up his nose if he's given a little sniff. She had lost her first real boyfriend to Andrea this way. Though she was only a teenager at the time, the memory still haunted her and deep inside she never forgave her friend for the hurt it caused. Since then, she had become possessive about her men, refusing to allow them the slightest possibility of a sniff. Like all men, Thomas's ego swelled any time a woman offered herself up to him. He couldn't turn it down. No, come Angie and Dawn or any other women as they may, Beverly told herself, she was ready for them. She didn't intend to give up her new husband without a fight.

"Mum!" Beverly heard Ashika call. "Mum, Ken keeps kicking me. Tell him mum, he just keeps kicking me for no reason."

Beverly turned towards her daughter who looked radiant but

distressed in her bridesmaid's outfit.

"Kenyatta! Just leave Ashika alone! Alright? Behave yourself! If I hear her crying once more, you'll have to answer."

"What did I do?" Beverly's son cried sulkily from across the table. "I didn't touch her. I didn't do nothing. Why do I always get the blame for everything?"

"Oh don't make out like you're innocent. This isn't the right time to be playing games. Just keep your feet to yourself, or you'll have me to deal with."

Still sulking, Kenyatta got up.

"I don't want to be at your stupid wedding anyway. I hate you! I hate you!"

He turned and walked away from the table.

"Kenyatta! Just turn back and sit down," Beverly commanded, but to no avail. The young boy was already halfway to the exit.

"I'll go and talk to him," Merlene offered, going after the kid.

As Beverly watched her son leave the hall, she wandered whether he would ever accept Thomas as his father. Ashika had readily embraced the idea of a replacement for her absent father. Her four-year-old mind no longer had any memories of Levi. As far as she was concerned Thomas was her father. But Kenyatta was two years older than his sister, and had become increasingly troublesome since Thomas moved in to their household. That wasn't through lack of trying on Thomas's part. He had bought the youngster gifts and had always made an effort to take him out. But apart from going to see Crystal Palace play on the odd Saturday afternoon, he seemed to be disinterested in anything Thomas did for him. Even that common ground vanished after Palace striker Egan Rowe, was transferred to Arsenal. Thomas's allegiance lay with the striker, while Kenyatta was a diehard Palace fan. Since then, Kenyatta's hostility towards Thomas had come out in the open.

"We got a different type of loving, girl. I don't want to let it go," Thomas had assured Beverly repeatedly. "I'm going to give my love to you and only you."

Before she was prepared to consider them as an item however, he had to convince her that even though he loved his car and his money and t'ing, he loved his browning above all else.

"The loving me have for you, no other can take," he assured her. Beverly didn't fall for it immediately, but how many female egos can withstand a barrage of sweet talk from a man?

"You I love and not another, you may change but I will nevah. You are my special lady...my special, special girl." He had gone on like this for weeks before she allowed him to sleep with her. Finally, she relented. She called him on the phone saying, "If you want me, then come and get me..."

Once they had decided to marry, Beverly's only concern was that if Thomas was playing away from home, she didn't want to be the last to know.

"I don't want to hear them whispering everywhere I go," she remarked. "I've got my pride."

"How could I be unfaithful, after all the things you have done for me?" Thomas had said.

A woman who has got two children sees things differently from a woman with only one child. The more kids you have, the bigger a deal it is to get married quickly. It's seen as a prestige thing. Women who get married quickly and then get divorced are looked upon better than those who just have many lovers.

Merlene returned, hugging Kenyatta. He was smart enough to avoid his mother's angry eyes which spelled 'fire'.

Beverly looked around the table at her closest friends Merlene, Andrea and Maxine. Really, they were in the same position as she was. None of them could be certain of their men. She hoped that marriage would make a difference, but deep down she knew... Marriage or no marriage, she couldn't be a hundred percent sure her man wouldn't play away from home. Though she felt sure she had chosen wisely.

Thomas returned to the family table slightly ruffled from his 'business trip' to Pastor Mason.

"I gave him ten pounds and he said, 'the usual is twenty'!" Thomas sounded annoyed. "He taxed me twenty pound! Cho!"

"Well he did do a good job at the church," Beverly replied, thinking Thomas was acting unnecessarily mean for a man on his wedding day.

"You look really beautiful," she whispered sweetly in his ear. I was so proud when I saw you waiting at the aisle this afternoon. I hope you've had lots of rest, 'cause tonight, I'm going to be at my best."

Out of the corner of her eye, Beverly could see the luminous electric-green of Angie's dress approaching their table again.

"Well big boy...." Angie spoke directly to Thomas, completely ignoring his bride. "I must leave now. I can't stay. You know I nevah eat food from strangers' kitchen. Here is your present!" She handed him a lightly wrapped parcel. "It's a

52

basket of your favourite toiletries - after shave and dem business. So....come up and see me any time." She planted a parting kiss squarely on Thomas's lips.

Angie intended Beverly to see and hear everything. Beverly was furious, but decided to keep her composure. She had hoped in vain that Thomas, would have made some effort to cut the slackness down. That he would at least defend her honour. But he didn't. He simply stood there, taking it all in and smiling that stupid, self-important smile, she had seen him smile so many times before. Angie had challenged her at her own wedding! She made a mental note to get even with that bitch one day.

Guests were still sauntering into the hall. The sound system boys were still humping their heavy speaker boxes on to the stage at one end of the hall. As sound boys always did at these functions, they felt that they were the highlight of the occasion, looking upon the wedding as a minor distraction.

"Pastor Mason...what a way dat man can deliver a wedding speech," said Mrs Henderson to nobody in particular. "It's the third wedding speech I've heard that man say, and I've not known him to go wrong. You can tell he is man of...*h*uplifting qualities....A man of standing in the community. A man to look up to."

"Mmmn-unh," agreed Mrs Brown. "It's true. You nevah speak a truer word. An' you could see how the young people dem were....were um....were dumbfounded," she said finally, struggling for her words.

Mrs Henderson looked at Mrs Brown, as if to say, '*dumbfounded?!*'

"Yes! You nevah hear that word before? You nevah know seh I could speak posh?" Mrs Brown added enthusiastically. "Yes, dumbfounded. You could see how the seriousness of the occasion rested on their shoulders."

Nobody at the reception cared for Mrs Brown's words. Even if they had heard them, they wouldn't have known what she meant. But it sounded good to Mrs Brown.

The two ladies were members of the pentecostal church which both Beverly's parents attended, her mother more diligently than the father. A group of a dozen or so older ladies from the church had got together to help organise the reception. Mrs Brown and Mrs Henderson would have continued their little banter all night long, if not for the rude interruption from one of their colleagues walking past with a tray piled high with food.

"While you're both sitting there commenting on Pastor Mason's sermon, I could comment say you're not doing nothing with your mouth, other than fe work it. Just get your bottom off the chair and help me with these trays!"

The reception was held at a local junior school a mile away from the church where the service had been held. Cars were parked tightly in what was normally the playground. Other cars were jammed together on the pavements around the school. There were at least 300 people at the reception and none of them had walked there. The reception was held in the assembly hall, which was able to accommodate everybody comfortably. There were people everywhere. Some standing around, some observing, some gathering in groups. Groups of men, groups of women. Some women with their children, some of them scolding those children. Girls oozing sex all over (some of them simply wanted sex, others used their sexuality in a way to entrap the men present, so that maybe, just maybe, one of them would utter those three magical words, "I love you." The women would then lead them by the scruff of the neck to the church, where there would be a big wedding, attended by hundreds of admiring friends and family). The sound system men were up on stage, assembling the hi-fi, carrying boxes, posing, strutting and checking out the women.

You could see that everybody had been barbered that morning. The women had all been to the hairdressers. Andrea only just managed to cope with the twenty or so women who had booked appointments that morning. It was the same every Saturday morning, because in the community, wedding season is all the year round. On Saturdays, some Brixton women had to go as far afield as Streatham and South Norwood to find a black hairdressers who would give them an appointment.

Stronger than the faint aroma of Caribbean cooking, was the smell of cigarette smoke and the heavy scent of expensive perfume. This is a wedding y'know. The attitude of most black people at weddings is that you can afford to splash out a bit. The alternative is to be a laughing stock.

Everybody dressed their best for weddings. Sometimes, people would spend hundreds of pounds just on clothes. Apart from anything else, you had to look your best because you might meet somebody.

At Beverly's wedding, there were women looking over their shoulders, checking there were no ladders in their stockings; making sure that their shoes were still shining and that their kids' noses were still clean.

Andrea and Merlene came respectable, the former in red and the latter in cream. They were hoping to attract maximum attention, but without upstaging Beverly the bride, who looked

like a five foot three earth angel behind the veil of a good size
ten lace white wedding dress with a long trail. Beverly looked
the business. At the front of her dress was a daring split, going
up to her knees. She wore dropped pearl earrings, which
matched her necklace. She had taken Andrea's advice and piled
her hair on top, giving her a much needed height increase - as
Thomas was a full twelve inches taller. Andrea was unable to
resist poodling about in Beverly's hair every chance she got. She
was constantly pulling out a comb from her handbag, to add the
finishing touches to the bride's hair. Beverly's mother had made
up a small bouquet which the bride wore pinned to her dress for
the finishing touch.

Everybody agreed that she was a beautiful bride. Some of the
older ladies could be heard muttering praises that she had
finally married. Merlene imagined throughout the church
ceremony that she was getting married to Winston, her 'ideal
man'. She thought about how they had first met, just after he
moved in with Andrea, and how they had taken time to know
each other, courting in the old-fashioned way. She thought about
their wedding and beyond. How, if he had lived, their first child
could have been born a year later.

"Ah two kids she have now by two different man," said Mrs
Brown.

"How the frock did look pretty," Sister Wright added.

Mrs Henderson cornered Beverly's mother and congratulated
her on the occasion.

"You know Betty, your daughter look real nice today,
y'know! I must say she look *real* nice! You must feel proud?"

Mrs Johnson turned to look at Beverly, realising that her
daughter was now a respectable married lady....What she had
always wanted.

"Yes I am proud," she replied turning to Mrs Henderson,
"but I have to say, it is all due to God's strength, why I'm here
to see my one daughter in her greatest moment of happiness."

Before Beverly's mum could wallow in her pride, Mrs Brown
interjected with a snide remark.

"It's a shame it couldn't work out even a lickle bit different,
you know," she said with a tone of insincere sympathy.

The remark hurt Beverly's mum. The fact that her daughter
had given birth to two children by two different men (neither of
whom she had married), had caused her great embarrassment in
her church circles. But she had accepted it nevertheless.
Determined not to allow Mrs Brown's comment to upset her, she
retorted, "Mmmn-humm! I know exactly what you mean. But
that is in the past and we are looking towards the future now.

And with God's blessing and my guidance she will be alright."

Beverly certainly looked stush. Though, they should have known that Max wouldn't dress appropriately for the occasion. No matter what the event, Max always dressed to suit her own moods. Once you've been in the spotlight, as Max had since she became a beauty in her teens, you still crave the attention even when you're way past your sell by date.

Wearing a short, short, *short* skirt with matching blouse and jacket and knee-length suede boots, Max seemed indifferent to the gasps and sniggers of the male guests. She wore a silver necklace, with a dazzling diamond teardrop centred on her cleavage. In her ears, were matching diamond teardrop studs.

At the head table were the immediate family and friends of the bride and bridegroom. Beverly's posse were naturally there as were her two kids. The bride's closest friends, Maxine, Merlene and Andrea were as good as family.

Beverly's father, sitting in the middle next to his daughter, was rapidly becoming drunk on his own lethal mixture of Jamaican rum laced with gin. On the other side of the bride, Thomas the bridegroom, had been watching the father casually.

"Go an' watch Beverly father. Go an' make sure seh him nah drink no more of that rum," he said nudging his best man. "Because once him taste the rum punch now, we're finished."

Thomas was the living black Adonis. A tall redskin man with an athletic physique, the gods had blessed him with more than his fair share of good looks which, complemented by a pinstripe moustache, made him irresistible. His near-perfect features were only marred, by an unfortunate scar under his left eye. But that didn't put the ladies off. He was too good-looking to be true. Moreover, he was a charmer. He dressed to kill and had a deep sexy voice, with which he could use one and two slick words to turn a girl's head. Even now as he leaned back relaxed in his chair with his loosened tie and the top button of his shirt undone, his pose was studied and worked out. No sheer accident.

Though he was born in England, Thomas preferred to chat in the yard style he had learned while schooling in Jamaica in his early teens. But more often than not, he switched at the drop of a hat, like all the rest of the Anglo-Jamaicans at the wedding, to a cockney/yardman mixture.

Red-skinned men are currently in vogue and Thomas had never been short of women, which is why his friends were surprised that this urban Casanova was willing to give it all up to marry this girl, Beverly. Why would a man who had women falling over him get married...? Right now, though, he was happy. Marriage gave him some kind of pride. For a long time, he had felt that there was something missing in his life. That something was a woman to call his wife. He felt like a man now, however. Marriage proved his manhood.

Beverly's father stood up to make the first speech, microphone in hand. Slightly light-headed from the rum-drinking, he was filled with deep, tender emotion for his daughter.

"I'm so glad to see so many of my friends, and my wife's friends here today, with my daughter and her friends, and her husband's friends."

It was the typical long-winded speech, going all around the houses to make a point. You could already see people rolling their eyes thinking 'here comes another daddy about to make a fool of himself.'

"I feel it's only fair to seh," Mr Johnson continued, "that I am very proud, very honoured, very....TOUCHED....yes, that's the word I'm looking for....TOUCHED!"

Thomas's best man whispered loudly enough for the people around him to hear.

"Yes, you look touched," he grumbled with reference to Mr Johnson's unsober condition. A ripple of laughter followed the outburst.

"Yes I am touched, by the overwhelming emotions of the day....I feel, as these two young people embark on married life, they must realise the seriousness of the situation. That when...."

Amongst the guests were some downright rude people. Mr Johnson must have heard quite clearly, the comment coming from one of the men and directed at him: "Tell the man to shut up!" But Johnson continued undaunted, with his wife punctuating his every word with a rejoicing, "Oh yes, oh yes!!" in acknowledgement.

"The seriousness of what you are about to go into," Johnson continued, "....Marriage is a very serious situation to get into...."

"You telling me boss!" came the disinterested cry from one of the hungry guests.

At this point Beverly's mother urged her husband to hurry up. Unruffled, Mr Johnson continued. This was his party and he was going to enjoy it and speak 'til he was done.

"Beverly is my last child, y'know....me lickle baby. And I feel happy to know that I can hand over the reign of responsibility to um....um....um....Terry....Terry, that's it! So I can hand over the reign of full responsibility, to my new son-in-law Terry...."

There was a sudden hush, followed by a great roar of laughter from the guests. Johnson's wife screamed hoarsely into his ear, "Thomas! The bwoy name Thomas! Your new son-in-law name Thomas!"

Realising his mistake Mr Johnson composed himself quickly, diffusing the situation, by laughing at his own mistake.

"Yes, yes! Ouno thought I was drunk, innit? Yes, yes....but I was only fooling you. I meant to say Thomas....my new son-in-law Thomas. Now, I would like all of you to join me in raising our....um....rum glass....glasses and give a cheer to Beverly and um...Thomas. Yes, I wish you all the very, very best, of the very best," he said, toasting and sitting down. He quickly got up again, and turned to Thomas adding seriously with more than a hint of a threat, "She's my lickle baby, and I'm putting her in your trust. So please tek care of her, or you'll have me to deal with!"

There was polite applause from the seated guests, some of whom couldn't resist adding their own little bit:

"The rum isn't even flowing strongly yet and the man drunk! It's a damn disgrace, enh? Why man mus' stay so?"

"Dem know seh that the man can't hold his drink, an' still dem let the rum talk fe him!"

"Typical innit? Typical!"

Some people just had to make their comments to downgrade the occasion. There are times when people do not think a wedding is a wedding, unless they can complain about something.

Mr Johnson passed the microphone to Thomas's best man. A long time spar of the bridegroom, Danny was Thomas's bosom buddy and by now he had gotten over the shock of losing his boyhood friend to a woman. Thomas had assured him that nothing much would change in their life style. That this was a marriage of convenience in a way. The woman had a nice house and Thomas needed a bit of respectability. Those words had a calming effect on Danny, who had at first been reluctant to play an active part in the wedding. Indeed, the pentecostal women had all remarked at the way he had organised his part efficiently.

Taking the microphone, Danny began to speak. Sheepishly at first, in a mix of cockney and patois.

"Well, I'd like to say to everybody that...um...Thomas is my mate. I've known him, y'know, we've been running around the streets from time. I just want to say to everybody that I never thought that this day would come," he said with a knowing wink for the benefit of those who knew Thomas from time. "Seriously....I'm just joking....seriously. When Thomas said, 'come and be my best man,' I had to say 'to who?' So, you ladies out there who've wanted Thomas....you can't have him. He's spoken for. And I as his spar, will defend him. And I will fight off any woman for you," he continued turning to Beverly. "So just to let you ladies know that Thomas is no longer available, but I am sure that I can fill all your requirements...." Danny sat down, passing the microphone to Thomas.

"Hello....I just want to say to everybody that I'm glad you came here today to celebrate the wedding of me and Beverly, who was my woman and is now my wife. I just want to let everybody know seh, I'm not doing this under no pressure, y'know. I'm doing this under my own steam, because I'm my own man, y'know. I've come to realise, that there are certain qualities I admire and want from a woman. And I've come to realise that Beverly is the woman who possesses those things."

The female section amongst the guests began to fire up in agreement with Thomas' tender words, expressing their approval with shouts of "gwaan!", "tell the people dem seh you love her! Just tell everybody seh you love her!!"

"Well, yeah I do..." said Thomas, in response. "I'll say this to all the men out there....I am not standing here under any pressure, I'm standing here by myself to honour my woman, right? 'Cause me an' her is one. We're a unit, we're a unified force. And if anybody wants to come and tear that force down, they'll have me to deal with. Beverly is the only woman that I want. No other woman out there can match her."

A stream of sunlight flooded in through the windows at the side of the auditorium. A dazzling flash of light resulted, as the sun exploded on an object in the auditorium. Thomas caught the dazzle in the corner of his eye. It made him squint momentarily. He lost concentration. Turning his head towards the light, his eyes locked on the sparkling diamond teardrop, dangling seductively on Max's chest and which now, with the aid of the afternoon sun, illuminated his thoughts. Every colour in the rainbow was filtered through the diamond, resulting in a sparkle of magnificent proportions. Thomas began to salivate, as his eyes followed Max's cleavage line. She observed him intensely, a mischievous twinkle in her eye. Their eyes met and locked. Only for a moment, but a moment was enough. Thomas thought he detected a half-smile in her eyes. His eyes half-smiled back. He knew she was a friend of Beverly's, but they hadn't yet been introduced. She was the sexiest girl he had ever laid eyes on.

Remembering himself, he began searching for words. Above all the group of beautiful women at the wedding reception, Maxine alone had the power to send a hunk of a man like Thomas gasping for air as he spoke. He couldn't help noticing that aura she had about her. Aura, or ambience....whichever. His voice wobbled as he spoke, and his words become slurred. He had a reputation for being flash with words, so he wanted his speech to get respect and charm everybody. He didn't want his guests going home and mocking the bridegroom's speech. But the more he struggled to find the right words, the more his voice quivered as his thoughts were distracted by the sexy black Cleopatra with 'wicked in bed' written all over her face. The guests, hanging on his every word with baited breath, realised something was up. But they didn't know what.

"I....I....thank you....all....thank you....I....I...." he stuttered. "Beverly is the woman I want....and adore....and....I....respect her...."

Realising that he was faltering, he adjusted his tie and excused himself.

"I must apologise....the rum's gone to my head....I am overwhelmed with emotion by the occasion. Sorry I sound a bit off, but that's how emotions get you, when you're feeling and talking about someone, straight from the bottom of your heart."

He was unwilling to meet Beverly's gaze as he spoke. She, knowing him, realised that something had disturbed him and knew that it wasn't what he had claimed it to be.

Max felt the intensity of the situation, and lowered her eyes. Still standing, Thomas had begun to look foolish, when Beverly saved him by standing up and taking hold of the microphone.

"I'm glad that all my friends and Thomas's friends are here today just to celebrate our union," Beverly interjected. "I can only echo what Thomas has said. For me personally, he's the man I've been looking for. He's my Prince Charming, my knight in shining armour." She looked in his dark eyes and smiled. This was indeed her Prince Charming. She didn't think of herself as his Cinderella, but rather a feline temptress who would this night, be engaged in passionate married love with her dream prince.

A sympathetic ripple could be heard amongst the women guests as they simultaneously whispered, "aaahhh ain't that sweet." Also audible were the cynical voices of some of the male guests who murmured, "ah nah rubbish, eenh!" One or bitchy females added their own comments by exchanging glances and skinning teeth as if to say, "what kind of foolishness is that..? Which prince? You see any man ride harmour? He ride 'ooman, he nah ride shining harmour!" The sound men, still setting up their system on stage, stopped and sniggered as Beverly spoke of her devotion for Thomas. With his back bent almost double as he heaved one half of a gigantic sound box, Slim the sound's main deejay, couldn't resist laying a wager with his partner.

"I bet you fifty pounds this wedding nah see out six months. I bet you fifty pounds it nah last. Mek me tell you now, you can mark it down, the wedding nah last!!" The pair were interrupted by one of the trusted ladies from the pentecostal church.

"Shhh!" she snapped. "If you don't want to say anything civil, you must leave the area!"

Still standing, and undeterred by the interruptions, Beverly continued.

"Yes, Thomas is my knight in shining armour and I know that he will treat me like he treats his mother...."

"Well I hope not," came a loud voice in the middle of the auditorium, "she don't want no baby!!"

The guests roared with laughter. Even Beverly's father joined in the merriment. Beverly got the joke, smiled and continued.

"I am happy that now...we can now go forward....that we're now respectable and that we're not now just living together. Because this means that Thomas has made a full commitment to me. He's telling all the world that he loves me. And I love him."

Again there are romantic gasps of 'aaahhh' from the sympathetic female guests. Beverly's mother took over the microphone as her daughter sat herself down.

"I would like to take this opportunity to thank everybody who has assisted my good self and my husband, in preparation of this wedding of my daughter Beverly and her new husband, Thomas. Please go ahead and enjoy yourself. Dinner is served!"

Barely had she uttered those last words, than there was a mad rush towards the long line of buffet tables along one side of the auditorium. But the bigger the wedding, the harder it is for you to see people ah *nyam-nyam*, as you're doing the speeches. Beverly had a big wedding. At big weddings, the queue for food could last hours. And it was first come first served. It was comical to see the free for all as the men, forgetting their manners, rushed to be at the front of the queue. The usual mutterings of, "Look how long you have to stand up and wait for food, y'know," and "Boy, me t'ink seh Beverly coulda organise t'ings a lickle bettah, y'know!" could be heard from the guests at the back of the queue.

The calypso smell of curried goat and fried fish wafted through the air as one by one the guests sat down, with plates piled high. Every aspect of the wedding feast, was chosen to put people in mind of the bride's Jamaican heritage. The hard dough bread known as 'duck bread' (because at weddings it's shaped as a duck), is staple diet at any Jamaican wedding. Beverly's mother had also added jerk chicken, white rice, tossed salad and watermelon. As the guests ate, the ladies from the church wandered between the tables, offering pieces of wedding cake.

Some of the men were reticent about eating too hard, because they didn't want to get any curry on their clothes. They would rather starve than dirty up their new shirt.

The sound system boys were ready to take over the reception. They didn't bother to hide their impatience as the guests dived into the feast before them. At such occasions, the sound system boys reluctantly left their ragga clothes at home, and dressed sheepishly in slacks, well-starched white shirts rolled up at the sleeves and fancy waistcoats, to blend in with the wedding atmosphere. Every few minutes one of them would disappear backstage and out the back entrance to charge up with a spliff. At a normal dance they might skin up right in front of the amplifier as they spun records. But wedding was formal. Beverly's parents, like most black parents, wouldn't appreciate the sweet aroma of sensimilla at their daughter's wedding. So the sound system boys congregated at the back of the building, smoking spliff with the other bad bwoys.

Beverly and Thomas took to the dancefloor alone for the first number. The sound system boys knew they would soon get to play their hardcore ragga music, so they settled with a popular lovers tune for the couple. *Here And Now* by Luther Vandross soon had the guests singing along, as the newly weds held each other tightly across the dancefloor:

"Here and now I promise to love faithfully
Here and now...."

Whistles and cheers followed the bass intro to the next lovers tune. Omar's *There's Nothing Like This*, had every man, woman and child who could walk joining Beverly and Thomas on the dancefloor. Once the floor was packed, the newlyweds were cajoled into dancing with each other's best friends.

"I can't let you dance with this gorgeous man all evening." Maxine interrupted the newlyweds. "Ease up nuh?" She playfully shoved Beverly out of the way and whined slowly with the bridegroom for the smoochy tune. Thomas' old school mate LaVern grabbed Beverly by the waist and shuffled smoochily away with her in the opposite direction.

A lazy soulful lovers rock tune followed. An otherwise tacky cover of an American soul hit, it was the perfect excuse to hold your dancing partner tight, without offending moral decency.

"Are you down with O.P.P.?" Thomas asked cautiously.

"What's O.P.P.?" Maxine enquired.

"Haven't you heard that tune....that rap tune, *O.P.P.?*"

"No."

"You nevah hear that tune....how it go?*You down with O.P.P.?*
Yeah you know me?"

"Oh that one....yeah I heard it so many times. But what does
it mean?" Maxine asked.

"Other People's Property!" Thomas replied hurriedly, still
unwilling to commit himself.

"Other People's Property?! Behave yourself Thomas. On your
wedding night and all!" Maxine laughed.

"O.P.P. don't have respect for wedding an' t'ing. It's the
cheating game. *You down with O.P.P. yeah you know me,*" Thomas
hummed the tune in Max's ear.

Maxine stared at him directly with a look of mock horror. She
admired his tall athletic physique and his hunky good looks.
Beverly had married a gorgeous guy. I could even fancy him
myself, she thought. Then she thought better of it, remembering
that this was Beverly's husband she found attractive.

She slapped his chest playfully. "I said behave yourself!"

The dancing was still going on six hours later when the
newlyweds sneaked off to their honeymoon suite at an
expensive hotel in the West End.

Beverly looked at Thomas and smiled. "Darling, close the
door. Turn down the lights. Come over here and squeeze me
tight. Give me what you gave me that first night."

Thomas staggered out of the bathroom, feeling the effects of
the rum he had drunk that day. From the vacant look in his eyes,
Beverly realised that her wedding night was not going to be the
most romantic night ever. He stumbled onto the bed and passed
out.

Thomas slept, snoring loudly. Beverly lay still but awake,
praying that now they were married, Thomas would continue
showing the warm, loving side he had previously always shown.
Tears welled up in her eyes. Thomas continued snoring.

FIVE

The two naked bodies lay sprawled out on the bed side by side, sweaty and exhausted after a seventy minute sex session. Maxine's eyes were open, staring almost lifelessly at the mirrored ceiling which reflected their contorted bodies, still tense after the climactic end to their physical passion. Her long and slender body, in colour the dark velvet of the midnight sky, contrasted against his light suntanned torso, like ebony and ivory. His eyes were closed, as men's are after an orgasm.

Andrew was Max's *boops*, her sugar daddy. He was a handsome, slim but muscular man in his early forties. Good looks and good manners. His courteous disposition, correct posture and received pronunciation had been learned at one of the country's top public schools, a million miles away from the Streatham comprehensive which Maxine left with an 'O' level in art.

Everybody teased her about having a lover nearly twice her age, but it didn't bother Max. Naked or clothed, Andrew looked good for his age the result of a daily workout. Max loved sex too much to pick up with any lazy body.

Max loved sex, but uncomplicated sex. She liked to be in total control of her own pleasure. It was pointless relying on a man for it. She was sure of that. Andrew was unlike most of the men she had met before, however. He put himself out to satisfy his woman. That was unusual. Even though you ultimately have to work at deriving your erotic pleasure yourself, it's a nice gesture when a man puts himself out.

For a moment, she let her mind wander to thoughts about the future. Would Andrew be part of that future? If so what role would he play? What role would she play? Though they had been together for three years they were only a couple, in the sense that they had good times together. Theirs was no ordinary relationship. There were no bad times. They met up only for the good times. It was either sex, or parties, or going out to dinner, going off on holiday together and having laughs together. They never really fought. Their relationship certainly never got violent. And there was never any need to break up. It was not so much a permanent relationship, more a permanently transitory relationship. For when she thought about it, she hardly knew him and though she was as open with him as was possible, she knew deep down that he really didn't understand where she was coming from.

They had met a few years previously, when Max had auditioned for a role in a television commercial Andrew directed for a well-known French perfume company. His jaw had dropped open, as she entered his studio dressed in little more than nothing and with an attitude that men will always interpret as horny.

He was besotted with her. But as hard as he tried the perfume company refused to use her for their television campaign, and chose another model. Andrew wasn't to be put off. He called her regularly and took her out for drinks away from the office. She was a bit hesitant at first, but she found him too charming and witty to resist. And he certainly knew how to make a girl feel good. After a long courtship, they finally consummated their relationship in a bout of frenzied intercourse in a bedroom, at a party Andrew had invited her to. It was nerve-racking. The party was at the house of one of Andrew's film business contacts, but neither he nor Max could resist the urge any longer. They excused themselves one after the other, as if they needed to use the bathroom, but quickly ran into the bedroom and jumped onto the bed.

"Quick, quick," he had whispered anxiously, "pull down your skirt....someone's coming....anyone could burst in...!!" It wasn't the greatest sexual experience, but the element of danger turned Max on. Their subsequent relationship was based on whatever turned her on.

What she didn't anticipate, was the possibility of being addicted to the luxurious lifestyle Andrew could offer. She had never known so much wealth and financial decadence. But it didn't take her long to get a taste for it. Now Max was so accustomed to the champagne lifestyle they enjoyed together, and she often wondered whether she could live without it. The big test for Max in their relationship, was to see if she could deal with it on a physical level, without taking her emotions in with her. When they first started dating, she planned to go in there, enjoy the ride and get out. Without anybody knowing about it. But six months down the road, she realised things could work out quite sweet. She liked him. She was attracted to him. And at the same time he was willing to splash out on her. Because he was white, she had initially held back her emotions. Had he been black she wouldn't have hesitated. For his part, he took his time when courting her. The beginning of the relationship was all the more intriguing for Max, because he took it slowly, instead of trying to get his leg over quickly. She did, however, realise that she was being moulded. He dropped subtle hints and gradually began to change her. He introduced her to a life she was unfamiliar with, took her to restaurants with four course meals, seven spoons this side and two spoons that side and expected her to leave some of her coarser street culture at home when they went out. Though her modelling career hadn't really taken off (besides cameos in Andrew's television shows), she no longer needed to work as a legal secretary if she didn't want to. The secretarial work, was how she made her living before she met Andrew. Now, she would temp for two or three days every month just to keep from being bored and to give herself some semblance of economic independence. In reality though, Andrew took care of her.

After three years, Andrew still felt a slight lack of confidence around Max. She wasn't to know, because he kept it all to himself, while outwardly displaying the over-confidence of an ex-public schoolboy. When they first met, he didn't believe that he stood a chance with her. That kind of attractive girl would never go for me, he thought. Since their relationship began his confidence in himself had grown tremendously. He had a guilt complex because if Max was a white girl, he would have probably set up home proper with her by now, or even asked her to marry him. But because of the high-powered position he was in, he couldn't go around with a black woman, not as his partner. He would lose big business if he was seen standing up there with a black woman on his arm as his legitimate partner. So he did the next best thing, by becoming her *boopsie* and setting her up in a luxury flat (Andrew had installed her on Brixton Water Lane, where the prettiest houses in Brixton are to be found), with jewellery and more than enough pocket money to satisfy her every whim. But this man did love her. For whatever reason. The curiosity that white men have about black women, was there initially, but that wasn't the main thing for him. His motivation in checking Max was that he saw it, he liked it and he started thinking, well, maybe they could pick up. It took a long time to get her, but it was worth it. Andrew fondly remembered the subtle dinners with Max and how he held back. It took about eight months, because for eight months Max was thinking, 'am I really prepared for this?'

Andrew came along and was willing to wait. Max had never had a man sit down and wait for her. No man had sat down and said, "mek me wait my eight months", while driving himself crazy trying to get this woman into position. Moreover, Andrew was experienced - 43 years old, yet physically fit.

Max knew exactly why she was allowing herself to be a kept woman. She loved that four-poster bed she slept in. She liked not having to struggle or worry about money when she went to market. She could go to market now, if she felt like it. The money she obtained from this guy enabled her to send regular money home to her mother in Jamaica. Max lied in letters home, saying she was now a big legal secretary in London and that the money she was sending, was just part of "the 'x' amount of money I can earn!" If she pulled out now, how would her mother survive? The thought of going back to her nine-to-five life, making ends meet on an average salary, was enough to remind Max that bread was tastier on the buttered side. Unless she could find somebody who could, physically and emotionally, tear everything out of her, she would stay with Andrew.

Their relationship could go on the way it was for a very long time. Max wasn't bothered. She would enjoy the ride while it lasted. In her own eyes, she was properly 'his girl'. His woman. She was more than a bit of fluff.

Suddenly, without warning, she found herself thinking of Thomas.

Most of Andrew's friends were visibly taken aback when they first met her. Max was dark-skinned, so they couldn't miss the fact that she was a black woman. She was also undeniably attractive. His friends knew they didn't stand a chance with her. Andrew enjoyed the fact, thinking to himself, 'yeah, you'd like to touch her, but you can't.'

On the matter of black guys trying to check his woman, Andrew was philosophical. "You can't offer her what I can offer. I've got the money, you haven't. I can open her eyes to a world you can't even imagine."

He wasn't streetwise. He didn't know street cred but, nevertheless, he managed to turn around a girl who any of those guys on the street would want. It was a power thing. Anywhere they went men ogled her. They could look but not touch her.

Things would have been a lot easier for the couple, had he been a black man and she a white woman. Some of the guys in the community weren't yet ready to deal with a black woman and a white man. What people thought didn't bother Max too tough. But Andrew, on the other hand, was always nervous and decided to keep a discreetly low profile whenever he drove to Max's plush apartment. It was alright going uptown together, but they rarely went out together in the community, at least not since a twelve inch machete was thrust in front of Andrew's face, on the corner of Atlantic Road and Coldharbour Lane, when the couple were out shopping together one Saturday afternoon.

As far as her crew was concerned, Andrea and Beverly were surprised that Max had allowed this 'old' man in as her sugar daddy. They had only met him twice - each time at a launch party that Max had invited them too. But they were like sisters. Whatever Max did was fine with them. They would back her to the hilt.

Merlene knew Andrew quite well. She understood why her sister was living as a kept woman. She had always encouraged her baby sister to continue in education. But more importantly, she had tried to instil in Max the need to jump at any opportunities she was granted in life. "Women don't get too many chances," she had often said. "Take what you can get and set yourself up with pride."

She could see how happy her sister was. Andrew wasn't roughing her up, he wasn't milking her dry and she seemed to be enjoying herself. Max had always had difficulties finding the right guy, because she wasn't meeting anybody who could match her. Merlene wanted more for her sister than she was able to attain for herself. The fact that Max wasn't a baby mother was down to her elder sister's influence. She took every opportunity to give Max a run down of the things in life she could forget about once she had kids.

"You've still got a lot of time to have kids," she assured her sister. "I should have waited as long as you and longer. Tek your time, sis."

Max had been doing a lot of thinking. In three years with Andrew, she had amassed over twenty grand in her personal savings account. That didn't include any of the jewellery that she had received from him - jewellery which, it was understood, she would not have to give back. Twenty grand! Twenty grand just sitting there!! Twenty grand! Any woman would be laughing if she knew there was that sort of cash just sitting there in her bank account. Twenty grand she didn't need to touch. Max was truly safe, by anybody's standard.

To her, the relationship with Andrew started out as a business thing. She had a lot of fun along the way, but it was first and foremost a business thing. She was discovering however, that the boundaries of the relationship had begun to be blurred. It wasn't just a cold, unemotional business deal anymore. She had begun to like him. She had begun to have feelings for him. That was something she wasn't too happy about. She didn't like that at all. She liked Andrew a lot, though love was not quite the right word. She simply didn't want to complicate things by falling in love with him.

There was the question of her future with Andrew. She didn't want to have kids with someone who was not prepared to marry her. Merlene had taught her well, so she wasn't about to be a baby mother for any and everybody. She had no intention of bearing a man's child on the same terms as her sister. She was always more than a bit careful when she slept with Andrew. There was no risk of any accidents happening.

Max could have been a younger version of Merlene, but different experiences gave the two sisters a different perspective. Merlene was serious, she had to be. She had been forced, because of their family's economic circumstances, to grow up fast, leave school in a hurry and had started a family while working to support a no-good baby father. Max's life on the other hand, had been a laugh a minute. She lived for the moment. Merlene had tried to mould Max into her own image, but the younger sister's experiences, in a world where fairy tales seemed to come true, gave her whole outlook a different slant.

Thinking about it, as she did this morning, Max didn't know much about Andrew. He seemed to have unlimited funds to provide for her. He had explained that, as well as his television producer's income, he had an allowance from a fund his grandparents had set up for him as a child. His parents were landowners out in the country. But Max had never met them. He had already cleared the air by saying that he didn't intend for her to meet them. Meeting his mother was a no-no. "She's a bit funny," he had explained, preferring not to expand on the matter.

Andrew awoke from his slumber to see Max's glittering eyes smiling down on him. He kissed her softly and casually looked at his watch.

"Listen," he said. "I'm away on business for a few days, so I've topped up your account. It's balanced now."

She looked at him smiling. He looked at her seriously.

"There seems to have been a very large purchase on the account...." He paused, looking at her intensely. Max averted his gaze.

"But that's cool," he continued, "as long as you don't keep going over the limit."

"Oh, I had some really major problems with the car," she lied, "and I had to take it to the garage. They did everything on it."

She didn't have to lie to him, but she preferred to not let him know her business too tough.

Max made him breakfast. Freshly squeezed orange juice.

"After all that exercise, you don't want to put it all back on again," she teased. Andrew's doeful expression persuaded the cook to relent. She tossed some eggs into a bowl and fried the most basic of pancakes, with a twist of lemon and some almonds on top.

Andrew got up to shower. From the kitchen, Max could hear the rush of water through the pipes and couldn't resist the welcoming sound. With one swift movement she removed the flimsy nightie from her body. Dumping it on the ground, she joined Andrew in the shower, a mischievous twinkle in her eye. He smiled, caressing her ample but firm breasts, with their bullet-size nipples standing to attention, revived by the morning shower.

With what they were doing in the shower, they couldn't have hoped to hear the phone as it rang on the bedside table. Half an hour later when they both emerged, still steaming from the shower, the flashing the red light on the answering machine brought their impassioned antics to an end.

"Max, Andrea here," came the tape recorded message. "Do you still want that appointment later on this afternoon? 'Cause if you do, I'll stay in to do your hair personally. But if you don't, I'll go home early. Call me at the salon."

Max observed Andrew closely as he got up to wash the dishes. She admired his tennis-trained physique thinking, "Mmm, his bottom is still tight, his legs are still firm." But again, without warning, she found her thoughts drifting to Thomas.

"You seem a bit distant," Andrew offered. "Your mind's not all there.....Do you need a bit more playing money?"

Max shook her head. "No, no. I've got enough." Then she changed her mind. "Well, I actually need about £100 extra a week. I was thinking of finding more temping work," she lied, knowing that it hurt him to think of her slaving in an office for pin money.

Andrew looked at her hard, wondering what she had on her mind. He had known her long enough to sense when something was troubling her. He suggested having her nails done.

"Take some time out at the health farm, you might feel a bit better." He added that it might do her some good, as she seemed to be putting on a bit of weight.

The comment irritated Max. She felt it lacked tact.

"Some individuals on the set.....," Andrew began, ".....there's too much time wasting and all that. I don't want it! The guys are acting so unprofessional. Coming on the set late and all that....They keep mucking me up, with no respect for my time!"

Andrew often talked to Max about his business. He came into regular contact with black people on a work level, as his company had earned a fortune producing programmes with and for the black community. Having Max's insight was a great asset for him.

Max looked at him frustrated.

"Set the time! Tell them if they don't like it, they can get get out!"

She sat down beside him, filling Andrew's glass once again with orange juice. She snuggled up close against him, nestling her head on his chest.

"So apart from the problems with the artists, is everything else alright?"

"Yes," he replied. "I think I need to take a break from all that though. Get away from everything."

"Well, I'm ready when you are," Max offered.

Andrew paused. It would be a good idea. But it was one thing wanting to take a break and it was another thing actually finding time to do it. His relationship with Max had to revolve around his job. He was the breadwinner. As much as he wanted to spend all his time with her, he found that his social life was increasingly at a premium.

Looking at his watch, Andrew realised he would be late for work. It was already ten-fifteen. He dressed quickly and rushed out the door.

Alone, Max's thoughts flashed back to Beverly's wedding. It was a grand affair. She thought, that's the way to get married. If you're going to do it, do it in style. She thought of Beverly and Thomas on honeymoon together, locked in a hotel room, with a 'do not disturb' sign on the door. Max envied Beverly for having found a soul mate. Even if he was rather naughty, he was still Beverly's soul mate. Andrew would never do for her what Thomas was doing for Beverly.

Back from her wishful thinking, Max phoned Andrea to make an appointment to have her hair done later that afternoon.

"Andrea's popped out for a minute....Can I do something for you?" The voice of a bored teenager came down the phone line.

"I'm Andrea's friend, Maxine. I want you to book an appointment for later on this afternoon."

The feisty girl at the end of the line didn't know Max and simply replied, "Sorry, we haven't got any appointments spare."

"Look, just book me in!" Max spat the words out.

She slammed the phone down and slipped a tight fitting lurex jumpsuit over her naked body before calling a cab.

SIX

Merlene awoke in a cold sweat. It was day, but her dreams were like a nightmare. It was always the same dream, detailed and concise. She would find love on a one way street, but lose it on a highway, alone and abandoned on the hard shoulder with fast, powerful cars zipping past her.

She found his charm irresistible. He was a *maaga* man (*maaga* mean *maaga*, it nah mean slim), with sweet words and even sweeter moves. She was flattered that he had picked her over all the other girls. There were some good times. Times that felt better than anything she had ever felt before. Michael had made her feel like a queen. She was his queen, he was her king.

In the beginning of the relationship they romanced like a honeymoon. He was the attentive lover who couldn't do enough for her. They would cook and eat dinner together lovingly, then share a night of passion. He'd sweet her so much, she didn't want anybody else. After that they were like strangers.

Merlene soon witnessed all the little things about him that added up to flaws in his character. On their own, these things didn't mean much. Put together, they formed a picture of a man who was an incessant liar, a cheat. A man who was vain, conceited and at the very least, irresponsible. He never took responsibility for his failings and when confronted with them would invariably back up against a wall and lash out violently. Her battered and bruised body was testament to that. She became a regular visitor to the casualty department at the local hospital, once spending three days in intensive care.

She always took him back. When the police came to make their report, she would lie and say she fell down the stairs. She never understood why. It didn't make any sense. Meanwhile her inner voice would echo from the land of reality, shouting, "the moment a man raises his hand against you, walk out!"

Merlene reclined on the leather settee, sweat dripping from her forehead. She had lain down hoping against hope, that she could think her way to purity. There had to be a way.

She had thrown her morals out the window in the last six months, in an attempt to stave off the alternative nightmare of a prison cell. She always imagined the same empty, cold, dirty cell. She dreaded the lack of privacy. She was ashamed of what she had become but now understood the meaning of survival.

She felt so weary, she didn't bother to move when she heard Marlon's key turning in the front door. Neither did she respond to his call of "mum!" After a moments silence, her son poked his head around the living room door, and greeted her.

"I was calling you, mum, and you didn't even answer me!" he sulked.

Merlene grunted. This was not the time for a toe-to-toe with her young son. He was going through puberty. That's bad enough for a mother at the best of times. Marlon entered the room, stepping aside to reveal a pretty young girl of roughly his age standing behind him. Merlene looked at the young girl disinterestedly. At Marlon's age, it was good to be seen with an attractive young girl. Or be seen to have a girlfriend. This was the third girl Marlon had brought home this school term.

"Mum, can I go upstairs with Melissa? We've got something to talk about."

Merlene would normally have said it was alright. But something stopped her. Something....something about the young girl that seemed vaguely familiar.

"Why do you have to go upstairs?" Merlene barked irritated.

Marlon looked hurt. He couldn't understand why his mother was being so difficult and asked whether something was wrong.

"Why you ask me if something's wrong? I can ask anything about any young girl you bring through the door. I do not have to justify myself to you." Then she relented. "I'm going to see to the dinner," she concluded as she stood up, "so do feel free to discuss, whatever you have to discuss, in this living room."

Merlene gone, Melissa looked at Marlon and asked whether she should come a different day, rather than upset his mother. She was a sweet girl.

They were classmates, at the secondary school they both attended in Kennington. They had gone to the pictures with each other a couple of times, where they sat in the back rows learning to neck and French kiss, so that they could return to school and lecture their respective friends on how to do it.

Marlon couldn't believe that his mum was suspicious about the two of them going up to his bedroom. They really were only going to talk. If they had anything more 'interesting' to do, they had enough opportunities to do it elsewhere.

A stream of tears poured out of Merlene's eyes as she chopped the onions. She was filled with fear. She could hardly concentrate on the dinner. Everything she had worked for was falling apart. She needed desperately to hold it together, especially for Marlon.

Her mind drifted back to the missing money. She hadn't gone fifteen minutes in the last six months without thinking about it. This was the kind of thing that happened to other people, not to her. She now realised she should never have let Winston talk her into stealing the money. The temptation had been too great. It had proved so very easy to move the money around, awarding college grants to fictitious students.

Winston had a sweet way with words that some would call 'persuasive'. He could have got her to do anything for him. It could have worked. Now that Winston was dead and the money gone, she was headed for disaster.

"Mum!" Marlon's voice startled her. "I'm going to walk Melissa home. I'll have my dinner later."

"Okay, okay, whatever!" Merlene just wanted to be left alone. "I've got to work tonight, so you'll find your dinner in the oven when you get back. And don't stay up too late!"

She kissed her son hurriedly on the forehead.

"Thank you Miss Livingstone," Melissa murmured.

Merlene turned to face the girl. Yes, Marlon had chosen well. There was no doubt about it, the girl was pretty, she could see the attraction for a young boy.

"Oh, yes....I hope you come again. Yes come and have a chat when I.m not busy," Merlene offered. She couldn't put her finger on the button, but there was something about this girl....

Melissa cast Marlon a coy glance. You could see in her eyes that Merlene's young son was stirring her feelings.

"I hope so too," she smiled. The smile lingered long enough to torment Merlene. Why did that innocent smile torment her so?

Merlene emerged from the subterranean twilight zone of Piccadilly Circus tube station and walked aggressively towards the neon haze of Soho. After a short walk up Shaftesbury Avenue, past the kerb artists turning out portraits of tourists by the truckload, she took a left turn into a seedy narrow street. She stopped at the gate to a basement club. The flashing neon lights above the entrance displayed the words The Bowler Hat Club.

This was London. Sex City, UK. Soho, the sex capital of London. A billion pounds a year changed hands here, just for a little pussy. With a bit of luck, a girl who's prepared to spread her legs a little, can get a raise and walk away after a couple of years with a nice little bundle. Some girls have all the luck and some girls have none.

"Hello Sugar love," the cashier greeted Merlene as she wandered through the reception area.

"Y'alright Venus?" Merlene answered.

"Can't complain," Venus shouted after her. Ozzie, the club's burly bouncer, nodded casually as Merlene swaggered past. She returned the gesture and made her way to the tiny office behind the bar, which doubled as a changing room for the girls.

The Bowler Hat Club was ostensibly a gentleman's club. In fact it provided a discreet atmosphere for gentlemen with lots of money to entertain ever-willing young ladies. In short it provided everything that real gentlemen's clubs didn't.

It was a scam. The 'hostesses' would pester the wallet-packing punter to buy them drinks ("Oh, I only drink champagne, dear!"). The bubbly cost the club a fiver a bottle, but they resold it at £80, of which the "hostess" would get twenty percent. A girl could make a hundred quid a night. The real money however, was made providing 'extras' for the generous male 'guests' at a hotel nearby. The hotel concierge, who got tipped on a weekly basis, was always willing to turn a blind eye.

The Bowler Hat was popular, particularly amongst Arabs and Japanese businessmen, who were given 'free' membership to the club by taxi drivers retained by the club on a permanent basis.

It had happened a few weeks after Winston's funeral. Merlene had found a letter from Fitzroy waiting for her when she arrived home one evening. She was only mildly surprised to read that he was in prison on remand, following a gun incident at a night club. Fitzroy ordered her to make her way up Brixton Hill to pay him a little visit. The threatening tone of the letter sent Merlene into a panic. It was quite plain that he was blackmailing her with his knowledge of her misdeeds. She didn't waste any time in making arrangements for the visit. He was a desperate man, and there was no telling what he was capable of doing with the information about the skank she had pulled.

It was the first time Merlene had been inside a prison. She had known people who had spent time within its walls, but she had never had the courage to go inside. Bad news carries fast in Brixton. As a precaution against bumping into any of her fellow visitors who might recognize her and carry word back ah street, Merlene had disguised herself in blue jeans, a black leather jacket, dark sunglasses and a baseball cap.

Her dread of prison was confirmed once she sat inside the large visiting room, alongside the other relatives, girlfriends and a few screaming babies. As the inmates filed in one by one to greet their visitors, she saw the pain in the eyes of each one of them. Their manhood now taken away from them, the mostly black inmates were only a shadow of the usual swaggering personas who liked to hang out on street corners.

"Y'alright, Merle?" Fitzroy asked her, when they finally located one another.

"Well, you should know," she barked sharply. "You're the one who sent the letter. You're the one trying to blackmail me. You must know how I'm feeling."

Fitzroy simply smiled. He hadn't expected Merlene to take his thinly veiled threats lightly. He viewed her as a snob, who felt her pride had been dented by his written warning. He was a prisoner, who didn't have much to lose.

"Yeah, well...," he grunted. "You know how long me sit an' wait for my court date? I can't take it any longer. I want to spend Christmas with my woman and the pickney dem." He told her his story about the incident at Concrete Jungle.

"Well, I don't see what that's got to do with me," Merlene interrupted. "Why don't you get to the point. Why have you called me up here? What do you want from me?"

The inmate looked at her hard, taking a long deliberate drag from a cigarette.

"You evah find that money?"

"No Fitzroy. You can forget the money. It's disappeared, and I've still got to find some money to replace it."

"Well, now you have to find money to get me out of here."

Merlene's face turned to stone. She had been expecting something like this, but the shock was still too much.

"I don't have any money, Fitzroy!" The words came out slowly and deliberately. "For the last time, I don't have any money. If I did, I would be getting myself out my problem."

"Your problem is your problem," Fitzroy interjected. "And my problem is your problem. £10,000 for my bail money, or I talk to somebody. You lucky it's not more. If I had bullets in the gun it would be more. Remember, before Christmas or else!"

He got up to go, but Merlene raised a hand to stop him.

"Look Fitzroy," she implored. "I would do anything to help you, I would do anything to stop you saying something. But what can I do Fitzroy, what can I do. I haven't got any money."

Fitzroy stood for a moment, rubbing his chin and thinking to himself.

"Well, I have a fren....," he began. "He can help you. He has a little runnins, y'know. I know he's always lookin' for people and he pays well. Go an' check him."

"Fitzroy, I'm not interested in any illegal runnins, y'hear?"

Fitzroy smiled. He knew she was going to do it. He had been in similar positions himself. He knew that she didn't have much choice but to check Barrington. All she had to do was show up and Barrington would personally sort out his bail money.

"Don't worry," he assured her. "Barrington's safe, y'know. Him legally legal."

He told Merlene how to get hold of Barrington and got up to leave.

"If you see Rosie, my baby mudda, tell her I hope she's taking care of the children," Fitzroy concluded, "....an' tell me idren up a street that I soon step forward again. And hail up Michael for me!"

Merlene was damned if she was going to extend his greetings to her ex.

The next two weeks were tense ones for Merlene. Bereaved, dispossessed, and in peril of her freedom, she suffered extreme disorientation and teetered precariously on the very edge of mental collapse. When you endure misfortune, you reveal your true self. Every moment Merlene spent at work was spent in terror. She feared that the auditors would arrive unexpectedly at any minute and the game would be up. Every moment she spent at home was spent with the torment of seeing herself stoop so low. She suspected Andrea had found the £34,000, but her immediate concern was now to find the £10,000 to cover Fitzroy's bail money. She had bumped into his woman, Rosie, in the part of the market down by Brixton Rec. Rosie had passed on a message from Fitzroy.

"Fitzroy tells me that you're going to put up his bail money for him," Rosie had said enquiringly.

"Oh well, I don't know...," Merlene began.

"Why would you do that for him, enh?" Rosie asked. "What have you and Fitzroy got to do with each other?"

"Nothing, really. Look, Rosie, he's just an old friend. I never said that I would put up his bail money, but if I can get it I will help him out."

"Well, he says you've only got four weeks to Christmas."

After that meeting, she had written an urgent letter to him stressing that she had tried everything but she couldn't get the money together. Fitzroy wrote back with vaguely disguised threats. *"Barrington will borrow you the money. If you go and see him, no distress will come,"* the letter had concluded ominously.

Since Winston's death, she had been playing the pools in hopeless desperation while her mind played tricks on her. When she least needed to be reminded of the shame of being caught with her hand in the till, she kept getting flashbacks from the time Sonia, a second cousin, had been caught bringing half a kilo of cocaine through Gatwick Airport. They had sentenced her to eight years in jail! Merlene remembered vividly, how the whole family had felt disgraced, and how Sonia's two kids had been passed from one reluctant member of the extended family to another, in a desperate attempt to keep them out of care. Marlon was better off in care than with his father, Merlene concluded, but she had to avoid either option.

Had Max been around, it would have been no problem. Merlene knew that her sister could have lent her the cash. But Max was still in Jamaica. Andrea was the only other person Merlene knew of who had that kind of money. She couldn't ask her to lend the money, without explaining how she knew about it. Her relationship with Winston had to be kept a secret at all costs. She had already lost her lover, she didn't need to lose her friend in the bargain.

On this particular evening, Merlene would rather not have been sitting with Mr Akiri, the Japanese businessman who was now ordering his fifth bottle of champagne.

"You show me good time after," he insisted, raising his glass for another toast.

Merlene smiled and promised that she would, but her mother's instinct kept sounding its alarm. She didn't know why she couldn't stop worrying about Marlon.

On entering the club earlier, Merlene had changed into a tight rubber dress, black fishnet and black stilletoes, and a long, straight black wig that were the trademark of her alter-ego, Sugar Brown. Merlene had invented the elegant, slinky character of Sugar Brown as a way of dealing with her moral objections to the type of night job she was doing. As Sugar Brown, she could swallow the shame of it all, by wearing a long, peroxide-blonde wig and red stilettoes. Sugar Brown was a totally different person from Merlene Livingstone. The customers loved it, and what's more it was a good disguise. Just in case.... Fortunately for Merlene, most Brixtonites preferred to stay south of the river during the weekdays (raving up west was strictly a weekend thing). As Sugar only went to play on Mondays to Thursdays, there was little chance of bumping into someone who recognised her.

Merlene's work colleagues had noticed the change in her. She had started coming to work with dark shadows under her eyes and would often nod off during office hours. But nobody could explain how this previously diligent bookkeeper had become so shoddy and slack. Her boss had called her in a couple of times and given her official warnings for coming in late and dozing on the job. But everybody knew that council employees never got sacked. Merlene gave an excuse about going through some heavy domestic scene. Six months later, the excuse was wearing thin.

By now, Mr Akiri was more than merry. He had thrown off his jacket, pocketed his spectacles and loosened his tie. With sweat pouring from his forehead, he was determined to have fun. He only needed half an opportunity to break into an off-key karaoke. Beverly did her best to smile and pretend to have fun. She hated working there, but she had no choice. She had to pay Barrington back the money and this was the best way to do it.

"I tell you something," Akiri began. "In Osaka, I have a very big house. You must come to Osaka and be my guest."

"What about your wife?" Merlene asked half-teasingly.

"Oh, you know, Japanese wife is very obedient. She do what I say. My wife is very good Japanese woman."

"Well, if you want me to come to Osaka, you'll have to buy me another bottle of champagne." Merlene purred.

"No, no more champagne!" Akiri suddenly turned angry. "I drink too much champagne already. Now, you show me good time!"

"Look, relax man. No need to get uptight. Of course I'll show you a good time. But sightseeing is extra. It'll cost you £50."

"Ahhh money is no problem," Akiri hissed dismissively. "In Osaka, I own big factory."

Merlene asked Ozzie to call a mini cab and started getting her things together. She pushed her day clothes into her handbag and got Venus to sign £80 to her credit. She was £80 closer to getting Barrington off her back, she thought. Not bad for a couple of hours work. And it was early yet. There was another fifty quid coming in before the night was through.

Outside, Akiri held the mini cab door open as Merlene jumped in. The night had turned chilly, and few but the most ardent prowlers were walking along the narrow street. Merlene took a drag of her cigarette and looked around as tourists, kerbcrawlers and idlers passed around her.

"Just drive us around for an hour," Merlene directed the mini cab driver. "We want to do all the sights, London by night. Buckingham Palace, Trafalgar Square, Houses of Parliament. Everything."

The cab driver nodded, casually eyeing Merlene's nervous and heavily painted face, in his rear view mirror. He was used to shunting whores around town with their gullible punters.

The driver pushed the gears into drive and screeched away heading south. They passed prostitutes and the seedy signs of sex shops in Soho, in the direction of the the Statue of Eros, with the bright lights of Piccadilly Circus' Coca-Cola sign high up on their left. At Trafalgar Square, Merlene pointed out Nelson's Column, for Akiri's benefit. He craned his neck to see the figure at the top, all the time remarking "ah so!" in wonder.

The Houses of Parliament, Westminster Abbey. West towards Buckingham Palace, then back east again, over to St Paul's Cathedral, the Tower of London and Tower Bridge. Merlene glanced repeatedly at her watch, puffing anxiously away at her cigarette. Finally the hour was up and the cab driver was instructed to head towards Akiri's Hotel on Piccadilly.

Akiri pulled out his wallet.

"Oh, I have only £20 left!" he cried out in dismay.

Merlene gritted her teeth. She was tired and couldn't wait to get home.

"It's alright, Akiri continued. I have more money in the hotel. You come."

Merlene cursed under her breath. "Why you nevah come out with enough money?"

"I use credit cards everywhere!" Akiri protested.

Merlene cursed again. "Alright!" she said reluctantly. "Pay the man. I'll get out with you."

The cab driver took the £20 note and said they were evens. As Merlene and her companion climbed out of the car, the driver called out:

"Merlene! Ah you dat?"

The South London patois of the young Anglo-Jamaican, hit Merlene like a bullet through the heart. She stopped dead in her tracks and turned slowly. She looked hard at the driver, narrowing her eyes to focus. The face looked vaguely familiar, but she didn't recognise him.

"It's me, Tony. You know, Pat's brother."

"Pat!" Merlene exclaimed jumping back. It hadn't twigged before, but now there seemed little doubt. Melissa's smile, the dimples on her cheek, it reminded her of Pat! Pat, was one of Michael's many baby mothers.

Merlene paced up and down impatiently, casting her gaze from the window to her watch and back to the window. Each glance was followed by a scowl as she kissed her teeth. Typical, she thought. You tell Michael to come at a certain time and you can guarantee that he's not going to show up until he's good and ready - if he shows up at all! The man's forty years old and still can't keep an appointment!

'Cause long time she deh and ah sit down steady. This wasn't the first time she had waited on Marlon's father, Michael. Their relationship had been one big long wait for something that never happened. She had given up on him since they split up, and very rarely waited more than a few minutes. Sometimes however, there were domestic issues to deal with, issues which he knew were too important for her not to wait. For all she knew, he was late on purpose, because he knew that she had no real choice but to pace up and down.

Pacing up and down in the tiny living room was tiresome. There wasn't really room to swing a cat, between the three piece suite, the stereo, the huge colour television and the drinks cabinet. Two paces this way and two paces that way. She eventually sat down. Standing increased her tension. She had a fever and fresh cold, from so much tears on her pillow. Tears like a flowing river....

Her stomach was tight and getting tighter, she was angry. Here she was, eight years out of a relationship with the guy, and he could still determine how she used the little free time she had available. She really didn't have time for this. Not this time. She had things on her mind. Waiting 'pon some man just didn't figure in the scheme of things.

Easing back into the armchair, she recalled the relationship with Michael. She thought back, wondering whether the position they were now in - the animosity, the anger and the contention that was there - could actually have been avoided. She had loved him at one time. That fact was irrefutable.

When they first met, she was convinced that it was the big one. That Michael was the man she wanted to spend the rest of her life with. But then along came the bad times.

The things you said you loved, you're gonna lose. Michael showed very early on that he had a short temper and an almost cruel streak (although obviously, he would have denied it). Looking back on the relationship, she couldn't actually remember too many good times after the first couple of months.

After the first two months, Merlene and Michael never did anything together as a pair. He didn't take her out, he didn't even remember her birthday.

Yes, in the beginning he was good to her. But Michael was not unlike a certain type of man. Not all men, but a certain type, who use their physical side to subdue their women. This type of man shows his true colours very early. His cruel streak will manifest itself five months down the road. What usually happens is that his true nature reveals itself by way of isolated incidents which individually don't make sense. It often takes a woman several inexplicable, isolated incidents, before she'll accept that the guy she's hitched up with has got serious problems....sometimes dangerous problems. That his character isn't all there, or worse, that he is psychologically unbalanced.

When Merlene and Michael first met, she was still inexperienced (people said she was too young to be his lover, and they were often castigated for the ten years that separated them, yet the two of them seemed to have something in common, which she called 'love'). She was unable to read the warning signs. Or if she did, she misinterpreted them as insignificant, rather than seeing them for what they were - scenarios that would be repeated indefinitely.

He didn't take her out, and yet she didn't see it as anything, because she didn't particularly want to go out. He would disappear for days on end, but she didn't mind, because it meant peace and quiet. She even allowed herself to accept his habit of spending all his earnings on clothes and raving and cars for himself, while any extra money she had was spent on Marlon. What she hadn't realised, however, was that deliberately or not, Michael was slowly taking away her self-confidence. She only had eyes for him. She never contemplated going to look anywhere else. But at the same time, by channelling all her emotions and thoughts to him, she neglected her own self.

Merlene was as gullible as the next woman. Despite all the sound advice to her sister, she used to let men walk all over her when it came to love.

With inexperience you've got nobody to learn from. You use your instincts. But this problem can be avoided. If you have a solid confidence thing from your parents, you'd soon realise that this kind of man is no good for you. Merlene didn't get any of that stuff. Her father had run off with a younger woman just before Max was born, and their mother heartbroken, had returned to Jamaica ten years after, believing that to leave her daughters in England with their strict relatives was better than taking them with her to the Caribbean.

That's not to say the confidence thing works every time. So many women today will stay in a relationship even when they know it's no good. Behind every 'successful' relationship, there must be a woman.

Some women'll say they're staying in a rotten relationship, because they can't resist the physical. And that's fine. As long as they admit it to themselves. Usually, though, they're not even getting enough of the physical, in which case they'll say they're in it for love and meanwhile, the guy abuses them. If not physically, he'll abuse them emotionally.

Merlene lacked personal confidence, and Michael was able to exploit that. He was able to convince her to have a child within their relationship, despite having already had several children prior to it, by getting up on his soap box and talking about how he was a righteous man and how he could do no wrong, and how he knew about this and he knew about that.

A man has to be judged by his deeds, not his words. Michael's deeds stunk. Yet he could always attract women. He was forced to admit that he already had five kids by three different women, yet Merlene decided it would be different for them. She shouldn't have ignored that kind of track record.

For a couple of years, she was willing to give everything of herself. But Michael would take little time with her. She tried to be the sweetest girl in the world, but she got nothing back in return. There's nothing worse than remembering your boyfriend's birthday every year, giving him a card, and buying him presents until it dawns on you that this man has forgotten your birthday. Michael was that certain type of man who feels it's a woman's right and duty to remember things like birthdays. As far as he was concerned, birthdays were not his role in life.

Birthday cards are vitally important where certain women are concerned, because they shows some sign of imagination. Even if you don't give a present, to actually take the time to go into a shop, pick a card and write something in it would smooth over a lot of creases. It doesn't matter if that man had beaten shit out of you the week before, you'd be willing to give him a squeeze if he'd just remember your birthday. A lot of guys are quite clever at this. They'll spend a lot of time demoralising and abusing women physically, mentally and emotionally. But they diligently perform the small gestures which keep a woman under their thumb. Even if they forget the birthday, these men will always do some silly little things, like coming in with a box of chocolates. Now, when you balance that box of chocolates against all the times you've cooked dinner and had to chuck it in the bin, or when you've had girls ringing up who don't want to speak to you, or you pick up the phone and the phone goes dead; balance that against a box of chocolates, and it's pitiful.... But it catches the woman every time. If it's not a box of chocolates, you've begged him and begged him and begged him, to go out with you and he doesn't want to go anywhere, y'know. He doesn't want to go anywhere with *you*. And the one time out of the fifty occasions that he's come with you, you think that you've got through. But you had to beg him and beg him and beg him.... What's the point of that?

Merlene remembered the nights she sat in by herself, watching paint dry. Waiting and waiting for Michael to come home. They were supposed to be living together, yet he was hardly ever home. When he would finally show up, she wouldn't question him. She would play the other game instead, which is, keep quiet and don't rock the boat and you'll eventually make things better.

When she looked back on it, Merlene realised she ought to have had it out with him. She ought to have torn shit out of him whenever he came home without a reasonable excuse. A man is only stronger than you if you let him believe he is. He might have physical superiority over you, but there are lots of ways women can put the fear of god into their men....

As far as their once hot sexual relationship was concerned, Merlene had learned to go through the motions without Michael being aware that she was passive. She knew exactly how to push the right buttons to make him think she was involved. She wasn't trying to avoid hurting his feelings. But she wasn't prepared to allow Michael the excuse of blaming her for their decaying relationship. He would probably have accused her of being frigid or some other stupidness. When they made love, he would roll over afterwards, while she lay passively. It was a long time since he had satisfied her. As far as she was concerned, there was nothing worse than a man on top of you once you realise you could have had more fun by yourself.

Slowly, she began to wean herself off him, until she finally gained the knowledge and the attitude to throw him out.

She had since had a couple of other relationships with reasonable guys, so she knew there were real men out there. You just had to search for them. There were men who showed warmth and generosity and gave her something. What she had with Michael did not compare.

Having somebody else to care about had made a difference. With the birth of their child, Michael changed in some ways. Merlene wondered how things would have been if she had given birth to a girl instead of a boy. Michael would have been less elated, and unable to make the same proud comments after she gave birth, such as, "yeah, my seeds strong," and "this will keep my line going." The fact that Marlon was born a Leo, like his father, also seemed to have some mystical significance for Michael.

Merlene worried about having Michael as a role model for her child. She didn't want a rough, tough boy, with all that physical stuff. She wanted her son to grow up into a strong man, yes, but not to live just on his wits, but to realise that there were only a few occasions when you had to resort to using the physical. She wanted her son to grow up respecting women. She didn't want him to grow up, have children and not know why they were there, or to notch up another child that he couldn't feed. On the other hand she felt that Marlon needed to have a relationship with Michael. But she wasn't too sure that Michael needed to have a relationship with Marlon. She knew what Marlon wanted, but as for Michael, what he wanted was beyond her. He changed his stance so easily.

As soon as he heard the familiar rhythm from the door knock, Marlon ran down the stairs to greet his father. He was happy as children are when their fathers come to visit. It was Marlon's thirteenth birthday. His father had rung during the week to say he wanted to take the boy and to keep him for the weekend. He had told Merlene, that as he would be in the area, he would pass by and pick the boy up.

Merlene stood behind the front door, waiting for Michael to step in. Dressed smartly and sporting designer sunglasses, he approached the door cautiously. He knew he was late and therefore, likely to get cussed. Cho! He had his runnins to do and that's that. As far as he was concerned, he was big enough to take a cussing. Anyway, he and Merlene were no longer an item. She could cuss the house down if she so wished.

Michael tried to enter, but Merlene stood stubbornly in front of him.

"You know somebody here?" she asked sarcastically. The edge on her voice put him on the defensive.

"Listen, right," he blurted, "Here I am and here I stand. When a man have something to do, him have to do it. I don't run my life by timetable. Right? Me said me gwaan come, I come! Me reach....Me late, but me reach! You should be lucky seh me come here in one piece."

Merlene stared at him angrily.

"Time is getting rough man," she said. "Me nah have no time to sit down 'pon corner an' wait 'pon any man." She didn't want to engage in a full length conversation with him.

Marlon stood innocently between his parents. He knew what was coming. He had seen it so many times before. He accepted it. What burned him, however, was that some other kids in his class who had been brought up by single parents, still had some sort of relationship with the absent parent. Marlon struggled with the fact that he had no relationship with his father. He was old enough to know that, though they didn't live under the same roof, his father could still turn up at Christmas, or on birthdays, or even at times in between, to say hello and pass the time of day. Even to talk rubbish to him. Santa Claus comes to town and all the estranged man's children gets are promises.

Marlon was at the age when he needed his role model. He wanted to experience the stuff that the other kids were experiencing. He envied his classmates when they drove about in their dad's new car. To them it was nice to say, " Cho that's my daddy!" That's what it's about for kids. Marlon had really looked forward to his daddy coming. He stayed cool and collected all day though, because he knew his mum would get worked up if he showed too much enthusiasm.

The vibe between Merlene and Michael was cool.

"This ain't good enough," she said finally. "What are you here for? We haven't seen you for ten months, and even then, you only popped in for a couple of hours. Do you intend to take on the role of supporting your son? 'Cause if not, I can deal with that, that's no problem. I'll have my son to myself, I know how to keep him....Well, what d'you want?"

"Don't carry on like that, Merlene. Stand still. Nah you pay me light bill! This man nah trouble no one, but if you trouble this man, it will bring a bam bam. You well an' know seh me come fe take my yout' out fe the day."

"What you mean you come fe tek your yout' out fe the day? Nuh you seh you want the boy fe the weekend? You come tell me seh you want the yout' fe the day?! Tell me what it is you want Michael? Tell me what it is exactly that you want in that brand new car that you have out there?"

"Now listen," Michael rejoined, "I didn't come here for no isms and schisms. If me wan' tribulation, me go dung a bull shop, right? Stokey police station just love me!"

"You should have been here from morning, you only jus' reach, an' now you're telling me you're only taking him for the day!!"

"Well me have runnins fe do. I don't want to hold up no argument with you. I just want to take Marlon out and spend the day with my son."

"You mean one of your sons don't you?!"

The door still open, Michael kicked it furiously, slamming it shut.

Merlene realised seh the temper a start. He wore dark glasses, but every now and then he had to take them off. She could see in his eyes that this was going to be a fight. Michael loved t' cuss raas an' to pop a lickle style.

She hadn't meant to lose her temper, but she found herself getting angry. Just looking at this man, seeing him roll up in a brand new car, while she was worrying herself sick trying to pay Barrington back, as well as supporting a kid.... She felt that Michael could at least, not so much for her but for his son, make the effort, regardless of any feelings he may have for her. Whether he liked or hated her, he should make the effort for his son. He didn't have to make a great show of it. He had never fed the child or clothed him. He was never around when the child was sick. He wouldn't even know if the child, his child, was taking penicillin.

Merlene decided that the best policy was to keep as calm as possible. She could feel Michael's temper rising. Marlon, totally ignored until now, looked up at his dad, saying, "Hi dad."

That burned Merlene. She kissed her teeth as if to say, "Ungh, ah dat what you call dad?" She decided to let it go, however.

"Marlon, go back upstairs, I just want to say something to your father."

Merlene led the way into her front room, followed closely by Michael, who again slammed the door living room door shut.

Merlene reminded him that he was in her house, her home.

"Personally, I don't give a shit about fe your house," Michael replied. "I don't give a shit if you're sleeping with man, or the whole sound system posse. Right? You're still my baby mudda! Because right now, I'm telling you, I don't like the way you talk to me. I don't like the attitude you ah show me!"

Merlene shook her head, her mouth open incredulously.

"I heard someone talking down the road, saying they saw you just the other day, an' you was talking about how you come back in my house to run t'ings same way. There ain't no stopping you, is there Michael? Well let me tell you, you can forget all that nonsense. This is my house, and as long as I'm around, there's no way you're coming back in!"

Michael cursed. "You better show me some respect!" he warned again.

"Show respect? You seem to forget Michael, that respect has to be earned. How can a man who has so many children who he doesn't maintain, by several women, know respect? How can a man who can drive on the same road that his child lives on and not even come in and pass the time of day with his pickney, know respect? How can a man, who cannot even remember or acknowledge the day his child was born, know respect? How can a man who drives around in a new car, when he knows that his child needs something to aid his learning or to widen his horizons, and not even bring forward the money or the time to help that child, know respect?

"'Respect' Michael, is a word you cannot spell? Therefore, you have no right to stand up there in front of me and tell me about respect. You can't spell the word! Go back ah school."

Michael fumed.

"Look Merlene, any time I want I can just take my son and go about my business. Any time!"

"Come! ....You come take your son, you come *feed* your son, you come take your child to school. You come speak to the teachers and make sure he's learning. You make sure that your child has the right clothing on his back. You make sure that your child has the emotional, the physical, the mental, the moral support that is needed day in, day out, to make that child grow. To bring that child through adolescence into manhood and to make his way through this world. Right? If at any time you t'ink seh you bigger and badder and broader than me, you come and you do that.

"But we both know seh you do not possess the skill, nor the knowledge to do that fe your own child. You only sit back in your easy chair and make like you care."

Unable to withstand Merlene's verbal onslaught, Michael picked up the ornamental marble ashtray on the coffee table, flinging it across the room. It smashed against the wall, and broke into thousands of pieces.

Merlene, suddenly afraid, realised that she may have gone too far, however true the words. She realised that she would have to backpeddle slightly to pacify him. She knew that he was riled up and like any man who is riled up and angry, he wasn't thinking straight. He was flexing his muscles.

She finally managed to calm him down. He moved nervously from one chair to another as he paced the room. Pulling out a cigarette, he lit up and threw himself on the sofa, with his feet sprawled across the arm.... He searched inside himself for insults he could throw at Merlene, whether they were true or not. But he couldn't come up with anything.

"Just tell me something Michael," Merlene began cautiously. "Just how many children do you intend to have? An' tell me, how you feed your pickney?"

He sucked hard on his cigarette. He wasn't in the mood to exchange pleasantries, or discuss his failings. 'Love is all I have, so love is all I bring,' he told himself. As far as he was concerned, in the eyes of every other woman, he was fine, okay, charming, physically and emotionally there for them. Merlene was just a *ginal*.

"Listen," she continued, "I don't really give a shit how many children you intend to have. But the one thing you should do is tell your children of their other brothers and sisters. The earlier you do, the better it will be for those involved."

Michael simply kissed his teeth. He really didn't want to hear all this crap. Merlene could see his indifference. He felt she was ranting as usual and that this was just another one of her moments.

Merlene studied Michael hard, trying very hard to restrain herself.

"Marlon came home last week, with his girlfriend...."

Michael kissed his teeth. What did this have to do with him?

"Listen, Michael, you think I've got nothing better to do with my time, than run over old arguments and old issues with you? Your son, our son brought in a girl to my house as his girlfriend, and this girl is called Melissa...."

Michael froze for a minute, unable or unwilling to figure out where Merlene was coming from.

"So de gyaal named Melissa....So what?!"

"Yes Michael, and the girl as far as I can see appears to be the same age as Marlon."

"Yes Merlene, the girl was the same age as Marlon, and she named Melissa. So what?!"

"Bwoy, you're a big fool y'know, Michael. Seriously to God, you are one of life's biggest fools. Out of all dem gyaal that you did run around town with, how much of them you breed? Or have you forgotten that you have a child called Melissa?"

Michael looked at Merlene, it registered now that she was talking about his daughter, but the implication still didn't connect. Merlene sighed heavily and walked away from him.

"Yes Michael, as I was saying, one of the world's biggest fools. Your son, our son, brought in a girl....That Melissa is your daughter."

Michael said nothing. He simply wiped his brow and stood up. He took his hand to his jaw and rubbed his chin, pacing up and down the room.

"How you know it was my daughter, enh?" he countered finally.

"Listen Michael, let me describe your daughter and you tell me if it's the same person. She's got relaxed hair. She's a little taller than Marlon and of a dark complexion like myself. She's got a strong resemblance to Pat. Same dimples when she smiles." Merlene saw the realisation dawn on Michael. "Yes," she continued, "the sowing of your wild oats has come to haunt you. But let me tell you something. Let me make myself loud and clear.

I don't want your stinking shit on my doorstep! You shit

anywhere you want, but just make sure it don't reach my door. I can't rely on you to take an active role in your son's upbringing, or his moral standing. But you make it clear to Melissa what the connection is. I've already told Marlon why nothing cyaan't go on."

Michael didn't say anything. What could he say? Merlene was right. He had ruled out the possibility of an incestuous relationship between his various offspring by different mothers. But here it was, it had happened. As a rule, Michael made sure that his baby mothers didn't know each other. But Merlene had found out about Pat by chance years ago.

Well, what was done was done, Michael figured. The important thing for now was not to allow Merlene to get one over on him. He had to somehow put a dent in her armour.

"Look Merlene, I don't know why you've come here with some bee in your bonnet. The boy come home with some girl, an' you assuming it's his girlfriend. It might be one of them boy girl things that don't lead nowhere. What's the point of telling Melissa seh Marlon's her brother? All you want to do is go bus' up in the hornet's nest, innit? Why gyaal, you love to get sting, innit? You just love to see my life mash up. Innit? You nah know seh dere are times when certain t'ing nah fe move? An' all this just because I have pickney with different woman! All dat sump'n deh happened from time. We've talked about it, you've raised hell about it, you've cussed about it. I shout 'bout it meself.... it done, it finish. I'm not telling Melissa nut'n. It don't make no sense. What am I telling Melissa for? How do I know she's looking at Marlon as boyfriend? The boy's thirteen. If she wants something to go practice on she'll choose somebody older, innit?"

Merlene looked at him and shook her head in dismay. Which fool did this man think he was talking to? Melissa was his daughter, Marlon was his son. The man was so blind, he couldn't or wouldn't see the importance of telling Melissa that Marlon was her brother. She made her way to the door, turned around and looked at Michael.

"I hope you reap the very best of what you sow. *The* very best. You see all like you now Michael, your dick should just drop off when you think of woman. It should just drop off, because you don't have no use for it. Forget about how you feel, or how your reputation is going to stay. Think about two young children living in close proximity to each other, and how they feel, when they find out they were not told they were half brother and sister. You certainly didn't think about your shame when you was fucking Pat, so why fret about it now? That's

90

your shame, you take it on your head, and you live with it. A'right? But I don't want my son to live like that. I don't want my son to pick up the dirty standard of living that you've elected to live."

"Well before you talk woman, you mus' learn to behave yourself. I hear seh, you was out all t'ree o'clock at night with some man in the West End. Tell me, where was our son then? Alone by himself in the house! So what kind of mother are you, enh? Answer me dat, Merle?!"

It was a low blow and it hurt Merlene. She had nothing to say. She had dreaded that Tony would mention their late night sightseeing tour to Michael. The two men were friends. But she hadn't prepared herself to have it thrown in her face moments after cussing Michael out for his behaviour. It was checkmate.

After a while, Michael collected Marlon and father and son departed, leaving Merlene to ponder her situation some more.

She had a vision the night before that she was walking on a beach of golden sand. This beach that she saw was where she should have been, with Winston. Instead, she had ended up owing thousands of pounds to Barrington.

Mr Akiri had persuaded her to follow him to his room in the expensive hotel on Piccadilly. She wanted the £50 he owed her so she didn't want to let him out of her sight. She felt safe and secure in the hotel.

Inside his room, Akiri had immediately reached for a pouch in the bottom of a suitcase, from which he pulled out a bundle of notes and dutifully counted out £50. As Merlene turned to leave, he called her back.

"I give you fifty pounds more if you show me your titties," he declared.

The offer threw Merlene off balance. Clients were always asking for the 'extras'. She had always refused to provide them. Most of the other girls at the club chose to sleep with the punters, because it was easy money. Merlene didn't mind the hostess bit, but she wasn't prepared to whore herself for any amount of money. So Akiri's offer peeved her.

"Look, I don't do extras, alright?"

"No, not extras," Akiri insisted. "Just show your titties. One hundred pounds?" He counted out another hundred and pushed the money towards her.

Merlene looked at the money and kissed her teeth. It was easy money though.

She hurriedly lifted up her blouse, exposing her naked

91

breasts. Akiri's eyes lit up as he ogled her, saliva dripping from his tongue. Just as hurriedly, Merlene pulled down her blouse and grabbed the hundred pounds from Akiri's outstretched hand.

Again she turned to leave and again Akiri called her back.

"Wait, please! I give you two hundred pounds if you let me just touch your titties!"

Merlene was furious. But Akiri calmed her down as he counted ten twenties and pushed the money towards her. Merlene decided that the request wouldn't do much harm. She had already gone this far and the money seemed so easy. It wasn't as if she was actually whoring herself. She snatched the money from Akiri's outstretched hand and lifted her blouse up, this time more cautiously.

Akiri didn't need any more encouragement. He pounced on Merlene, pinning her against the wall and grabbed one of her breasts with an iron grip, pushing it up towards his face. He dived in immediately, biting the breast roughly, mercilessly. Merlene struggled, trying to push the man's head away. But it was impossible. Akiri clung to her breast like a vice. The pain was unbearable. She eventually managed to free herself sufficiently to direct a perfect hit with her knee. Akiri bent over double holding his crotch as he howled in pain. With her breast throbbing like it was on fire, Merlene turned quickly and rushed out, still clutching three hundred pounds in cash in her hand, to hail a black cab.

Once she was safely home, the full distress of what she had gone through hit her. She broke down crying, trying hard not to wake Marlon. She couldn't allow him to see her this way. She rushed into the bathroom and turned on the shower, stepping under the warm water, still dressed in her party clothes.

She felt dirty. She despised herself for what she had become. Oh, if only Winston had driven more carefully on that fateful night, she wouldn't be in this mess. She didn't know how she would manage to repay Barrington, but she resolved never to go back to the Club again.

SEVEN

The Four Musketeers met up the next evening. Beverly had just arrived back from her honeymoon in Jamaica and there was lots of gossip from back-ah-yard.

They sat at their usual table at the back of the bar in Dunn's River, each woman sipping from a different cocktail.

"Max, I hope you haven't sold that beautiful car while I've been away," Beverly enquired about her friend's customised Beetle.

"Nuh worry yourself," Max reassured, "'Cause it's criss and clean and waiting for you, when you're ready."

"Well, I can't exactly say that you look like a married woman Beverly," Andrea offered. Look like you've put on a little bit of weight. I thought honeymoon was to make you shed weight....?"

Dunn's River was packed to the brim with its curious mix of buppies and white trendies. The Four Musketeers stood out amongst everybody. They could steal any show dressed the way they were. However, they ignored the attentive glances from the lecherous men in suits doing their lizard thing at the bar.

"How can you ask the girl a personal question like that?" Merlene interrupted. "Beverly, did you enjoy your honeymoon?"

Beverly hesitated before answering. "Yes, it was really wonderful, a bit strange at first, but things worked out nice. We were a bit distant, but you know.... Things are cool."

"What do you mean 'distant'?" a surprised Merlene asked. "It was your honeymoon. Y'know. You don't have no children 'round your heels. What do you mean 'distant'?"

Beverly simply shrugged her shoulders.

Merlene studied Beverly's distant eyes long and hard, before asking, "Do you think you've made a mistake?"

"Of course I didn't make a mistake! I just told you, things were fine and he was just a bit, y'know, a bit nervous. I know it sounds silly, but...."

"Well, if I get married and my husband's acting a bit distant on our honeymoon, I'd have to ask the man why!" Andrea warned casually. "So Beverly, you start turn fool now. Since when you can have man in your quarters behaving this way? What kind of rubbish is that?!"

"You just want to read something into nothing. It's no big

thing," Beverly countered, wanting desperately to get off the point. "I mean we've been together four an a half months.... I'm just saying that the man was a bit distant, that's all. Maybe he was finding it a bit strange, that's all. No big deal. Everybody's entitled to a little bit of nervousness about being married. But anyway, since we've been back, he's been cool. There's been no problem. He loves me madly, and I must admit I feel the same."

A sudden silence fell over the girls. In their experience, men who were distant were usually playing away from home.

Beverly broke the silence by adding, "Well, we did manage to go out to Port Royal and Ocho Rios, and we even climbed Dunn's River!"

"I don't believe you, Beverly!" Andrea retorted. "How you can manage to climb Dunns River, when you're too afraid to go on the big wheel at the fair ground? You've managed to climb Dunn's River?"

"Yes I did. But you have to remember that I did have my husband with me," Beverly added mockingly. "I wasn't frightened, because I did have my *husband* with me."

"It's alright," Merlene interjected. "You don't have to say 'husband' so many times, like say you is the only person good enough to get married."

Beverly began to talk more about the holiday. About the food they ate, and what they didn't eat, who they saw and so on.

"Every time I remember Jamdown, water come ah me eye," she reminisced.

"So," asked Andrea, "how you get on with him people? How him people stay?"

"What a Waterloo! If I had stayed in Jamaica I might have lost my life!" came Beverly's exaggerated reply. She was relieved that she had successfully changed the subject.

They all started laughing because the girls knew that here, was a bit of juicy gossip.

"Well come on, what happened? What were his people like?"

"Well, they never liked me," Beverly began. "Let me tell you the truth, they never liked me. When I got through the door, his mum, who I had to call Sister King, because believe it or not, she belongs to the church.... Thomas never told me his parents belonged to the church, y'know? So when I came along and started forgetting myself - big shame and disgrace! You know what his mum had the cheek to ask me? She said Thomas had told her that I had two children. She had the cheek to ask me if they were from the same man!?"

"She what!?" Merlene asked incredulously.

"No, she nevah?!" Andrea couldn't believe it. "What you seh

to her?"

"I looked her straight in the eye and told her yes, they were for two different men and what about it? I simply told her that I love my children and they are well provided for materially. They will want for nothing. When she realised I had two children, as far as she was concerned, I was bringing her son down and fire, brimstone and whatsit would hail down on him for fraternising with me....and associating himself, with a low life woman. That's the way the woman saw me, I'm telling you, I could see it in her eyes. There's no way I could mistake it. She even wanted to tek me to church to baptise me! You ever hear anything so stupid so? You go on your honeymoon, and your mother-in-law wants to baptise you!"

"Well," said Andrea teasingly, "there's no redemption for you now. Two pickney by two different man!! And now you're getting married and you're bound to have baby, that is three baby for t'ree different man!!!" she giggled holding up three fingers to stress the point. "So, she could baptise you, but the water will have no use!"

They all started laughing. Even Beverly saw the funny side of it.

"Even when I got up in the mornings, you could hear the woman saying her prayers," Beverly continued. "When we had breakfast we had to have one long prayer over the food. By that time the food cold!"

Beverly paused for a moment, reflecting.

"I love him, and I'm glad that I married him. But I have to admit, the way that his mum treated me - and she treated me a way - and I know he listens to his mother, whatever she says.... To him, its important that she likes me, so I tried hard. But it didn't matter what I did for this woman.... The woman just did not like me. Her son chose me as his wife, so she will have to accept it."

"What about his dad?" Max asked. "How did the dad treat you?"

"Now I come to think about it he was hardly there.... It could have been a woman. But I do not wish to get involved in people's dirty business. I keep myself to myself."

"For somebody who keep dem self to dem self," said Merlene, "you love wash you mouth 'pon people."

Beverly's eyes narrowed. Merlene's passing comment with the sting in its tail had burned her. She waved her left hand dismissively in front of Merlene, seemingly emphasising the wedding band on her finger. It was a simple gold ring with two interlocking hearts set in diamond. The other women marvelled at it, but resented Beverly's emphasis. Beverly was telling them that come rain or shine, joy or pain, at least she was married.

Beating teasingly about the bush with a glint in her eye, Andrea asked the newly-wed, "Well listen, we're your friends and we'll do anything for you, but I want to ask you one question.... you don't have to answer me if you don't want to, but did erm.... did you.... We's your friend and we'll do anything for you and we love you bad, yeah....? But the one thing that we would really like to know.... truly.... does Thomas eat off a two-foot table?!"

The other girls were horrified. Andrea had gone a bit too far.

"How could you....?" Merlene stuttered. "....That is too strong, that is too strong, Andrea. Because if you evah ask me such a question, I would lay you out same place. All 24 of your teeth would box out and lay down at the bottom of your stomach."

The four of them roared with laughter. But though they laughed heartily, Max, Merlene and Andrea still wanted to know.

Once the hilarities had subsided Beverly replied loftily, "As I am a married woman, you should respect the privacy of my marriage."

"You just full of fart, Bev!" Andrea retorted mercilessly. "Either the man eats off a two-foot table, or he don't."

"Him eat off a two-foot table," Max interjected triumphantly. "'Cause from when she says 'respect the privacy,' that mean fe seh him can eat off a two-foot table."

"No, I want Beverly to answer me dat," Andrea demanded.

"I'm a married woman," Beverly repeated snobbishly. "So therefore, anything that happens within the confines of my marriage is....private."

Andrea wasn't going to be put off easily.

"If you don't tell us whether Thomas eats off a two-foot table, I will put him to the test."

"That is out of order you know," Beverly replied coldly. "That's like incest."

Realising that she had overstepped her mark, Andrea decided to let it go.

The girls talked for an hour about the pros and cons of men who eat off two-foot tables, a term denoting a man who is willing to practice oral sex with a woman.

Oral sex is still taboo in the community. Few men will admit to going down on their women orally (although they don't mind the other way around). These four experienced women each knew the opposite to be true. The very same men who, on commencing a relationship will remind you forcefully that they don't eat off two-foot table, are the same men who will practically think that they've been cheated if they're not given a blow job. They'll feel as if you've robbed them.

Yes, they enjoyed oral sex and their men enjoyed giving it as well as receiving it. Still, cow nevah know the use of him tail till the butcher cut it off.

The conversation continued in the general direction of men's sexual inadequacies.

"Men don't mind the woman doing all the work while they stand back and simply enjoy it."

"In the case of some men, foreplay is just like saying, let's go for tennis. They're not aware of what the word foreplay is. Especially men who have this habit of doing the job mechanically and snoring afterwards. Literally, they gone completely fast asleep. Some guys will swear blind that the adrenalin that's flowing causes some chemical reaction which puts them to sleep."

"They just use that as a damn excuse, because as soon as they've got what they're concerned about, that's it. It releases them from any physical commitments afterwards. As far as they're concerned, 'I've got there, I've reached, I've conquered. I don't need to play around now, I can just go to sleep, and everything's cool!'"

They talked about the lack of sensitivity of some men.

"Some of them have to be taught to eat off a two-foot table," Andrea offered. "They're not aware of what they're doing, so you do have to teach. But that's only if they're prepared to be taught."

"Some men's egos are so fragile that it takes loads of sessions And it has to be done very carefully, because if a man suspects that you're guiding him, or you're teaching him, or you're doing different moves, he'll think you're either sleeping with somebody else, or you're saying there's something wrong with the way he performs."

"It's true though," Merlene interrupted. "Some of them don't know how to perform. As far as they're concerned, any mistake, they never made it. They simply woke up one day at the age of sixteen and knew how to do it perfectly."

"You have to be very careful," Andrea continued. "You can't just turn around and tell a man that what he did was rubbish. Not unless you're very brave, or unless you really don't want that man."

The women's convivial banter was interrupted only by Beverly's abrasive enquiry directed at Max.

"What's it like, sleeping with a white man?"

"What is what like.... A man is a man." Max was unwilling to be drawn into Beverly's line of questioning.

"No you cannot just come with that and expect us to take that," Beverly insisted. "You're screwing a white man. That is big 'tory for anybody. You're screwing a white man, so what's the difference?"

Andrea couldn't resist a little tease.

"Oh please Max, the thought. Y'know - pink?! No please...."

The four women burst out laughing.

"Come on....does it look the same?"

"It's a man. A man's thing is going to look the same, unless its smaller, bigger, taller whatever," Max assured them. Her three companions sat contemplative for a moment, until Beverly pursued the issue.

"Are you trying to tell us that this white man, just does the same thing as a black man....? If so and he delivers the same goods as a black man, then why are you with a white man? You might as well have a black man. What's the difference?"

"Well, there is a difference," Max said trying to be frank. "Not a lot. But there is just a little difference. I can't really speak for any other white man, because I don't know a lot. But this particular man, he's sensitive and caring. He's prepared to take time. It's more than just a screw. There's more than one way to skin a cat. There's a limit to how many times you can do the same thing in the same way at the same time, y'know, week in week out. That's not enjoyment, that's not learning, that's not.... discovering one another's bodies."

"Discovering one another's bodies?" Andrea couldn't believe the stupidness she was hearing. "Nut'n nah go so. A fuck is a fuck! What is that?"

"You don't have to put it like that!" Merlene rallied to her sister's defence. "When she says 'discovering one another's bodies,' she means making love."

But Andrea wasn't giving up.

"Me fail to see what she means by 'discovering one another's bodies.' A fuck is a fuck is a fuck, right?! There's no two ways about it."

Max turned to Merlene for more support. The elder sister simply rolled her eyes helplessly, finding the subject a bit too close to the knuckle. Anyway, if she got entangled in it, she might have to divulge her personal tastes, which she was not prepared to do.

With too many black men unwilling to treat their women with respect, where white men are concerned, some black women are no longer prepared to say nevah again.

Beverly looked at Max, unable to let the subject drop. It wasn't her business who Max dated, she just felt that a good black woman could always find a good black man.

"Well look, why have you got a white man in your bed? There's black men out there. I'm married."

"Only five minutes...." Andrea added.

"Yes, I've been married five minutes, but I'm married to a black man.... 'Cause that's how things are supposed to go...."

Beverly fumbled for words. She had never been able to express herself quite as eloquently as her three soul sisters. "Yes, that's how things are supposed to go. You're supposed to marry your own black man. Just tell me what your white man is delivering that my Thomas couldn't do? The only thing that man's giving you more than the black man is money."

Max looked at Beverly hard, with pain in her eyes. That was the point that hurt her most. Andrea was anxious to hear Max's response.

"Well, is it money?"

Max hesitated before finally giving in.

"The money is a big factor, I'm not going to deny it. The money is a big factor. But what I'm saying is, at the beginning the money was a t'ing, it did entice me. Yeah. To get all the things I never had before. Yeah. Of course it did entice me. Now, it's a bit more than that. Now, I feel a bit more for the man than just straight sex and money."

"Are you saying that you actually love him?" Andrea asked.

Max didn't answer.

"Well I'm sorry," Beverly continued. "I don't agree with you Max. There is no way I would pick up myself with some white man, knowing there's some serious looking black man out there. Some serious looking black man and you go and pick up some middle aged white man, who just because *he* can eat off two-foot table, you go and give him credit! You're not telling me that when you turn over in the morning you wouldn't rather have a black man in your bed!"

"Well," Andrea added, "I know seh, if I pick up with white man, him have fe go cook, clean, wash. Do everything fe me. He'd have to offer me more than a black man. He'd have to put himself so high up, that no black man standing up on ten man could reach...."

"I would agree with you Beverly. There is good black man out there, but I can't find one. So what you going to do? You can't sit down and wait forever," Max interjected.

It was two against one. Merlene being the eldest felt she had to come down on the side of Max, not just because it was her sister, but to keep a balance.

"Max says she went with this man first of all for the money," Merlene chose her words carefully. "You can't judge her for that. Beverly, when the father of your first baby disappeared, you were cleaning floors to make extra money. That man didn't keep you. You've got two children, two different fathers. That's your black man for you! And what have you got for it?"

"Yes, that's true," said Beverly defensively. "Things didn't work out. But I now have a black man who I'm married to and I'm happy to be married to him. What I'm saying about Max, is that I don't see how she can really in all honesty seh the white man is better. Bettah she turn to Bajan...." she added in humour.

"Don't seh that," Andrea added mischievously. "Can you imagine, turning over in bed to hear some man tell you in that squeaky Bajan voice, 'me love you!' Well I don't know, y'know. If me have to wake up every morning to a Bajan man, I would go to white man. That's enough to turn you to white man!" The girls all laughed.

Merlene thought long and hard, before concluding on a serious note:

"I would have said before that I would never go out with a white man, but I would never say never anymore. It just doesn't seem right to say never anymore. It's cosmopolitan out there. If I can't get no man at all and I'm on my own and a white man comes and offers me his time, then I can't categorically say that I wouldn't take him up on his offer. Let's face it, white or black man, they're all dogs. Once they sniff it, they're there. Nobody questions the black man going for white women. Everybody says 'Cho dat common now, that's no problem! You just deal with it.' Well what's the problem with a black woman going out with a white man, if that's what she really wants? Don't only talk about the problems in the world, you've got to help solve them."

Beverly bowed to Merlene's greater wisdom, but with one reservation.

"I agree with everything you say, but speaking for myself, I'm going to say I would never go with no white man. I would rather take the worst of the black man, than take myself and put myself in some white man's bed. There is no two ways about it. My parents never came to this country to work hard and suffer so much, so that I could just turn round and say, 'Here mummy, look at my blond hair and blue eyes man!' It just doesn't wash. In Jamaica, some lickle white man come and said he's going to try and do a thing with me. When Thomas saw him he just cussed the man's b/c and his d/c and told him, if he wanted to live, to get out the area and never come back. In Jamaica people don't ramp with those things!"

"That's not saying anything!" Merlene said drily.

The other three women were irritated by Beverly's childlike self-righteousness.

"If you were put to the test.... Let's just get this open now....If you were put to the test, right...Supposing Thomas nevah come along and you did physically check for that white man? What would you say?" asked Merlene.

"No way!" Beverly insisted. "There's no way I would have gone with that man. Or even begin anything with that man."

"No, no, no. What we're saying, is suppose this man's exactly the type of man you're attracted to, the only difference is the colour of his skin. What we're asking you, is whether you would you have been able to say categorically, with your hand on your heart, that you wouldn't check for this white man?"

"I wouldn't have checked him. I would rather check any other black man walking on that beach. You've got to stand up and fight for your black man, or you ain't gonna get no culture."

"The white man is no different from all those red men that you take a particular liking to," Merlene reminded her.

"That's rubbish! That's rubbish!" Beverly's voice had taken on a hint of rage. "What's red man got to do with this?! I am telling you that I don't go for white man, you come and tell me about red man!"

"What's the difference between a redskin man and a fair skin man? With your preference for red man how can you say you wouldn't go for white man?"

"I don't have a problem with colour, so I don't know how you can say I only check for red men?"

"Beverly, since when you evah go out with any dark skin man? Because in all the years I've known you, you have nevah, *nevah* picked up any. If I am wrong, be not afraid to say so...."

"Anyway," Merlene continued. "We are all sisters, so what are we fighting for? Nuh skin up! We can't skin up. We've got to work things out together. Forget what colour you may be. Begin to check the blood and you will find out that, we are all one.... So let us talk about love and forget enmity."

A heartless observer aware of the problems on Merlene's mind, may have felt that she had an ulterior motive in commending unity amongst her sistren.

"We've got to stick together, it's a crazy world. It's rough out in the streets where our children go and play," she concluded.

This was the last happy evening the four women were to spend together. Dark secrets were tearing at their relationship.

101

EIGHT

As usual, the annual Afro-Hair and Beauty Show afforded an opportunity for the ladies to parade their new style and fashion and to criticise those who had not quite got the right dress sense.

"But wait...look 'pon Sharon now?!" one girl dressed to impress in a micro-miniskirt and halter-back, whispered to her friend in matching attire. "Whoever told her that dress look good 'pon her?"

For many women, the show was the important calender date of the year. Forget Christmas, Easter and birthdays, giving the mid-summer Afro-Hair and Beauty a miss was like missing out on the most important opportunity to model and pose. You can't just go in anything, either. You had to dress up in the latest style, with 'nuff jewellery and make-up on your face like an Apache Indian. A lickle dis, a lickle dat, and a touch of beauty.

Few women can resist posing at 'celebrity' events. For some, these events are a way of netting the right calibre of man (generally, buppies and buppie wannabes are in demand). Women will claim to their friends that they're not going to bother putting on anything special for the occasion. "I'm just going to pick something out of the wardrobe....anything I put on will do." But that's a load of rubbish. Nobody's going to an event dressed in just anything, because 'nuff men and women will be there, ready to criticise what you wear. If something ain't right about your clothes, the punters at the Afro-Hair and Beauty will comment. You'll hear someone commenting about how your outfit's holey-holey for example, or that it tear. Or you'll here someone else cuss you for wearing "cheap clothes" to the event. And the people who criticise you, are more than likely your friends. The very same friends that talk behind your back, but want to borrow your frock to wear at the Afro-Hair and Beauty. Some girls are just too deceiving and conniving.

To turn out in the best outfit possible is so important, that some women in a class and category will even ask to borrow their friend's best frock for the show. The point is, you want to look good, yet you want to look as if you have made no effort at all. For years, Jamaican girls have run that style twenty-four seven. Whether they live in Jamaica, London or New York City, Jamaican girls love to lead fashion, they do not follow fashion.

Men pretend they're different, but the reality is that they love crissness as much as the women. If you don't look good, they'll be the first to say you nevah ready, and yet still they'll talk 'bout *you* love vanity!

Max knew before she got there that she'd be head and shoulders above the competition - quite literally. The fact that she was tall and dark always stood in her favour at these events, where the emphasis was on a middle-class, Afrocentrism. Though dressed simply, she looked stunning as usual. A dark-skinned ebony princess in white cotton jeans, and bold African jewellery. She felt that this was her year and that nothing, nobody, no woman, could stop her, no matter how much they big up their chest. She certainly didn't feel like competing with the new kids on the block - those young ragamuffin girls who are prepared to wear practically anything and do anything to themselves in the hope of looking appealing to a man.

Things had changed a lot since the days when Max was the unofficial Miss Black Brixton. In the past few years there had been a massive increase in the amount of girls going around in posses dressed identically. These girls were generally not even size 10 let alone size 12. They're often a size 8! With lanky limbs!! And all because they don't want their man to say, "Eh baby, you ah put on a little bit of weight."

Max kept in trim. She didn't want to hear anybody calling after her, "Bwoy you nah see how the fat suit you!"

In the old days the Four Musketeers would have gone to the Afro-Hair and Beauty as a posse. But Beverly had been unable to get a babysitter in time and Merlene had given some excuse at the last minute. Andrea however, had to go. In her new role of salon proprietor, the Afro-Hair and Beauty would be both business and pleasure. She would get a chance to see which new hair products were coming in from the United States, and check out the creative hair designs. And Max, of course, wouldn't dream of missing the event. Miss Ready and Waiting (Andrea) and Max (Miss Ready To Go), made quite a fearsome combination, something that didn't go unnoticed amongst the attendent men.

As they entered the venue (an ultra-modern business design centre in a trendy part of North London), the two women checked everything a final time to make sure they looked their best. Their hair was in place, make up in place, lipstick matted, stockings without a snare and heeled shoes still gleaming. Andrea with her usual habit took a comb from her handbag and made slight adjustments to Max's hair.They pushed their way past the bouncers without paying, by an inviting wink of the eye and a seductive lick of the lips, the hint of very expensive perfume trailing behind them.

Max always wore the most expensive perfumes, but even Andrea had thought it wise to pull out a bottle of Chanel for this event. As she caught a glimpse of herself from the reflection on a glass door, Andrea was secretly pleased to see the effect of the ten-day diet she had embarked on, in order to look just that bit trimmer for the Afro-Hair and Beauty. She hadn't mentioned the mini-diet to Max, who noticed the difference and commented that her friend did look "particularly nice."

Andrea's outfit was a little more daring than normal. She revealed a lot more cleavage than she normally would, with her hemline a mere wisp above the knee. She was quite clearly out to get a man. But not just any man. Andrea was on the hunt for a sensible man.

She could no longer cope with younger men. When she told Max this, the more extrovert woman was astonished.

"I don't know how you can say that," she had remarked.

But Andrea had a point. Older men are more experienced than the younger boys. If nothing else, they've used the same lines over and over again. The young men haven't had time to learn their lines properly yet. Also, Andrea was determined not to be the old bike for any young man to ride.

Winston was two years older and she was confident that, had he not died, he would have grown old quickly. If a man's older, he'll still find you attractive when flab has long since turned his belly into jelly. Young men on the other hand, are ignorant, immature, and generally can't see beyond an equally young woman. If you pull up your blouse and show a young man your stretch marks, he won't even know what they are. He'll say something like, 'what somebody take a knife and cut you?'

The vast and cavernous venue, lilted slightly to the mixture of soul and reggae that floated freely in the background. There were women everywhere you looked and the atmosphere was tight with the aroma of various scents. In truth, it was the ideal ground for casual liaisons. Unattached men stood around, circling the available, fit women. In return, the women threw inviting glances at the fit, unattached men. Those who got there early were those who were desperate for action. As all late comers know, the trick was to arrive late, composed, confident and ready for that unexpected stranger.

The girls came in all shapes and sizes. Tall, short, stout, fit and pencil slim, each woman mingling amongst her particular posse. Naturally, the younger girls were there in force. Girls who hadn't yet kissed puberty goodbye. Girls still holding hands with each other, yet intent on doing battle with their older counterparts. Uninhibited by their small, rounded, pert breasts, their lack of hips and their undeveloped calf muscles, they pouted for a man, craving for the excitement and maturity they thought the older girls enjoyed. Girls of fifteen and sixteen years of age. Little teenagers, who believed they were ready for womanhood. Despite their lack of hips, calves and chests, the little they had they made sure was out on parade, standing to attention. Accompanied by boyfriends playing 'big bout yah,' sporting tiny little *yabba-you* chins and posing with their arms around their waif-like girlfriends, while staring nonchalantly over their sunglasses at the latest piece that walked past.

Groups of older guys stood around with their hands resting lightly across their mouths as they whispered things conspiratorially to their friends. Like, "see dat piece over dere so.... hey, check the gyaal in a de red pants now.... yes, she look fit," and the usual derogatory remarks that come from men who think they are ready to pick up something, yet know seh they've got nothing to offer really, other than the eternal chat up line, "haven't I seen you somewhere before?"

And every hairstyle imaginable was in effect. From the girls with short-cropped hairstyles with a pattern going round, to the full length weave-ons.

The pungent smell of people having their hair done filled the hall. There were some eighty stands, selling a variety of hair products. At some stands women were having their hair done with protein conditioners, to enable the different exhibiting salons to do their 'before' and 'after' demonstration thing. A couple of stands were selling food - patties and cold drinks. At the far end of the hall, a fashion show was under way. Hair conditioner and hair spray freebies were handed out and a lucky woman screamed with joy as the winning raffle ticket was called out. Up on the stage, minor celebrity guests were paraded to a lukewarm response from the audience, and before long the PA and t'ing was brought back, to the approval of everyone present.

Everybody who was anybody was there. Some had turned up just for the sheer hell of seeing the thing collapse, because sometimes that's entertaining enough. Men go to something like the Afro-Hair and Beauty, even though it's a female event, because they know there's a whole heap of women there, and they're bound to pick up sump'n.

For the men, the Afro-Hair and Beauty was a talent scout. It was high summer and every man wanted to be seen cruising around in a sweet convertible car, with something squeezable in the passenger seat.

Once the guys realised that they could get a much better view of the local talent from the gallery above, up they went, each one pretending that he was going up to consume alcohol in the gallery restaurant. Several of the women responded to the men's newly discovered bird's eye view, by flirting from a distance - tossing their weaves back on their shoulders and their plaits from left to right.

Women who are the consumers in the community, have slightly more reasons for attending such events. Some will go just for a good laugh, because there's bound to be people making fools of themselves. Others go to see who's gone with who, or more to the point, who hasn't taken who with them. Then there are the starfuckers who go to meet celebrities and chill out. Before he disappeared following the scandal over a steroid-laced urine sample, 100 metre champion Danny Henry was a regular at all these events. He knew he could always score amongst the women who were only too happy to oblige. Just like the men, a good portion of women attended because they knew 'nuff men flock to such events.

Thomas's eyes were the first thing Max saw when she and Andrea emerged from the ladies' room. He was standing way over on the other size of the hangar-sized hall, but even at that distance, his eyes melted any resistance she could have put up. They were locked in eye contact, all sorts of emotions and sensations running between them. She remained paralysed for some seconds, before quickly composing herself, remembering she was not alone.

Loosely followed by his posse, Thomas walked over to the two girls. He was dressed in deep green balloon trousers with matching waistcoat. The usual array of sovereigns hung from his neck, while his hands glistened from the gold rings on his fingers. Thomas, knowing that he looked good, swaggered that bit more. His crew were dressed equally sharp. There were even a couple of two-piece suited super dudes amongst them.

Thomas's crew were slick teasers. They puffed up their chests, confident about the way they looked and admired the women present, talking loudly about "what a girl have a sexy body," and about "how her hips are broad and her batty nice and big." They would call out to the talent and if the girls didn't stop, they would turn an cuss them, in front of their boyfriends if necessary. As far as they were concerned no other posse could test them. Not today anyway. They were sure they could pick up plenty of women, 'cause they looked better than the competition.

It was clear to Max and Andrea, having powdered their

noses, that the two guys hanging lecherously outside the ladies didn't hold a fresh before they went out that morning. As one of them went up to Max and rested his arm on her shoulder, she became acutely aware of the repugnant smell that oozed from his armpit. Andrea remarked that the boy " 'tink". Max turned around, addressing her admirer in a low but audible voice.

"Unless you have the dollars to entertain this merchandise, remove your hand from the equipment!"

Andrea roared with laughter. It was quite clear from the 'cuff-up shoes he was wearing, that the man couldn't afford her. Max's condescending expression was enough to brush off the unwanted admirer.

Thomas walked up and greeted each girl with a kiss on the cheek, asking them how they were doing. They exchanged pleasantries, and both groups remarked on the event. The atmosphere between them was light hearted. Thomas was cool as ever on the outside. But inside, he was not at ease. He knew that what he had made up his mind to do, could backfire with unforeseeable consequences. But he had always been a chancer, especially when it came to affairs of the heart, or more precisely, affairs of the sexual kind.

Max acted casual, while deep inside her a tingling sensation told her that she was anything but relaxed. She was fully aware that the slightest hint of any sexual chemistry between Thomas and herself would be picked up by her companion and give the game away. Max always preferred to be discreet, especially when playing with other people's property.

The two groups merged into one as together they walked around the exhibition hall. Gradually, Thomas managed to separate the two women. While Andrea's attention was drawn to an Afrocentric bookstand, where copies of Victor Headley's *Yardie* were selling like hot patties, Max sneaked off at a discreet distance behind Thomas, looking over her shoulder to check as she did so. The pair went to a great deal of trouble not to be seen together as they slipped out of the building.

Outside, the warm summer evening had drawn crowds out of their homes and into the many restaurants around Islington. Magic was in the air - and what men call love and the gods adultery is much more common when the climate's sultry.

Thomas and Max made their way to a little wine bar half way down Upper Street. They sat opposite each other in a booth near the back of the bar, where they were only partially obscured from the people around them. Neither of them knew what to say, so they began by talking about anything but what was on their minds. They were both unsure about how far the other was prepared to go.

After a couple of hours of talking about nothing in particular and sharing some polite but false laughs, Thomas made the first move. He took Max's hand in his and caressed it slowly, nervously. Max felt the smoothness and warmth of Thomas' hand as he massaged her fingers and she wanted it to go on. At the same time she wouldn't allow herself to admit it to herself, so she hastily removed her hand.

Thomas couldn't make out the gesture. Was she game or wasn't she?

Max regretted withdrawing her hand and wished she could take that move back, but all the time, her conscience was telling her that this was her best friend's husband.

In the meantime, Andrea had become aware back at the Afro-Hair and Beauty, that they had lost Max and Thomas, but she was not unduly worried. Besides, she had herself found something to engage her amorous inclinations. Something in the shape of a youthful but mature man called Spence. Andrea loved nothing better than a flirt.

The show was coming to a close and the event had turned into a dance with a deejay spinning the tunes.

"Give me some of your somet'ing and me give you some of my t'ing," Spence teased as he took her on to the dancefloor.

Andrea had been standing by herself watching the dancers all doing the latest dance to have taken the community by storm. Originated in Jamaica by the lame legged man from whom the dance took its name, the new reggae dance had swept like a tempest through the community. The poor guy who had originated it had all but missed out on cashing in on his invention, because while the dance took off with unprecedented momentum, he was sitting in the General Penitentiary back-ah-yard after an unfortunate altercation with the law.

The best way to do the dance (a variation on the old 'mating dance' theme) was to pretend that you yourself had a lame leg, as the infectious reggae dancehall rhythm which popularised the dance, pumped out from the speakers. The dance had become so popular that if you couldn't do it, or a variation of the original, you had better not even try to step out on the dancefloor.

With some guys, if they see you standing by yourself at a dance and they don't see any other men dancing with you or going up to check you, they think there's something wrong with you. Because how come no other man is checking you, if there's nothing wrong with you? Women do the same too. If you see a man standing there by himself and no other women are interested in him, then you don't want to admit that you are into him.

So, Andrea stood around, waiting for a man to have the courage to come up and beg her a dance. She occupied the time by marvelling at the sheer lack of clothing on some or most of the women there. It was a new fashion style, to go with the new dance style - the object apparently being to have as little clothing on as possible while only just remaining decent.

Spence finally plucked up enough courage to ask Andrea if she'd like a drink.

"Yes," she answered after allowing for a respectable pause, " I would like to have a drink or three with you, if you're paying." Spence turned to his friend standing close by, announcing, "You nah see how dis gyaal renk and feisty y'know! Offer to buy her a drink, and she come tell me one or three...."

"She will feed 'pon your pocket like termite feed 'pon carpet," the friend warned. But the advice came too late. Spence was already smitten, he just wanted to find a way of getting round paying for the drinks.

He turned to Andrea and said, " Haven't you heard, this is the modern day, love.... are we going Dutch?"

Andrea looked at him from his toe to his slightly receding hairline and kissed her teeth. She had forgotten how tight men could be when it came to buying a lady a drink.

Nowadays Andrea expected men to pay for everything. She didn't have too much extra cash to go out raving and paying. No that was the man's job. In no way did this influence her newly-found independence. It was just that the hairdresser's salon took all her available money. Like any new business she had cash flow problems and she wasn't actually earning much. But she had accepted the decision. Because she felt she had to move quickly, before she hit thirty. So she decided not to go out raving anymore, unless a man was prepared to pay for everything.

Unlike a lot of girls who go to clubs and are really into it, for Andrea it was no big deal. She could go to a dance without meeting any men and still feel good. She could go to a dance without dancing with any men, and that's alright by her. She certainly didn't need the tight-fisted aggro that Spence was coming on with.

Women are tired of pushing men to do things that they should be doing anyway. Buying drinks is the man's responsibility from time.

"Dutch? Dutch not in my vocabulary you know *dahling!* If you cannot afford to buy me a drink, I suggest you keep your mouth quiet."

Spence found the loud-mouthed girl irresistible, and decided reluctantly to get the drinks in.

Spence and his friend Roger escorted Andrea upstairs to the bar. Roger was a great deal more attractive than Spence, and for a moment Andrea considered him as a possibility, but he had an unfortunate stammer, which convinced her that he had little chance getting off the starting block. Andrea was likely to devour him. She was never really into unsure men, and least of all one who couldn't even get his words right. He tried unsuccessfully to broach several subjects with her but to no avail. Andrea, fully aware of what his ulterior motives were, turned her attention completely to Spence, as a way of giving Roger a polite brush-off. They observed the crowd down below, and proceeded to pass their worldly knowledge on how people should or should not dress.

"Check that girl over there for instance," Andrea observed, "....the one in ah the blonde wig, you're telling me that you don't think that looks good?"

Spence looked at Andrea to check if she was serious. How she could think a black woman dressed in a blonde wig, with those clumpy boots that she was wearing, could look alluring to a man like him....? He had to do a double take. Was she joking or was she deadly serious?

"Is that for real, man? Are you trying to tell me that looks good?" Spence enquired.

"Well yeah, it nah look bad," Andrea insisted. "I've got one."

"You an' God one would be sleeping with that blonde wig," Spence said. "'Cause I certainly wouldn't go near no women with no blonde wig!"

Andrea didn't believe him.

"Are you telling me that regardless of how sweet or how good the woman was, you still would ignore a woman if she had a blonde wig?"

Spence rubbed his chin softly, and finally concluded, "Weeeeeell, you know how it go, Andrea. If somet'ing sweet y'know, it nah matter what disguise it come in, you still ah gwine check it same way."

"Well, there goes my black man," Andrea thought. "Ever ready, ever still, ever foolish...."

They continued to slag off the crowd below, most of them now whining in rhythm to the music being played by Ladies Choice Hi-Fi, the most popular sound system of the day.

110

Jamaican girls are the sweetest whiners. When some girls whine, they will only move a hand or a foot, or their chest, and it still looks good. They can switch from whining fast to whining slow without batting an eyelid. Regular clubgoers will swear blind that they have seen some women doing the whine on their knees, but you'd have to see that to believe it.

How come Jamaican girls whine so good? That's one of the great mysteries of the world, and they're not prepared to reveal their secret. If you know you can't work up a storm on the dancefloor same way, then step aside. Leave the Jamdown girls to show you how.

"Won't you come dance wit' me again?" Spence begged, angling to turn his liaison with Andrea into more than just a chat show.

Andrea smiled, knowing what was going through his mind. On the dancefloor, he would want to come wheel and turn her, whispering sweet words of love. He didn't need to. Spence had bought the winning card in the O.P.P. game. She had already made up her mind that she would allow him to share her bed this night. But she had a particularly sadistic pleasure in seeing men sweat it out.

"You ah the best," Spence whispered in Andrea's ear as he escorted her on to the dancefloor. "You ah de best. You deh 'pon me mind. No girl can test you.... Well right now girl, I'm full up of action. But me's man who like to know where me stand in a line. Do you want to be my woman?"

"Do you want to be my man?" Andrea asked in response.

Spence laughed a little. He knew now that he had got a result, so he was cock sure of himself.

"Well yeah, you tickle my fancy. If your love was currency, I would accept bribes."

Remarkable what a sweet woman and the right music can do to a man. Suddenly poetry starts emerging, from a mouth more accustomed to cussing bad word. Andrea did look fit, but she probably couldn't have achieved such eloquence without the help of Ladies Choice Hi-Fi, which was pumping its lovers music with a vengeance. The couples on the dancefloor, had abandoned the popular reggae dance for some serious smooching. Anywhere else, their dancing may have been considered obscene.

"You say you full up of action," Andrea teased, she had begun to take a real fancy to this guy. "Well, food soon ripe for you to take your bite. Now's your chance to prove yourself."

Spence didn't need any more hints. He hurried Andrea off the dancefloor, out of the venue and into his Ford Granada. He was lucky not to get pulled, the speed he was driving.

Nightfall had darkened the skies by the time they left the bar with little resolved. Thomas offered to drive Max back to Brixton. She accepted and he directed her towards a BMW convertible parked a short distance from the venue, along a dark, narrow back alley.

Inside Thomas's newly-acquired dream vehicle, the two paused for a moment. They knew what they had come there to do, and they had no doubt that they were going to do it. But each felt obliged to give the other a moment to opt out. It was exceptional circumstances. They were getting themselves into something bigger than the both of them.

Thomas broke the impasse, by kissing his conquest lightly on the back of the neck. Max enjoyed the oral caress a little too much. She dropped her hand down to touch his, very lightly, looking at him hard as she did so. At this precise moment, words were not necessary. The ache she had for him spoke much louder than words as Thomas's hands softly caressed her body.

Now let's get this clear, Max loved Beverly like a sister. But Max also loved good sex. It was like a drug to her. You know how it is with some drugs, you'd sell your own sister to get a bit. She had enough experience with men to see that Thomas was good sex. He was handsome, he was fit. Blood would run if Beverly found out, she warned herself. If she slipped up, she'd slide and break her back. But it was too late now. Something, like a stream, was running through her heart, making her as happy as she could be. No amount of good sense can rule when a woman follows her heart. Love was in the air, and she felt totally at ease with Thomas. She felt there was something quite fantastic about him. It was the perfect situation for a love affair. She would take the chance. All in love is fair, she concluded, as she began a brand new episode in her life.

"Oh no....it just can't work," she moaned as Thomas's hands slipped down the front of her jeans. "I'm gonna get hurt....'Cause if you mess with me, I tell you, it could be dangerous."

Thomas continued undaunted. His heat was on and he was in a hurry to lay it on. To his pleasant surprise, he discovered that she didn't have knickers on. He was ready, and when he felt her womanhood oozing wet on his wandering fingers, he knew she was also ready. He looked her in the eye and replied, "Hush darling. Even if it hurt, don't cry."

"But Thomas.... Beverly....? My friend....," she gasped.

"Please!"

"Me nah response fe dat, Max," Thomas insisted. "Ah jus' so it go." He wasn't interested in talking about Beverly. As far as he was concerned, none of his doings was ever wrong.

"I don't want the news carrying," she begged. "I don't want to lose Beverly. She's my friend."

He looked at her incredulously. "You t'ink seh I go telling everybody wha' me know?"

"Oh, just give it to me Thomas," Max sighed, a mischievous twinkle in her eye. "Just give it to me and do it to me. I've got to have you right away."

With that she pulled him towards her, diving into his warm and willing mouth, with her tongue. The course they were embarking on was one they would have to endure, come whatever the eventual outcome.

Love is not for the swift, but for those who can endure it. Max and Thomas had endured the long wait since his pass at the wedding, but only just. There was no time for foreplay. She had genuinely only intended to have a ten minute feel up, to release some of that pent-up energy. But once they had started, she knew it was going to be good and intensive. She intended to start from the beginning and take her time reaching the end.

One moment, he was reclining the seats and the next moment, he was easing his rock hard manhood into her inviting heaven, oblivious to the fact that they were parked in a public street.

They started moving in the groove. Slowly and deeply at first, then faster and faster and faster.... Then slowly and deeply again. They were just starting to get to know each other.

He made her respond to his every movement and she, incredibly frustrated as she was, wanted his body more and more with every thrust. She finally found out whether Thomas ate off a two foot table. He loved oral sex. It was wild, animalistic.... One position after another.

From the summit, they slowly, twitchingly, returned to the calm of complete satisfaction. They both lay perfectly still, she on top of him. Thomas had exploded into her like a Scud missile, though much more accurately. Her simultaneous orgasmic moaning had assured him that he was spot on. He never knew she could 'whine' so fine.

100% hot loving. Illegitimate loving, but 100% nonetheless. Neither of them was prepared to feel like a criminal.

"I will keep you warm," he whispered in her ear. "Whenever you want me...."

Max put her forefinger to his lips, telling him to hush, but he continued with the pose up.

"Just a few words....a few words. That's all I need to say, 'I love you.' "

Max hadn't completely recovered. Thomas had touched her soul, and the tingling hadn't stopped. Her pussy throbbed with pain, but tingled with pleasure.

"You sure know how to do it to me," she smiled. " There's no other lover quite like you. You do it so good that I really want more."

She had feelings for him she couldn't understand. The girls nowadays don't want no one minute man. She wanted his loving and wanted it non-stop.

He was only too willing to have another one for the road.

Andrew was asleep in the living room, when Max returned home late that night. He woke as she slammed the door shut.

"Oh!" Max exclaimed as she saw Andrew's silhouette rise up from the sofa. "Oh! It's you, Andrew," she said guiltily. "I didn't know you were coming by."

"Where've you been all this time," Andrew asked suspiciously. "It's after three."

"Oh, I was out with the girls. Remember I told you, I was going up to the Afro-Hair and Beauty. Well, we went for some drinks afterwards. You know how it is? How comes you came around?" she asked changing the subject quickly.

"I wanted to see you, because I've got to leave town at the end of the week for a few days, and go to my parents' place. My father is very ill, and I have to help sort out his business affairs. I spoke to my mother yesterday. She seemed quite distressed. He's been ill for a long time, but he's always managed to carry on with the business. Apparently, he's just bed-ridden now."

"Oh I am sorry." Max's tone turned to one of genuine sympathy. "You never told me that he was seriously ill. I hope he'll be alright."

"Parkinson's disease," Andrew answered. "He's not going to be alright, these things go on for years."

"I'll come up with you and help you!"

Andrew looked at his concubine seriously. She had overstepped the boundaries of their relationship. She was genuinely concerned, and didn't stop to think.

"You know that I don't ever take women to meet my parents," he replied slowly. "They....they're old fashioned....They'll start poking their noses in."

Max looked at Andrew hard. What was his problem. The

114

man's father is dying, and he's got to rush off, but he's not prepared to take any help from her. What was the big deal? Plenty men would jump at the chance of having their woman at their side during their time of grief.

"Come off it Andrew! How long have we been going out together, and you're afraid to take me to meet your family. Look, I don't give a toss about them and their ways, I'm big enough to take it all. But I'm not big enough to have you being ashamed of me, or whatever else is on your mind. If that's the case, you can forget it! I'm coming with you. It's about time I met your family, unless you think that I'm your prostitute, or somebody who just provides bed service....If you think it's only bed service I'm providing, and that is my only role in this relationship, then you can just get the fuck out of my life."

Andrew could see the anger boiling in Max's mind. What a drag. All he wanted out of life was a woman who would put up and shut up. Not this grief.

"I just don't think it's a good time...now...not a good time, that's all," he said.

"When then, eh? When? Come on Andrew. Your father's lying seriously ill, it's not like I'll get another chance to meet the guy, is it? Look, all I'm offering is to help. Don't pretend that you couldn't use me at your side when things are getting a bit tough. What's the big problem?"

"Alright, alright!" Andrew exclaimed. She didn't know what the big problem was, she'd have to find out. "Alright. We'll leave on Thursday. I need to drive all the way, because I've got some business in Manchester on the way up, otherwise I'd say we should fly."

"Fly? Where the hell do your parents live?"

"Scotland. Four hundred miles away. It will be a really nice drive. Have enough clothes packed for a week. Nothing fancy. Nobody up there would appreciate it."

Max looked at him long and hard, trying to figure out if he really wanted her to come, or whether he had simply given in under duress.

"I'm going with you to your family, because I want to see what you're family's like, I want to know them and I want them to know me....'Cause if I am as important to your life as you keep saying, I want a clear commitment. I'm not prepared to be hidden away. I want an acknowledgement of who I am and what I do for you, not just on a business level but on a personal level as well."

115

Thomas returned home at four o'clock in the morning. He was on a high after scoring with Max earlier that evening. But his high was laced with a feeling of guilt which he would rather have been without.

Making his way to the kitchen, he poured himself a glass of malt from the fridge, listening intently for any sound of Beverly moving about upstairs.

"She's asleep, so I won't have to face her," he concluded, relieved. He finished his drink and sneaked upstairs to the bedroom. Beverly appeared to be asleep. The thought crossed his mind that she may be faking it, but at that precise moment he didn't particular care whether she was or not. He began to remove his clothes and sat on the edge of the bed in his boxer shorts, contemplating the night's adventures for a moment. He knew that his feelings for Max were more than a passing whim. So strong in fact that he knew that he and Beverly could not continue living together. He had ceased making love to her the previous week, because he was tired of her. He didn't find her attractive any more, she was dead stock. Though Beverly was initially glad for the respite from the indifferent encounters Thomas had turned their magic moments into, after the third day she began to be worried. Sex, however dull, was all that remained of their relationship. And she knew how much Thomas loved his sex. He could hardly go through a day without it. If he wasn't getting any from her, he had to be getting it elsewhere. And if so, what was left of their marriage. She needed their marriage, to give her the respectability she craved so much for.

She opened her eyes and sat up in the bed beside Thomas putting her arms around him.

"Listen, is something wrong?" she asked innocently.

Thomas simply kissed his teeth. She tired again.

"Is there something wrong at work...or is there something troubling you that we can....talk about?"

Thomas simply climbed into the bed and turned his back on Beverly saying, "Right now I want to sleep. Seen?"

Beverly said nothing. In fact, she really just wanted to remain silent, but her heart was saying no. This was the third night this week that Thomas had come home in the early hours of the morning. No explanations as to why or where he had been. Considering they were newly-weds this was unusual to say the least.

The thought crossed her mind constantly that it could be another woman. Her previous experience with men suggested that Thomas's change in attitude, his changed manner, his continued indifference towards her, was to do with a woman.

But she hadn't seen Thomas with any woman. Nobody came to mind. And she hadn't been getting any mysterious phone calls from women asking to speak to him, or slamming the phone down as would be usual.

While Thomas fell asleep, Beverly stayed awake. As he slept, she listened to his deep, even breathing. She had previously found this very irritating because it kept her awake. Not tonight though, she welcomed the sound, using it to cradle her body as her heart cried silently.

There was something about his offhand, disinterested manner after coming home late without so much as an apology or an excuse, that alerted her feminine instincts. Close to him in bed, she could just about smell the faint fragrance of expensive perfume as it changed to his body odour. The perfume reminded her of Maxine, but she put aside the thought. No, not Maxine. Whoever it was though, had a taste for the best perfumes and probably a lot of money to go with it. Beverly laid her head gently on the pillow. She felt dirty and betrayed. How could Thomas do something like this to her? They had only been married a couple of months, and she was already sure that he had been intimate with another woman. She couldn't take it anymore, so she pinched Thomas awake.

Never wake a man in his sleep, not if you love your life anyway. Waking a man in his sleep is asking for trouble. Ask any black man, or ask their women who have had to learn the consequences. Thomas had a look of death in his eyes, and truly he terrified Beverly, but she tried to sound as casual as possible. Even to her own ears, her question sounded limp.

"Where were you Thomas?" she asked. "You know, you could have been anywhere. You could have fallen under the wheels of a lorry, you could have been in hospital. I'm not turning into a moany cow, I just want to know where you were. I don't want to make a big deal out of it."

Thomas simply stared at her, with murder in his eyes. Beverly continued, tense but undaunted.

"Look Thomas, what's the big deal? This is the third night this week that you come in after four in the morning. You know, if you have a woman, then I want to know about her. If you've got some other problem, then let's talk it out. Let's sit down and try and see if the two of us can work it out."

Thomas could feel the anger in Beverly and he sensed that she really wasn't going to give in. In fact, she was just warming up.

"Thomas," Beverly barked indignantly, "I'm trying to talk to you, man. Wha' do you? Can't you show a bit of manners and answer me?! I'm supposed to be your wife and you're treating me like I'm some stupid girl!"

Thomas eased himself off his pillow and towered glaringly over Beverly. But she was not about to let this put her off.

"Thomas, just speak to me man. I just wanna know where you were. You have to go to work every day, yet you come in....this is the third night in a row, and you come in at four o'clock in the morning! What kind of lifestyle is that? What am I supposed to say to the children when you come home in the early hours of the morning, and they can hear you? And then, when you come in, you just come bring in your stinking self, and park it in my bed?! But Thomas, that's not right! You're seriously out of order!!"

"Well Beverly, it look like seh you set for me t'night, don't it?" Thomas said menacingly. "But right now, all I want to do is go to sleep. And I suggest that you do the same..."

Beverly, aware that her husband was on the threshold of losing his temper, wanted to let the discussion go, but she just wasn't able to. Something inside of her was telling her that something just wasn't right in Thomas's behaviour, and she wouldn't or couldn't, let the issue go.

"Thomas, this can't go on," she insisted. "It's ridiculous. I thought that being married or taking the steps to being married, you'd want to...you know....We're supposed to be making a commitment to each other. This isn't making a commitment. Coming in, early hours of the morning. Not saying where you were. Stinking of cigarettes and perfume. It don't make sense. Have I done you something?"

Thomas kissed his teeth again.

"Beverly, shut the fuck up. I don't want to listen to what you have to say, I am going to sleep."

Beverly sat there for a few moments. She pondered. Should she pursue it, or should she fall asleep and let it go? But if she fell asleep and let it go, this would give Thomas the right to cuss her down whenever he felt like it. Whereas most women would have brushed off their husband's swearing as being a man just trying to talk his way out of an argument, Beverly saw it as a big insult. A major insult! A major spite on her as an individual. How could her husband tell her to "shut the fuck up?!" She got up angrily off the bed with her hands on her hips.

"Thomas, when I talk to you, I don't swear! So what makes you think that I, even though I am your wife, I should have to sit back and take that kind of rubbish?! "

She waited for a few moments, edging for a response from him. But the response she got wasn't quite what she was waiting for. Thomas got up quickly from the bed, and stood squarely in front of her. She looked up at him. Waiting. Sensing....

Before she could think of anything else, the blow to her face with the back of Thomas' hand struck her squarely on the face. She didn't even have the chance to raise her hand to protect herself. The blow had come swiftly and sharply.

Her crying had little effect on Thomas. In fact, it seemed to make him more angry. He looked at Beverly whimpering on the floor. He felt nothing. Nothing at all. He turned and got back into bed and fell into a cold sleep.

Beverly felt so helpless, there was nothing she could do. Thomas had never showed any violence to her before and his assault left her stunned. What the hell was going on? She did not understand any of it.

Beverly put a hand to her mouth. The throbbings from her lower lip seemed to be intensifying. She got up and went to the bathroom. In the bathroom mirror, she examined the swelling that had already developed on her lip. She looked at herself and shook her head. Even to her own eyes, this was unbelievable. She'd only been married months and already she was being knocked about by her husband. This was completely new to her. She had never been hit by any of her previous men.

She lowered her head into the sink and splashed some cold water on her face. She tried to rationalise what had happened and thought that possibly Thomas was under some kind of strain at work and therefore, not knowing how to get rid of his pent up frustrations, was taking it out on her. But even to Beverly it was a pitiful excuse.

Tears welled up in her eyes as she made her way timidly back to the bedroom and silently got into the bed.

Beverly stayed awake most of the night. What was she to do? As she considered her options, a deep sleep came over her and she slipped into dream land.

Beverly got up as usual at seven o'clock that morning to get the children up. Thomas had got up and left for work an hour before. She was baffled by Thomas' Jekyll and Hyde transformation. Pride would not allow her to think that it was another woman. After all, in her book, Thomas was supposed to be her knight in shining armour. Or the closest to it. Her heart wanted to hold on to the past, but her brain was saying, get out fast, there's danger!

NINE

Thomas picked up another heavy box, his brow breaking with sweat. This was his daily toil at the warehouse where he worked. It was good for the muscles and kept him fit, but it was a job he despised. Carnival was still a couple weeks away, but a rare tropical heatwave had put Brixton on a *'maas* alert' since the beginning of the month. Thomas would rather have been driving along Acre Lane with his top down than working in a steaming warehouse, where the temperature was 86 degrees in the shade.

After depositing the box full of alarm clocks on a shelf, he decided it was time for a tea break. Fari was already in the tiny alcove they called a tea room, immersed in his copy of The Voice with a cup of tepid coffee in his hand. Thomas sat down opposite the elderly rasta, hailing him up as he did so. They exchanged the usual pleasantries as one does at work. They discussed a dance that they were both at the previous week. Shaka the indomitable lion of Deptford was on the wire, and as usual the session had been rammed to the max.

"Fari, did you get any overtime?" Thomas asked changing the subject.

"Overtime? It's just like that fool boy Smith. I could just set for that boy, y'know. Truly, I could just set for him!!"

Thomas tried to calm his dreadlocked workmate down, "Cho, just let the man carry on about his ways. There's no problem, you know. That's how he stays, and he's the boss. There's nothing we can do about it."

The pair spent as long as they could get away with in the tea room, before going back reluctantly to work, the irate Fari even more reluctantly than his workmate who had had little sleep the night before. As they went about their job of picking up boxes and lifting them onto their allocated shelves, Thomas watched his colleague out of the corner of his eye. He was rather worried about him. The glazed look in the rasta's eyes suggested that he was stoned. But that was nothing unusual. Fari was a man who loved his lamb's bread. He was always stoned. But he could handle it. Today, though, there was something different about him. He was muttering loudly to nobody in particular about the boss, not caring whether anybody heard him or not. Fari was

120

ranting ceaselessly, like some of the characters that walk around
Brixton all day long screaming passages from the bible.

Thomas and Fari had worked together for about eight
months. In that time, they had become good friends and learned
each other's idiosyncrasies. Though from different backgrounds,
they were still able to meet on a level. They had a common
enemy (the management at the warehouse) and a common bond
(the management was giving both of them a bit of trouble). To
both men, it seemed like Smith, the foreman, was constantly
looking for a confrontation. Not directly, but indirectly. Smith's
tactics were so subtle that an objective observer wouldn't have
picked up on them, but as far as Smith was concerned, he was
paying these blacks good money and he expected them to "work
like niggers." As far as Fari and Thomas were concerned, he was
getting on their backs for no reason. It seemed to them that he
would prefer it if they didn't work there. For whatever reason,
Smith saw Thomas in particular as some sort of threat to his
manhood. All the secretaries at the company loved Thomas,
because he looked fit. The way the young black man swanked
into work every morning, dressed in some crisp clothing, made
Smith look like shame. He disliked the younger man's
confidence. He hated the strength of character he saw and
resented Thomas for his potential in life. The fact that Thomas
was filling in time at the warehouse, until something better came
along, irritated Smith even more.

Fari continued to ramble on, forgetting himself totally and
getting himself more and more worked up, as the shift ticked
slowly away. He didn't notice Smith walking up to him. He
stood for a moment, and listened to the abuse Fari was hurling
at him. Thomas tried to get Fari's attention, but the rasta was in
his own world. Smith walked up to him, his face red with fury
and told Fari that his allocated overtime was no longer available.
Fari said nothing. But when Smith turned his back to return to
his office, Fari hissed in a low, but audible voice, "You're full of
shit!"

Smith stopped dead in his tracks. He couldn't believe his
ears. He turned around and faced Fari.

"I beg your pardon?!"

"I said you're full of shit. You're just full of it. Listen, if you
have a genuine argument to come to me with, let me hear it. But
don't come and give me this kind of hassle. You're fuckries!!
You have a personal vendetta and you're ignorant. I don't know
what kind of inferiority complex you're suffering from, but
don't come and heap it on me, right?! And anyhow you come
and tell anybody that this conversation took place, only me and

121

Thomas is here to witness it. And I'll swear blind it never occurred. So you just take your two little short leg and fuck off! Seen?!"

Thomas had stopped working, and now stood beside Fari, to form a common line of defence. He could see that Smith's forehead had become moist and there was a trickle of perspiration rolling down the side of his face. Thomas enjoyed seeing Smith squirm. Thomas's first instinct was to box the man one time. But he decided against it. Though Thomas was unconcerned about losing his job, he wasn't sure that Fari was prepared, or could afford, to lose his. Smith tried to speak, but Fari wasn't finished yet.

"I've been slaving in this warehouse for so many years, y'hear?! Never had a chance to talk with the boss. So me nah really appreciate a lickle bwoy like you. Y'hear! And for so long I've been living in this dump yah! Me ready fe die you understand?

"But jus' t'rough you nah know. Udderwise, you wouldn't come trouble me."

Smith looked at the two men staring at him, waiting for him to make his move. He knew he had no move to make but to back down. There was no telling what they would do to him if he put up any resistance. He didn't have the bottle to sack them either. The last time he had sacked a black man for no reason, the guy had waited for him outside the warehouse with five of his friends. The nervous foreman decided to drop the whole thing, and walked back defeated, to his office. Fari didn't bother to savour his victory. He continued griping to himself.

"It's t'rough seh dat man don't know what I can do to him," he confided in Thomas, a menacing tone in his voice. "It's only because I'm trying to keep my spirit calm by standing firm. Anytime that I want to do that man, I can deal with him. There's more than one way to skin a cat. When me ready to rain in blows on that man, I don't have to use it a physical way."

Thomas listened. He had often wondered about Fari. The middle-aged rasta was old enough to be his father and had much wisdom, and worldly knowledge. Thomas always listened to him, and gave him the respect he would give his father. Although he was a quiet man and said little, what Fari did say, he meant. He wasn't a man to waste words. If he said something, he had a reason for saying it. But sometimes, Fari spoke in mystical sentences, that needed a mystic man to unravel. Thomas had an idea of what Fari meant, but he wasn't altogether sure.

"What do you mean?" asked Thomas.

"How you mean, what do I mean? You nevah hear what I said? I'm not going to repeat it. You heard what I said. So jus'...hold your calm, because I don't want me an' you falling out."

Thomas calmed Fari down. He could see that the older man wasn't in the mood for any games.

"I heard what you said. I don't disagree with what you're saying, either. Because if the man play with fire, he must get burned by fire, an' if you know anyway to burn him then that's fine. Anyway!" Thomas paused, allowing the old man the chance to say something, but nothing was forthcoming. He proceeded cautiously. "You know, I have a problem....Erm, me have somebody give me a lickle trouble, you know. An' try as I might, I just can't warn them off. I just want...I just want them fe lef' me alone....You know wha' I'm saying?"

Fari looked up at Thomas. Yes, he knew exactly what his young friend was saying. Although he liked Thomas, he knew that the youngster was just a bit too hot-headed. Ruled too much by his emotions. He never really took time to feel his way around a problem properly. He knew that the smallest power in Thomas's hands could lead to disaster. But he liked the young man too much to turn him down, so he decided, 'well, alright'.

"Well, Thomas, what you asking me?"

"Well if you know somebody, that could maybe put me on to somebody to...you know? I just want my path clear so I can see through an', y'know, carry on with my day to day living. Because I'm finding that this person is blocking my view, y'know. I can't make headway. You know when you feel seh crosses deh 'pon you? An' you find seh bad luck ah tek you an' you don't know why?"

Thomas did his best to explain himself without giving anything away. However, Fari knew what he was dealing with, and took a pen from his pocket, and wrote down a number on a piece of paper, which he handed to his workmate. Thomas nodded gratefully.

"Just tek in dat piece of paper and when you done, jus dash it way. This is a serious t'ing, not to be messed with," the older man warned.

"That's cool by me, man," Thomas assured him. The two men resumed their hard labour, as if the conversation never took place. Both relieved that they didn't need to continue such a dangerous conversation.

That night, Thomas rang the number and made an appointment for the following day.

He set off early, because he didn't know the area well, and because he had only asked for the morning off work. The address he had been given was in deepest east London, over by Plaistow side. He made his way down there, and pulled up in his car, taking the precaution of parking around the corner from the terraced 'two up two down' house. Sometimes, it didn't pay to leave your calling card outside the place you were going. He smoked a large spliff.

He was at least half an hour early, but the front door opened as soon as he had touched the doorbell. The large middle-aged woman who stood before him looked fearsome. She had a knowing sneer on her face. Thomas tried to look inconspicuous but he felt uncomfortable. As she ushered him through the door, he was greeted by an array of people. They all sat motionless. Nobody daring to look in the eyes of the other people, for fear of being recognised at a later gathering. He would rather not have been there, but at the moment it was his only option.

The house was not uncommon in the community. It was the type of place that many know exists, but nobody admits to ever going there. Many at some time or other, go to seek a little guidance, or a little help from a specialist, to give them some direction. The spiritual world is not something to scoff at. This is a serious world, no joke business. Even those who do not participate in it could not deny that there was a certain power to be had in the world of *obeah*, or *juju* as the Africans call it. Most people believed in it. Even the ones who treat it with scepticism are wary of it. The most committed Christians claim that their belief is the only spiritual belief they hold, yet they are too afraid to confront *obeah*. They would rather take the line, 'don't trouble trouble unless trouble trouble you.' Few would deny that there are certain forces in this world, that have no logic to them. There are those forces which no one understands.

The large woman held open the door to the back room. Thomas peered into the dark room, not knowing what to do, as he had never been to such a place before. He half-expected someone to come through the door, but nobody came. The door remained open. He could see a silhouette beyond the entrance, but nobody presented themselves. The large woman explained that she didn't have all day, and ordered Thomas to step inside or leave the premises. He thanked her nervously and reluctantly made his way into the dark room, taking fright as the door was slammed shut behind him!

Now, he was in complete darkness. He tried hard to adjust his eyes, but he couldn't quite make everything out. The silhouette had disappeared and now he couldn't tell whether the person was standing in front of, or behind him. The sensimilla on his brain was playing havoc with his mind. He tried to shake his head into full consciousness, but it was good weed, and he was now truly under its spell. His brain had expanded too much and his eyes were too relaxed to focus properly. Using the other senses available to him, Thomas noticed first that the room was filled with the smell of incense. Although he used incense regularly himself he had never smelt any that smelled of such a bitter sweet scent. Suddenly a voice boomed out of the darkness, "Please take a seat, and state your business!" A flash light appeared out of nowhere and shone its beam unto a chair. Thomas, grateful for the light, hurriedly took his seat, trying to seem as relaxed as possible. But he wasn't fooling anyone, least of all the man who was now shining the flash light directly into his face, and who could see the fear in the young man's eyes.

A cackle of laughter broke the silence. A wall switch was thrown, and the light from the overhead electric bulb threw its stark glare, illuminating the room.

The old man cackled uncontrollably. Thomas could see him clearly now. Dressed somewhat shabbily and eccentrically in a dark brown gaberdine two-piece suit, covered almost completely with small bits of mirrors. Thomas looked at him, and saw himself reflected a hundred times in the man's jacket.

"It works every time," the man giggled. "Every time. People expect mystery....so I give them mystery."

The old man smiled, observing Thomas from underneath a wide brimmed hat. Thomas was new at the spiritual game, and felt decidedly uneasy. He clenched his teeth together, sniffing nervously. He looked about the room. There were candles everywhere. Candles and bits of mirrors littered every available space. A plethora of other meaningless objects cluttered the small room. There was nothing in particular that Thomas could focus on. Apart from the junk, the room was simple and non-descript. He waited nervously for the man to speak. The old man also waited. He was looking for a sign of the hunger in Thomas's eyes.

"How can I help you?"

"I uhm...ahm...I'm not sure what you can do," Thomas stuttered.

The old man looked at Thomas through steely eyes.

"Well, if you tell me what your problem is, I will try and see what I can do. I'm sure you realise that this doesn't come cheap. But you must speak the truth. Conversations with clients are treated in the strictest confidence, like any confession to a priest."

Thomas nodded.

"Well, I'm in a relationship," he began, "....and I don't want to be in it no more."

The old man looked at him hard. Thomas felt that he was possibly being judged. But that was not the case. After all, there weren't many stories the old man had not heard. Nothing surprised him anymore. He got all sorts of requests. It was the nature of the business. The old man was however, troubled by the growing number of young men that had come to him recently, all saying that they wanted to get rid of their woman. He sometimes wondered why they simply didn't walk out and leave their girlfriends, instead of insisting that he should do things to make the women get vexed, and leave of their own accord. What never ceased to amaze the old man was the apparent contradiction in the manner of the men he saw. Despite their so-called strength, and their claims that they knew how to handle and deal with their women, men still flocked to him begging for help. If they really were as strong as they made out, they would simply walk away from a relationship that wasn't going too well.

"I just want to get rid of her," Thomas said finally. "Right? Because there's somebody else right now who I want, who I want to be with and she's the only person I want."

The old man looked at Thomas, searching for some doubt in the young man's eyes. If there was the shadow of a doubt, he could change the youngster's mind. He searched and searched, but couldn't see anything. Thomas was resolved to go through with it.

"Do you have something that belongs to your woman, or should I say your wife?"

Thomas looked down at his wedding ring. It had given the game away.

"Yes, we are married....But with your help, it won't be for much longer."

"I need something that belongs to your wife," the old man repeated. "Something personal. Have you brought anything like that with you?"

"Well no, I haven't."

"I need something personal from her. What exactly do you want to happen to her?" the old man enquired hesitantly.

"Well I want the woman out of my life. I want her out! I just want her out!"

In his dream world, Thomas wanted Beverly to disappear so that he could move in with Max, with whom he could make a

126

new start. He was crazy about his new-found love, the long-legged unofficial beauty queen of Brixton. He realised that he had made a mistake of his marriage, and right now, he couldn't stand the sight of his wife.

The old man asked Thomas if he was sure he wanted that. "Because what is done can't be undone," he stressed.

Thomas nodded his head in a slow, deliberate manner.

"Alright, maybe I can help you, but once you go on this road there's no turning back. Do you understand? I presume that you just want her confused enough to go elsewhere, yeah? But you have to bring me something that belongs to her, and when you come back, I'll tell you what you have to do. So if you don't mind, just leave the money on the table."

"That's cool, how much do I have to pay you?"

Thomas counted out the notes and left. After he had gone, the old man shook his head and smiled to himself thinking, "What a young fool! They just never learn." The old man was blessed with certain gifts, which he would rather have put to a positive use. But human nature being what it is, he made most of his living from the misery of others, by practising the old ancient crafts handed down by a thousand generations, in a bad way. Sometimes, people brought misery on themselves. These ancient arts had started out as a way for people to protect themselves and each other, but today were being used to do harm, in a world where people were prepared to do almost anything to someone they disliked. Most of the old man's customers were people wanting to teach their friends a lesson. It was a pity, the old man thought to himself, that more people didn't realise and learn that it's not your enemy that's the most dangerous to you, it's your friends. 'Cause only your friends know your secrets, so only they can reveal them. Only your friends have the inside knowledge of what you're doing and how you think. Only those closest to you can use that knowledge to do you real harm. Keep your friends close, and your enemies even closer.

The phone had rung several times before Max woke up.

"Max...?"

"Andrew. How are you darling?"

"I'm alright. And you?"

"Look, I haven't got time to speak very much right now, because I'm just about to go into an important meeting. I was trying to get hold of you all last night, but there was no answer."

"Oh, I must have been fast asleep," Max lied.

"Look, I'll pass by at noon to pick you up for the trip up to Scotland."

"What....? Oh, yes, of course." Max had forgotten about the trip to Andrew's parents place. She remembered the fuss she had made about accompanying him on it. Right now she wasn't in the mood for going up to Scotland. Thomas had been a regular thing for the past six days. They had such a good thing going, she had clean forgotten about Andrew's sick father. She preferred to stay in London, with Thomas in her bed the whole weekend. "Look, are you sure that you don't want to go up there on your own....if you feel it would be better?"

"No, not at all. You were quite right, Max. I ought to share my emotions and my family life with you a lot more. I just wish we weren't going up there in circumstances such as these. They say that my father's very ill."

"Perhaps it's not a good idea if I came this time?" Max offered. But Andrew insisted. She had brought it on herself by demanding to go earlier in the week, and now he expected her to follow him. There was no way out. Andrew couldn't figure out why Max suddenly sounded reluctant. Oh well, he had other things on his mind for the moment. They would perhaps have a chance to reason it out later.

The conversation over, Max replaced the receiver on its cradle, rolled over to the other side of the bed and pulled out a pack of Silk Cut from the bedside drawer. She hadn't had a puff in a month. But she could feel a nicotine urge. This was going to be a drag of a weekend. She just wasn't in the mood to play wife to Andrew's family. She resolved to take with her the whole quarter ounce of weed that she was saving for her sexual liaison with Thomas. She imagined that she would need all the help she could get to kill the boredom of a weekend in the countryside.

Max's travel bag was packed with the usual toiletries and waiting in the hall, when Andrew arrived to pick her up.

They drove off in his 3.5 litre Rover. It was one of the old ones, with thick leather seats and a walnut dashboard. In its earlier life, the car had been used by a former prime minister. The ideal car for a long journey. Andrew slipped the motor into drive and roared its 150 horsepower engine along the streets of Brixton. He headed north.

In all her twenty-five years, Max had rarely seen more of Britain than the inner cities. Locked in her own thoughts, she took in the country views. The air was fresher and clearer than she was accustomed to in South London. And as they got deeper and deeper into the countryside, she could feel that she was leaving the city tensions behind her. She was getting more and more excited about the prospect of meeting Andrew's family. She felt that in the mood she was in, she could take them on. Little did she knew that she was inadequately dressed for the occasion.

They stopped in Manchester for an hour, and then back on the road again. A few more hours, and the motorway gave way to a trunk road. Another hour or so, and they were on a tiny country road.

"We're really in Scotland now," he informed her. He had said very little during the journey. And almost nothing about what she should expect at his family home.

The roads got smaller and smaller. Eventually, the Rover was brought to a halt by a herd of sheep trying to cross the road. Max couldn't believe it.

"It's just one of those things you have to put up with in the countryside," Andrew explained.

The shepherd raised his flat cap to extend his thanks to the driver. As the Rover pulled alongside, the shepherd peered in and immediately recognised the driver.

"Oh.....hello Master Andrew," the man totally ignored Max. "Well, what a surprise....It's a long time since we've seen you up this way. I hope you'll be staying a while this time. Make sure you drop by and see myself and the old lady before you go back to London, won't you?"

Andrew assured the shepherd that he wouldn't dream of departing without popping in to see him. They bade each other farewell.

Max noticed that the shepherd had not acknowledged her presence. But she didn't know if it was down to her colour, or because he didn't actually know her and like some men, just speak to the person their addressing and not any other companion.

A road sign loomed ahead, indicating that the Fern Lodge Estate lay to the left up ahead. The South London girl noticed the sign, but it meant nothing to her. She simply eased herself comfortably into her seat as Andrew swung the car into the left bend. The Rover bumped along the gravel road. They passed a huge oak tree, beyond which Max caught her first glimpse of the huge mansion up ahead. She looked inquisitively to Andrew and back to the house up ahead. Andrew remained silent, saying nothing all the way up the drive to the house. He stopped the Rover in front of the great oak door of the mansion.

"Is this it?" she asked in amazement.

"Yes," Andrew answered solemnly. "Big, isn't it? Too big if you ask me."

Max sat motionless in the passenger seat, shaking her head slowly. She was expecting "to go ah country, to tek a lickle rest in her boopsie's parents' shack." Nothing could have prepared her for this. It began to dawn on her that Andrew was worth much more than his producer's salary. She felt like patting herself on the shoulder and saying, 'well done Max, you didn't just pick a sugar daddy, you picked the biggest daddy around.' She eased herself out of the car without taking her eyes off the house. With her hands on her hips she took in the full view from an upright position. She could not believe how wide the mansion was. All she could think was, 'this man doesn't make money, he is money.' She had surpassed her good fortune by having a man like Andrew fall for her. He got out, stretching his hand to her. They walked up to the house hand in hand.

Before they had even reached the great oak door it was swung open by an elderly man in a butler's uniform.

"Ah Master Andrew, welcome. We've been expecting you, and your guest!" The butler threw a cold half-glance in Max's direction.

"I see Wooton," Andrew remarked dismissively, "that despite your age, that your irreverence is as sharp as ever."

Max stepped into the huge hallway. In front of her, a magnificent curved staircase, divided into two sections, rose towards the left and the right of the house. She had to arch her neck all the way back to see the ceiling on which was a mural painted to represent scenes from the Bible. Max allowed herself to take in the sheer opulence of the place. Oil paintings which had no meaning to her, but were quite clearly expensive, hung on the walls. The marble floor she stood on was like a work of art in itself. The character of the house smelled money. There was nobody else to be seen, but Max could hear the hushed murmur of people talking in another room.

"My mother is here?" Andrew asked the butler.

"Yes she is, sir. She's in the drawing room at the moment, with your sisters."

Andrew gave Max a reassuring squeeze of his hand. Wooton sniffed at this open display of affection for the black woman.

"Dinner will be served presently," he announced, turning on his heels to collect the couple's baggage, and leaving them alone in the hallway.

"Servants," Max whispered to Andrew. "You have servants?!"

"Well in a house this size, you didn't expect us to do

everything on our own, did you?"

Andrew realised that this return home would be tense. It had been five months since he was last home, and he expected a certain amount of hostility from his family for not keeping in touch, although he had kept his eye on the family finances via their solicitor. If there was going to be heat, he'd have to take it, he decided, as he led Max into the drawing room.

Andrew's mother sat at the table, pretending to read a newspaper. She had already been informed by her daughters Lucinda and Abigail, that Andrew had arrived, with his black woman in tow.

Max stood in the gigantic room, feeling very uncomfortable. None of its occupants looked up to acknowledge the newly arrived couple. Lucinda sat motionless with her legs flopped over an armchair, pretending to read a book. Max noticed that the book was upside down. Abigail stood by a window peering out disinterestedly. Andrew could feel the tension in the air. His mother, Hannah, observed Max silently. Max got the message. She was unwelcome and wasn't sure how to deal with it. What she was sure of was that the next couple of days would be hell if this treatment continued.

Andrew's mother continued looking Max up and down, her nose in the air. The angle of her nose spoke contempt for the girl's dress sense; the slim heeled shoes, the very tight striped trousers, and matching jeans jacket and the fake gold jewellery or 'cargo'. Max felt the heat of the examining eyes, and looked to Andrew for some moral support. He took her by the hand, leading her across the room to his mother, for formal introductions. Hannah coldly looked at Max and said, "I'm not entirely happy about you being here, but there are certain matters that need Andrew's urgent attention, matters of legality which cannot wait. So I would appreciate your making yourself at home in the guest room. The staff will attend to your needs."

"Oh, thank you!" Max replied with overstated gratitude, a mischievous twinkle in her eye. Pulling Andrew towards her, she gave him a very long, intimate kiss. She turned to face Hannah triumphantly, executing a perfectly overstated curtsy followed by an exaggerated bow.

The shock on his mother's face made Andrew grimace. He knew that his woman would be unwelcome at the family home, but had hoped that Max would use her own sense of survival to deal with it. The heat was really centred on Max, but he was well aware that she could hold her own. Unless she was able to come out on top by herself, his sisters and mother would make licorice all-sorts of the unworldly Max.

Abigail moved away from the window. She walked around Max in a wide circle, looking her up and down as she did so. Finally, she walked out the room haughtily with an exaggerated gesture of disgust.

The gesture completely floored Max. She had come across prejudice before, but to actually have someone eye her up and down, and treat her with such disdain was too much. The girl was lucky to be standing up, because in any other situation, Max would have just hauled her back into the room by her collar and given her what for. The Scottish wilderness was unchartered territory for most Brixtonites.

Now it was the other sister's turn to deflate Max. Looking up from the book she was pretending to read, Lucinda addressed her.

"I presume you have a name?"

"I presume you have manners," Max retorted as she left the room. She had exchanged pleasantries enough. Now she needed to find a bathroom somewhere, and get to her room so she could enjoy a cool relaxing spliff.

Back inside the drawing room, Andrew's mother was fuming.

"What the hell do you think you're playing at? Your father's on his death bed, there are important papers and documents that need to be signed, the estate has to be sorted out; and you have the audacity to bring your black whore back with you! It may suffice in London, but it won't do out here."

"There was really no need to treat her like that," Andrew protested half-heartedly.

"I'm really not the slightest bit interested in which whore you happen to have picked up this week," his mother replied.

"She's not a whore, she's my er....."

"She's your what? She's your what?! For god's sake Andrew, don't tell me that is your girlfriend. She couldn't possibly....Your bed partner yes, but she certainly can't be your girlfriend?!"

Andrew didn't see the point of arguing with his mother on the issue. She really wouldn't have been able to comprehend his need for Maxine. Their relationship, for him, was no longer just a physical thing, he had an emotional investment in her. Emotion for a black woman, was something his family could not understand.

"She is my girlfriend," he insisted.

"She may well be your girlfriend today, Andrew, and she may well be your girlfriend tomorrow. But if she's not your girlfriend in a month's time, she's a whore!" Lucinda interjected. Not that she ever had anything of any consequence to say herself. Lucinda echoed her mother's every word like a parrot.

Andrew sat on his favourite stool and asked about the deteriorating health of his father. They had been expecting his death for some time now, but the old codger had hung on in there.

"My purpose here is to make my peace with father, sort out the estate's paperwork, and be here for the funeral," Andrew stated. "How much time has he got left?"

They went over the formalities for the old man's impending death. Andrew spent an hour looking over the legal papers, and felt quite drained when he left the room in search of Max.

On leaving the family to themselves earlier, Max had made her way up to her prepared room, escorted by Wooton. The butler had informed her that "M'lud of the house is an Earl!"

Though Max had an idea that Andrew's parents might be wealthy, she could never in her wildest imagination have anticipated that they were a titled family. It was quite an awesome thing for her to walk leisurely up the beautiful staircase, with large paintings of deceased ancestors peering down on her from the walls. She found the house quite breathtaking. Built in the late eighteenth century, its interior design belonged to the more recent Edwardian age.

The weekend was a disaster far worse than Max had anticipated. She was unprepared for the hostility that Lucinda and Abigail always found time to hurl her way, despite their dying father. Max decided to lock herself in her bedroom, in self-imposed imprisonment. Andrew had attempted to make love to her on their first night at the mansion. The fact that his father was lying down the hall on his death bed did nothing to suppress his sexual appetite. But Max wasn't having any of it, and played dead. It seemed no amount of caressing, kissing or other manipulation had any effect. She felt bitter that Andrew was not supporting her, and told him so. This led to a heated argument. "It's just not bloody good enough!" Max said angrily. "You'll just have to tell your posh family - your high and mighty family - that I'm not your whore. I'm not some black wench that you picked off the street, right! I'm a black woman who shares your bed, in your life, and who you care for. Because the way I see it Andrew, unless you tell your family so and that you're in love with me, and that we have a loving one to one relationship, I can't see where the fuck we're going."

Andrew rolled over onto his back and let out a heavy sigh.

"I don't need this right now, Max. My father's on his death bed, I've got mountains of paperwork which has to be done, and the last thing on my mind is to involve my family in my relationship with you. I know how I feel about you, I'm secure in that knowledge. I do not have to explain myself to my family."

"I don't give a fucking shit what you think," Max spat venomously.

"I know that the way your family's treating me....It's like a way of telling me, that we're not going anywhere fast. Are we? Can you imagine the look on your mother's face if you were ever to entertain the thought that you might marry somebody like me. You may not have noticed that I am black, but she has!"

"No, no no...of course I didn't notice that you were black Max, and I'm a bloody Chinaman!" he said sarcastically.

They went on for a while throwing small insults at one another. Max was deadly serious. Andrew tried unsuccessfully to defuse the situation by pacifying her in a low seductive voice. In the end, he was overcome by tiredness and gave up his amorous intentions as he slipped into slumberland.

The next morning, Andrew thought he was dreaming. Could this be the same woman, who last night played like the vestal virgin? He was laying on his stomach and woke up to the series of very gentle butterfly kisses Max planted on his back, his shoulders and his ears. Could this be the same beautiful young woman, who rejected his most amorous advances just hours earlier? He wanted to play hard to get, but Max knew better. He began to wriggle under her as she kissed and caressed him. She knew that his body was reacting to her.

"I've changed my mind," with a mischievous twinkle in her eye. "I want you to prove just how much you care about me."

Andrew turned to her and smiled.

"Your wish is my command. I'd be very happy to oblige....."

They showered and went down to breakfast. The morning of passion had put Max in a good mood, which evaporated the moment she clocked Abigail and Lucinda across the breakfast table. She could tell that they weren't going to let up. Lucinda enquired about the type of job she did for a living. Max's first reaction was to tell her that she worked in a supermarket, but she thought better about it because she felt it would only enforce the stereotypes Andrew's sisters quite obviously had.

"I do work," she answered guardedly. "I am employed, and it's none of your goddamn business what I do for a living!"

Lucinda responded to Max's outburst with a triumphant look on her face, but kept silent. She had managed to game, set and match the black girl with her first serve of the day.

Max endured the scrutiny throughout the long breakfast. Even though the sisters and Andrew's mother ate their breakfast in silence, Max clearly understood that her presence there was not needed or wanted. The whole episode made her feel somewhat insecure about her relationship with Andrew.

By the Sunday morning, Max had decided that nothing could be accomplished by remaining at the mansion a moment longer. The situation was quite intolerable. She tried on several occasions to strike up polite conversation with Andrew's mother, but Hannah was not forthcoming, reiterating rather that it would be best all round if Max returned to her "housing estate," in London. Only the fact that Andrew's father was dying upstairs had stopped Max from throwing an insult at the mother. They weren't going to let her in, she decided.

Everything came to a head early on Sunday morning, when Andrew told Max that he had to leave on business and that she'd have to spend the night at the mansion without him. Max told him plainly, there was no way she was staying there on her own.

"No way! This house? With your family, who have no wish to have a black woman at their table? It's just not on. It's just not going to happen? Andrew, you've been acting like a little boy all weekend. I'm supposed to be your girlfriend! You should be able to tell your mother where to get off!"

"Grow up," replied Andrew coldly. "If my father doesn't die today he'll more than likely be dead by tomorrow, or the day after that. There's a great many things that must be dealt with, in the meantime. If you don't like it, then go back to London."

Max looked at Andrew coldly.

"Drive me to a train station," she said. "I'll leave now."

Andrew was reluctant to oblige, but agreed. Nothing could be achieved by having Max stay any longer.

Max sat motionless throughout the bumpy ride down to the local railway station. Andrew could feel her anger. He had never seen her this upset. He hoped that he hadn't lost her for good. But he didn't exactly know what to say.

"People say I'm not the type of man to be your lover," he said slowly. "But Max, you and I are good for each other."

Max said nothing. Andrew decided that perhaps now was not the time for words. The two sat in silence until Andrew's Rover pulled up at the small railway station. Without a word, Max took her bag from the car and walked through the station entrance.

Back in London, she called Andrea's and booked an appointment at the salon. She was literally going to wash Andrew right out of her hair.

TEN

It was the day before Carnival. To Beverly, it seemed like the whole of Brixton was in festive spirits except her. She had become increasingly desperate about her marriage. She didn't know where to turn and found herself taking her anger out on the kids. She knew it wasn't really their fault, but as she had no one else to hit on, they were easy targets.

Beverly washed up and got the kids ready. She made a call before leaving.

"Hi mum".

"Beverly? Is you? What's wrong?"

"Does anything have to be wrong? I'm just ringing to say that I'm bringing the children down for the weekend if that's still okay. You can still take them down to the Carnival tomorrow?"

"If you say so, Beverly. I'm not going anywhere, so you can come."

Beverly slammed down the phone, irritated at her mother's self-righteous tone. She had put up with it since she was a kid, but felt like she was a big enough woman now. Her mother didn't have to continue treating her as if she was ignorant about life.

She got dressed, slipping on a pair of leggings and an oversized t-shirt. She looked around for the new pair of high-heeled shoes, but couldn't find them in the wardrobe. After a few minutes searching, she found them under the bed. She was puzzled as how they came to be there as she was certain she'd put them away in the wardrobe.

She slipped the left shoe on, but found it to be a tighter squeeze than she expected. It felt like there was something jammed in the toes. She removed the shoe and examined it, shaking out a clove of garlic as she did. She couldn't figure out how it got there, but thought nothing much of it. It was probably Kenyatta and Ashika fooling around, she reasoned.

"Why do we have to stay with grandma for the weekend?" Kenyatta asked angrily as they made their way over to Beverly's mother, his sister Ashika running behind them.

"She wants to see you that's why. She is your grandmother. Just behave yourself!"

"I don't like to go there!" Kenyatta persisted. "She's always singing prayers. All the time! And she tries to get me to sing too. I never get to do anything I want to do there."

"Well that's too bad!" Beverly gave him short shrift. "You're going and that's the end of it!"

Kenyatta looked at her with tears in his eyes. Beverly could see that he hated her as she had often hated her parents when she was his age.

Beverly looked at Kenyatta and remembered how difficult his father had been during her time with him. Wesley was a man who liked to get his own way and when he didn't, he would sulk for days like a child. Their eight month relationship was generally a happy one until along came another woman. Within weeks he had packed his bags and left with the woman. A month later Beverly discovered she was pregnant. The last she had heard was that Wesley was married and living in JA.

"Don't bother give me no screw face, either. I'm warning you, Ken!"

Kenyatta burst into tears uncontrollably, unable any longer to take his mother's verbal onslaught. His sister, unsure of what was going on, took fright at the sight of her elder brother sobbing, and began to cry herself.

"You're just making us go there!" Kenyatta sobbed. "I don't want to go and Ashika doesn't want to go. But you're making us and that's not fair."

Beverly finished her preparations and ordered the reluctant children out of the front door. Outside Kenyatta continued his protestation.

"It's not fair. It's not fair. It's not fair." He complained.

"Don't talk to me about fair," Beverly retorted, walking briskly and forcing the two children to run tearfully in order to keep up. "And anyway Ashika likes going, don't you darling."

Still crying, Ashika shook her head hoping that it was the right answer.

Beverly simply sighed. She realised that she was making the children suffer because of the emotional crisis she herself was going through. It wasn't their fault. But there was no way she could be responsible for them tonight.

"So, are you staying for dinner?" Mrs Johnson asked when her daughter arrived at the family home on the Stockwell Green end of Landor Road.

Beverly looked at her mother hesitantly. She didn't really want to stay to dinner, but on the other hand, there was nothing to go home for. Thomas didn't want her. He was quite obviously eating elsewhere....

With the kids occupied watching telly in the living room,

Beverly sat down in the kitchen, making small talk as her mother prepared the evening meal. But her heart wasn't in it. Her mum realised this, but couldn't figure out what was troubling her daughter.

"Where is Thomas now. I suppose he's gone to work?"

"Yes," Beverly replied. In truth, she didn't know where Thomas was. He had gone out two nights previously and hadn't returned home.

"So, you're definitely not going to The Carnival?" Mrs Johnson asked.

Beverly studied her mum casually, wondering whether she was the right person to confide in.

"No mum. I don't feel too good this weekend?"

"You know Mrs Morris's daughter is expecting a child?" Mrs Johnson announced.

"Is she?" Beverly answered disinterestedly.

Her daughter's indifference hadn't gone unnoticed by Mrs Johnson. She sighed aloud, guessing what lay at the core of Beverly's lack of humour.

"So you thought marriage was going to be easy?" the older woman began. "You made a choice, a decision and therefore, you should stand by those decisions. Well Beverly, nothing in this life is easy."

Beverly realised her mother was going to start lecturing her. At this stage, there was nothing to do except sit back and take it.

"I love you to my heart Beverly," Mrs Johnson continued, "but you must realise, it's two children you have by two different man. And now you've chosen this man Thomas to marry and the likelihood is that you will have more children. The likelihood is that the road will be rocky, but you will just have to grin and bear it. You have to deal with it as best you can. Like we all do.

"Just remember that marriage is a beautiful creation. If you choose the right man, and hopefully you have, then things will work out right eventually. Nobody put a gun to your head Beverly. You went into your marriage with your two eyes open. So now you've made your choice, you'll just have to stick with it.

"So, did you want my advice about anything particularly, Beverly?"

Beverly shook her head. What could she say. How could she tell her mother about how Thomas was treating her? She felt isolated, confused. She was going through was a nightmare, yet there didn't seem to be a way out. She couldn't wake herself up.

No one to turn to. No one to ask questions.

In her heart, she knew she loved Thomas despite everything. Physically she loved him. Mentally she adored him. Emotionally, he overwhelmed her.

However, the strain of the contention between them was beginning to show on Beverly. She was even beginning to lose weight, a fact that had not escaped her mother's attention though she chose not to mention it.

Home alone that evening, Beverly got increasingly distressed pondering her marriage. She eventually picked up the phone and dialled Max's number. The answering machine was on, but Beverly decided against leaving a message. She called Merlene instead. Marlon answered.

"My mum's not in, Auntie Beverly," he informed her. "She's always out in the evenings."

Oh, I didn't know that," Beverly said, looking at her watch. It was eight o'clock in the evening. "Just leave a message for her to call me when she gets back, or just to come 'round. I'll be in all evening."

"That's if she doesn't come back too late."

Merlene must be seeing a man, to be staying out all hours, Beverly assumed.

"Whenever. Just leave the message. You alright yourself, Marl?" Beverly enquired of the boy.

"A bit bored on my own, but I'm okay."

"Well, like I say I'm here all evening, so if you get too bored, just call up. You going to Carnival tomorrow?"

"Yeah," Marlon answered nonchalantly. "My dad's taking me."

"Oh that's good, isn't it? Alright? Take care Marl."

For a moment, Beverly wondered what kind of a man was so important that Merlene would leave Marlon alone by himself all night? Then she dialled Andrea's number. She was probably not in as usual. She had a good thing going on with Spence, who had turned out alright. He took care of her well and couldn't get enough of her. As far as Spence was concerned, every day was an Andrea day.

"Hello," Andrea's voice came down the line.

"Andrea? It's Beverly."

Andrea was the last person Beverly wished to discuss her private life with. Since they fell out all those years back, Beverly had excluded Andrea from her intimate thoughts.

"Hi Beverly, how's things? Enjoying married life?"

Beverly said nothing.

139

"Are the kids alright?" Andrea asked sensing that something was wrong.

Again Beverly said nothing.

"Are you in trouble, Beverly?"

Beverly waited a few moments before answering.

"Andrea, if you're not too busy, will you just call round and see me?"

"Yeah no problem. I'll be there in about half an hour!"

Beverly hung up the phone.

Andrea guessed that married life wasn't as sweet as Beverly expected it to be. She wallowed slightly in her friend's misery. Thomas had seemed to her like the type of man who would give trouble. He was just a little too slick. Nonetheless, that's who her friend chose as her partner, and at the end of the day she had to back her.

A mini cab tooted its horn outside the flat and Andrea left for Beverly's house.

On arrival at Beverly's, Andrea was shocked to see the dishevelled state her friend was in. Beverly had obviously been crying for hours.

"Just look at the state of you," Andrea said concerned. "Just look how tangled your hair is. The first thing we're going to do, is sort you out, Bev. We'll soon have you looking fine in no time."

Andrea always carried a comb in her handbag in case she was called on in an emergency, to draw on her talents. Beverly however, was in no mood for beauty tips.

"Please, just sit down, Andrea," she begged.

"I was going ask Spence to drive 'round tomorrow afternoon and pick you up for Carnival," Andrea said, throwing the unwanted comb on the coffee table.

"I'm not going to Carnival," Beverly informed her dispassionately.

"A lie!" Andrea exclaimed incredulously. "Since when you nevah go to Carnival?"

"I'm not going!" Beverly repeated, a little more determined.

Andrea stopped joking and looked deep into Beverly's eyes. This was serious, she thought. Beverly must really be feeling it.

Beverly offered Andrea a cup of tea.

"Yes, just make sure you mek it sweet, I need to keep my sugar level up," the guest said, trying to cheer her friend up. "Because a young lady like me needs all the energy that she can get."

Beverly poured the tea and they sat down.

Andrea waited for Beverly to talk, but nothing.

"Why did you call?" Andrea asked eventually.

Fresh tears welled up in Beverly's eyes. Andrea wasn't sure what she was about to hear, but as Beverly wasn't the type of woman to cry easily, she knew it was important. She sat there and waited, until Beverly regained her composure.

"It's not working, Andrea," she whispered.

"What's not working?"

"I'm talking about the marriage," Beverly persisted.

Andrea wanted to choose her words carefully, but her conscience wouldn't allow it.

"What do you mean it's not working? What's not working? The whole thing? The children? He's not working? The sex life? What is it, Beverly?"

"Well everything. He's not coming in any more, or he's getting home in the early hours of the morning, with no explanation as to where he's been. He won't touch me. Anything that I say or try to talk to him about, if I talk to him about it too strong, the man's ready to raise hand."

Andrea's mouth fell open.

"What did you say?"

"You heard what I said, Andrea. Stop playing fool."

"You mean...." Andrea stuttered, "....in the short time you're ....you...." She couldn't find the right words. "Are you trying to tell me that this man was hitting you prior to getting married and you still went ahead and married him? But Beverly, I thought you had more sense?"

"Look Andrea, he didn't hit me before we got married!" Beverly protested.

Andrea was not convinced.

"He never hit you before you got married, and now all of a sudden, for no reason, he's decided to hit you? That don't make sense, Bev!"

"You don't make sense!"

Beverly knew how far-fetched it sounded to Andrea, but it was the truth. Thomas hadn't been violent before the wedding. Yes he had a temper, but if she thought at the time that he would ever lift up his hand and hit her, she would have gone! She'd never been out with a man that hit her. She knew other women it had happened to, but she had always maintained that she wouldn't stay in a relationship where she was being used as a punchbag. The fact that she had married Thomas made it slightly different, however. She couldn't just walk away because he had hit her, after all the expense the family had been through for the wedding. It would burn her parents. And she would be made a laughing stock. Married six months and then divorce!

141

She had to try and work it out.

"Well, what do you want to do?" Andrea asked. "Because you're the one who's in this marriage. Decide what you want to do, and take it from there."

Beverly knew that Andrea was right.

"Well, has he got another woman?" Andrea asked.

Beverly said she wasn't sure. Maybe, but she couldn't say for definite.

Andrea felt uncomfortable about being alone with Beverly at a time like this. The two women's relationship had been strained during their days as students at Brixton College. That's when Andrea first got off with Winston.

He had no connection with the college, but he used to hang around outside with his spar Fitzroy, taking in the breeze as the female students went home for the day. Andrea had seen him a couple of times and hadn't really taken too much notice. But one day he called her over. She was just eighteen and happy to be seen with this cool ragamuffin.

Winston sweet-talked her into bed within a few days. He was a charmer when he wanted to be and gave her roses and chocolates, and picked her up from college in his red BMW. By the end of the week they were making love two or three times a day.

The following Monday, Beverly came in to college after being off ill for a week. Stepping out on Brixton Hill after classes, she couldn't help but see Andrea and Winston snogging openly in his car parked right outside. She freaked out, screaming and tearing at her friend's hair. The situation soon developed into a full-blown fight, fanned by students pouring out of the college to urge the girls on.

Winston managed to come between the girls, separating them. Beverly, still screaming, spat in Andrea's face.

"You bitch," she hollered. "You dirty bitch!"

Andrea was too dazed to take in everything around her. She didn't know why Beverly had attacked her, but friend or no friend, she was going to fight back.

"Oh just shut up yourself, bitch!" Andrea retorted.

Later on that evening, Merlene called Beverly. Max had told her about the fight. After speaking at length with Beverly, Merlene then called Andrea and explained that Beverly claimed to be going out with Winston. Andrea couldn't believe it. That was the first she had heard of it.

When she confronted Winston later, he admitted he had slept with Beverly just before he met Andrea.

"But it was only a one-off," he insisted. "Me nevah seh nut'n to her 'bout no relationship!"

It took Merlene weeks of mediating to get Beverly to accept that it was all a misunderstanding, but she finally succeeded. The Four Musketeers went out raving together and Andrea and Beverly made up.

Though all that was in the past, Andrea still felt uncomfortable talking to Beverly about her marital problems.

"I'm not going to tell you what to do," Andrea declared finally, "but first of all, you should find out if there really is another woman, just in case something else is going down. Maybe it's something to do with drugs or whatever."

Beverly looked at Andrea shaking her head slowly. Thomas was a 'one spliff and a Heineken' man, he never touched drugs. They both knew this was to do with another woman.

"If it's a woman, can you think of anyone it might be?" Andrea suggested.

Beverly searched frantically through her mind to remember anything about anyone Thomas had taken a particular interest in, but she could think of no one. She hadn't seen him behave funny towards anyone, and she had not received any strange phone calls - nobody hanging up suddenly - so if there was a woman, where was she?

"So you definitely didn't have these doubts before you got married?"

Beverly answered honestly. "No."

"But Beverly even to your mind, nobody can change that quickly. And if he has changed that quickly, then get out. Tell the man to fuck off and get out. Right? You don't have to sit down in this kind of shit. I know that if man lif' up his hand and say he's coming for me, him ha' fe dead. Him can't live.... My mother never give birth to me so that any man can come and just say lif' up his hand and box me down, like seh him a box pickney. I wouldn't take it."

Beverly knew this to be true. Nobody could get rid of men as quickly as Andrea could. It left her with a rather dubious reputation since Winston's death because she was far from discreet. There was no denying that in her relationship with Spence Andrea was boss. Ah she run t'ings, t'ings nuh run she!

"Beverly, if you won't kick him out, I suggest that you and Thomas sit down and try and reason this thing through."

"Andrea, you don't understand, the man won't talk to me. I've tried everything. I cook, I clean, I wash....I do everything I'm supposed to do and it....it doesn't make sense. Y'know?"

"But tell me something, what happened on your honeymoon? Was everything alright then?"

Beverly looked at Andrea and began to squirm a bit with embarrassment.

"Well, if you don't want to tell me, cool. But you brought me here to talk this out. What I'm trying to find out here is where this thing went wrong. Because it couldn't be no sudden thing."

"I can't even put it into words. The honeymoon was okay, but he was kind of rough. Y'know? He didn't handle me like he was supposed to. He was rough man, like one of those men who don't really care about you. I don't know.... On the honeymoon, I put it all down to the pressures of the wedding and getting organised and so on. I couldn't really put my finger on it. Since we came back from Jamaica though, it's been worse.

"We got married for better or for worse, and a few months down the road now, this man's decided that he wants to get violent.

"Look don't get me wrong, Thomas has hit me only on one occasion but I'm worried that he might do it again.

"I just don't know why this is happening to me? I need to know. I even phoned up one of them tarot card business, just to cheer myself up."

Beverly reached across for her handbag and pulled out a flyer advertising a tarot card reader. 'Prince Elijah's Tarotscope.'

Tarot cards? It didn't surprise Andrea who remembered that Beverly had always been superstitious, but at the same time dismissive of the pop mystics who read the cards.

"You phone them tarot cards?" Andrea asked incredulously, taking the flyer and reading it. "You who said they were rubbish? You who said only misguided woman will turn to those things? You who said they couldn't help anybody and said how could a sensible, right-thinking person phone up one of those places and expect another person on the other end of the line to put their life in order for them? Now, look who's calling the kettle black."

Beverly had to smile. Andrea was quite right. She had previously run them down. But she was desperately clutching at straws. She had tried everything else to no avail. So she tried the unconventional. All she wanted, was to be given some insight into what the future held for Thomas and herself. A little insight to ease the pain.

Andrea held the flyer up to her nose and sniffed it. "Boy, even their paper smells funny."

"How d'you mean?" Beverly asked.

"Well you smell that and tell me if you don't think it smells of garlic," Andrea said, handing the flyer over.

Beverly took the flyer and sniffed casually. She had to agree, it did smell funny.

Beverly had called and made an appointment for the Tuesday morning after Carnival. She was going to see somebody who would either tell her "yeah, 't'ings are going to work out," or tell her if there was a woman involved, or say if there was something she was supposed to do to make things better. She would put her life in the hands of the cards and let them decide.

Andrea admitted reluctantly that she had also gone for tarot readings, but she didn't want Beverly to think that she frequented such places regularly.

"From time to time everybody needs a little help, a little guidance," Andrea said. She had gone for a reading when she first bought the salon and business wasn't going to good. "I just needed a little luck, y'know. I was talking about that with Max just yesterday, when she came in to have her hair done. She reckons there's nothing in it, but let me tell you, there's more to the tarot cards than meets the eye."

The women joked together for an hour, with Andrea succeeding in cheering Beverly up a little. However, Andrea felt she had to ram home her advice.

"Beverly, it can't go," she began. "It's tough out there as it is. I'm not ramping over this. If you want to stay in this marriage and play stush, then cool, you stay there and play stush. But I know that if you come ring me in the middle of the night and come tell me seh Thomas box you, or I get urgent phone call from hospital to seh you in there and you're unconscious, you can stay there. I will come, pick up your kids and take them where I live or take them where your mother yard or somewhere else, but don't expect me to come visit you in hospital, right?

"I don't business what other girls want to do. If they want to stay in their house and mek the man beat the shit out of them, that's their problem, right? You is my friend, and as a friend, I'm telling you get out! If the man's hit you already, him done. Him finish. I don't care if it only happen one time, he will do it again. You know that and him still here!

"It can't work, Beverly. If you want to sit down and work it out I'll 'llow you and say well, alright, do it. But nobody else can get you out of this kind of trouble, but you.

"Look, you love Thomas and I'm sure seh before this, you thought Thomas loved you. But Thomas is a man and a man is a dog. Now I've had enough of man to know that what you've just told me shows signs that Thomas pick up with somebody. It's not important who it is. The fact is that he's done it. What you have to do is tell him that he can either drop her or get out."

Beverly knew that Andrea was right, but this was different.

This wasn't some man she picked off of the street. This was someone she had married. This was someone she had vowed to spend the rest of her life with. Beverly wasn't prepared to give him up without a fight.

Beverly shifted uncomfortably in her chair and toyed with her wedding ring, twisting it nervously around her finger. Tears eventually welled up in her eyes. Within seconds she had broken down.

"Andrea I love him, that's all there is to it," she blurted. "I want him, I love him, I want him to be daddy for both of my children. I know things are uncomfortable at the moment, but I'm just hoping that with a little commitment, with some effort from myself, it's going to work out. I know what you're saying Andrea, and I agree with you. But I can't live my life the way you live your life. I don't really think it's fair to say I'm being stush. What does stush mean, y'know? If stush is wanting a man....your lover to be your husband, your keeper, your soulmate, then yeah, I'm stush. If stush means to be part of one whole unit with Thomas, then I'll stand up to be counted. I can't....I can't explain it to you....I can't justify it....But Thomas is the man I love....For whatever reason....Maybe, maybe it's not another woman. Maybe it's just pressures getting to him. After all, he's only just got married....Taking on two children that are not his....so....For the time being I'm just going to cool, y'know. Just let things ride. There's nothing I can do. He won't talk to me. And really and truly he's not a big talker anyway. So....." Beverly's voice trailed off.

Andrea observed her friend closely and shook her head. All Beverly said was bullshit. Had anybody else been in the predicament she found herself in, she would have seen the stupidity of it.

"Let me know how things go, and if it gets rough then we'll just have to see what goes down from there. But I'm telling you straight Beverly, if the man is lifts his hand up to you again, set the police on him."

It was a sunny Tuesday morning when Beverly left home to make her way to the tarot card reader. Brixton to Plaistow was one of those long and complicated tube routes that made you wish you owned a car. Beverly made a mental note to give Max a call about her Beetle. She had the money and she wouldn't mind having a car to cruise around in during the last few weeks of the summer. It would take her mind off her marital problems and it would help with the kids and shopping, now Thomas was never around.

She emerged from the underground and with the help of an
A to Z, found her way to a terraced 'two up two down' house.

The front door was opened the moment she touched the door
bell, by a large, fearsome-looking, middle-aged woman who
ushered Beverly through the door and into the dimly-lit room.
An old man sitting down behind a desk opposite the door
welcomed her. There was a hint of mystery in his voice.

"Come in faith and seek the wisdom of the tarot cards and all
will be revealed. Sit down!" he commanded, pointing to a chair.

Beverly did as she was told. Seated, she folded her arms
anxiously and crossed her legs.

The man looked at her long and hard. He could sense that she
was tense and he knew why. People were always tense on their
first visit. They didn't know what to expect.

"Unfold your arms and uncross your legs," he ordered.
"Folded arms and crossed legs put up a barrier. You have to be
totally transparent. Nothing is to come between you and the
cards."

Beverly unfolded her arms and spread her legs slightly apart,
apologising as she did so. She was still tense and the old man
knew it.

"Just relax, gyaal. That's the best way."

On a desk in front of him was a pack of cards. The old man
picked them up and handed them to Beverly.

"Shuffle them," he instructed her.

Beverly nervously accepted the pack and began shuffling
slowly. When she had shuffled sufficiently, she looked at the old
man . He took the pack from her hands and placed them on the
table, cutting the cards into two packs, putting the bottom half
on top and vice versa. He handed Beverly the cards once again
and told her to shuffle some more. Beverly obliged and once she
had shuffled sufficiently, once again handed the cards back to
the man. He once again cut the pack in two and counted out
seven cards from the bottom pile. The seven cards were spread
out on the table.

"Pick a card," the old man ordered.

Beverly did as she was told. The old man flicked the card
over and studied it momentarily.

"There's a man in your life," he said. "And you're having
problems."

Beverly nodded her head.

He invited her to select another card. She picked it and
handed it to him. He glanced at the card.

"There is no bondage between you and your husband," he

147

said. "Are you living in separate houses?"

Beverly shook her head.

"But you don't share the same bed?"

Beverly nodded.

"Resolve your differences," the old man advised her. "Resolve your differences quickly, or he will never be in your bed again."

Beverly chose another card.

"Your man has been mistreating you...."

As sceptical as she was, hearing her marital problems being described so perfectly by this tarot card reader had twanged the chords of Beverly's heart. Tears welled up in her eyes. Unable to contain herself any longer, she broke down, crying uncontrollably.

The old man sat through her weeping dispassionately. He was used to this. A tarot card reading to some women, was like the confession to Catholics. People often got emotional.

"Never mind, dear...." he tried to comfort her. "I told you that this tarot was a serious t'ing."

"I just want...." Beverly blurted through the tears, "I just want to hear some good news. I need to hear something positive. What's going to happen tomorrow, next week, next month. Please...."

The old man got up and walked over to Beverly to comfort her.

"It's alright," he said with a sympathetic arm around her. He noticed the wedding ring on her finger. It reminded him of another ring he had seen recently. And then it slowly dawned on him....

"An' your husband...." the old man continued, "he mus' be six feet tall and maybe more?"

Beverly nodded.

"He's a light skin breddah, an' he has a cut, jus' a lickle cut under his eye, soh?"

Again Beverly nodded.

The old man looked at her incredulously. Could this be possible? Not only was it possible, it had happened. On one hand the world is a huge place, he thought to himself, but on the other, it's as small as your own back yard. Life is full of unbelievable coincidences. Some just dismiss it as chance, while others call it fate. Only the gods know. They alone would no why fate had brought Thomas and Beverly to the same house in east London.

"I'm....I'm afraid I've got some bad news for you," the old man stuttered eventually, studying the cards with a worried look on his face.

"Those that hate and persecute you, are lying awake, plotting to steal your soul. They want to mess up your life. Watch your step, child."

Beverly couldn't believe what she was hearing. She looked at the old man rambling on. He had gone too far. He had a manic look on his face, and he was sweating profusely. She shifted on her seat, wishing he would just stop talking. She was paying good money to hear something positive. The old man had succeeded in destroying any hopes of that. She opened her handbag and got up to leave hurriedly. She pulled out some notes from her handbag and counted them. A clove of garlic had stuck unto one of the notes. She shook it free, making a mental note to remind Kenyatta and Ashika to stay out of her handbag, and counted out the agreed fee.

"Tek care child," he warned her desperately as she departed. "Tek care! Nah lend anybody your clothes to wear go pose, 'cause that can bring sudden destruction. Tell your friends to bring back the clothes weh dem borrow. Once you get them back, throw them away or burn them. If you can't get them back leave it and only accept a new replacement."

The old man rambled on and on, but Beverly had already switched off. She got out of the house as swiftly as she could, and breathed a sigh of relief.

She made her way quickly back to the tube station. She had planned to spend the afternoon at Andrea's gossiping, but it was too early. Andrea would still be dealing with her early customers.

She decided instead to give Max a call to see if she could go round and give the Beetle a spin. If it drove well, she would stop by the bank and draw out however much they agreed on. She found a payphone that worked and dialled the number.

"Hello!"

Beverly recognised Thomas's voice immediately. She was speechless, her heart pumping so hard, she became nauseous.

"You bastard!" she exclaimed defiantly.

It was Tuesday morning after the Carnival. Thomas lay relaxing on Max's silk sheets after spending the night with her. They had a great time together at The Carnival, bumping waists with each other for hours, to the sound of the mighty Observer sound system over by Westbourne Park way.

Max knew what she was doing was wrong, but she could not deny how alive she felt when she was with Thomas. The fact that

149

he was married to Beverly didn't deter her. Beverly's two children did not matter, not when she felt like this. She had never been so elated. She not only wanted Thomas, she needed him, no matter what the cost. She ached from longing when she was without him, and she ached from pure pleasure when she was with him.

She was pretty sure that she loved him. He gave her the love she had craved for. The secret dream she had perceived, was now a reality. Who said life was easy? Nobody walks a straight road. Maybe the price to pay for Thomas was the cost of her friendship. If so, it was a price she was prepared to pay.

She stood motionless in the shower, allowing the rush of hot water to gently caress her body. She and Thomas would make beautiful babies, she thought. She would gladly allow her flat stomach to swell for the love of her life.

She wrestled with her thoughts, conjuring up pictures of a future with Thomas. Try as hard as she could though, she couldn't imagine a picture of the future without Beverly's familiar figure beside him. The dutiful wife. Nevertheless Thomas, in her mind, was still a free agent. Free to choose whoever he wanted to be with. He had chosen her.

Despite a tingling of guilt, Max's feeling for Thomas was stronger than any remorse she might otherwise have felt. For Max, everything about Thomas, his manner, his speech, his touch, his petting, reminded her of the things Andrew could not give her.

With Thomas there was a lot more spontaneity. A lot more rawness. Quite simply, Andrew lacked fun. Max allowed her mind to wander back to that morning's sexual encounter with Thomas. With Thomas she found it easier to let herself go and get passionate and start talking dirty. With Andrew, it was always, "oh do it again, please." She had to be a bit more 'refined.' With Thomas she didn't have to beg for it. She could just be herself and allow her animal passions to show through.

One thing about Thomas, he wasn't your usual street yardman, because like everybody knows, yardman just don't like to eat off a two-foot table. There are guys out there who still believe that as long as you 'lick' the neck of the womb twenty times, that's the sex done. Roll over and draw a snooze. You've come, so that's the end of the job. As long as the woman feels a bit sore, you've made it. But Thomas? Well, he was a different barrel of fish. He was sweeter than sweet so. He was strong, firm, tender, titillating, arousing, sexual. All of those things rolled into one.

He had woken her early that morning, whispering sweet

nothings in her ear. His warm seductiveness succeeded in pushing all her buttons. That was something she was unused to.

When you first start seeing them, men like to think, "Cho! Just get my leg over and it done." Whereas Thomas, with all his streetness, was sensitive.

He took time to engage in small talk, asking her how she was. She replied that everyt'ing was cool, y'know. He wrapped his hand playfully around her head. She could hear her heart beating fast. He talked casually about some hassle he was having with one of his spars.

"There are times when you shouldn't tell people all of your business," he remarked, contemplatively.

He tried to sound relaxed, but he had already decided that the relationship with Max was just too damned sweet to let it go in five minutes. Well hold up," he thought to himself. "I want to taste this. I want to savour it, I want to enjoy it." Thomas was one of those men who preferred to take his time when tasting something sweet.

One thing he had learned in all his years as a man, was that you take your time with a woman of pedigree. Pick up with a street girl and you can just raise your leg and go over. They're not going to mind. They're just happy that they've even got a man. Thomas had been taught by the very best. He knew that with a woman like Max, he had to take his time and make his move right. Make it slow and execute it with confidence. Despite his level of experience, Thomas trembled as he lay in the bed, Max in his arms. If I don't get hold of myself, he was thinking, I am going to squeeze up, and I don't want to squeeze up. 'Cause I have waited so long for this girl. I even dream about her.

Ever since that first time together after the Afro-Hair and Beauty Show, Max had followed him in his thoughts. Last thing at night and first thing in the morning, a vision of Max was always with him. He couldn't look at photographs in magazines without seeing her sexy body. He couldn't even pee in peace, 'cause Max was right there with him. He would be just about to go, when the vision of Max with no clothes on would appear. Then he would stiffen, peeing all over the toilet seat as a result.

Thomas turned and admired the sleepy beauty beside him. The girl has some nice legs, he thought. Those calves are well defined. She has a nice, rich, skin complexion. And the curve of her buttocks is tantalising. *Tantalising!*

Thomas didn't waste much time to go down on her. One moment he was resting his chin on her shoulder, with his arm slipped around her waist, and gently, very gently, nuzzling her. All the while, he was thinking about how much he wanted to put

151

his tongue in the water and test the temperature. The moment he got what he wanted, bell number one rang saying, "Mmm mmgh! The temperature sweet in here!"

Max meanwhile, was trying her best to look as cool and as calm, as she knew she should be. But Thomas could feel her convulsions and thought to himself, Yes! He had hit the right button. He looked up at her and saw the stars dancing in her eyes.

"I will take you to heaven and bring you back and take you there again and bring you back again....then we will glide together," he promised in a whisper.

He ran a finger around her eyes and with the same finger, caressed her nose and her lips. Then he listened for her heartbeat, which was so loud it echoed. With his tongue, he slowly caressed her lips waiting, waiting, until finally he thrust his tongue into her warm, inviting, salivating mouth. He kissed her so lightly, she shuddered. In that gentle movement, he had awakened all her senses. She could have sworn that she had found a new sense, because the feeling she had in her soul could not be explained by the others.

This man is good, Max thought to herself. Thomas looked inviting. Max sat on top of him gently, then even more gently rocked her hips up and down and round and round.

"You're heavier than you look, y'know," he teased.

She slapped his wrists playfully, and as she did so, Thomas could feel her hand trembling, ever so slightly. It was hardly detectable, but for Thomas it was enough proof that as for him, the feeling was so good for Max, it chilled her bones. He thought, bwoy this is good!

He hadn't felt this good for so long. What he and Beverly had, just didn't have that buzz. That buzz you get when you see somebody that you fancy. The buzz that gets the juices running. The buzz that makes you come alive. When your stomach hums "mmmn!" When your heart says "mmmm!" Thomas took her hand and very slowly sucked her fingers, one by one, then proceeded to kiss her on the arms and chest. She is lighting my fire, he thought. Everything she wants she can have.

It didn't take them long before they were having intercourse. For every thrust he made, Max would gasp in desperation. Thomas was taking her so high. It was like she hadn't been anywhere before.

Thomas had to use all his imagination to keep himself in the flow. Bwoy, if I take off now, I'll miss my timing, he warned himself. Bwoy, that would be such a sin with a gorgeous girl like Max. He unbuttoned the top of her blouse with his teeth. She was so eager, she reached behind her back to undo her bra, but he caught her and held her hand firmly in an arm lock. He nuzzled and nipped at her neck. Max wanted to take the initiative and she wasn't prepared to wait but he just held her down and took her steady, guiding her. She knew her business, but Thomas was now in the driver's seat. So she relaxed and allowed herself to be teased, thinking, 'Andrew could never have done this to me.' He couldn't have made this vibe happen.

Few words were exchanged between the two illicit lovers, the desperate sound of each other's breathing was enough conversation for their purpose. Thomas made Max feel so good inside. She would have given him anything he wanted. Absolutely anything. That's how good his sweet, personal touch was to her. All the time, he never took his eyes off her, as if he was only interested in her pleasure. Bwoy, she thought, this man can do some wicked things with his tongue, and yet he hadn't reached the serious parts of her body. He was going to get her going first. He wasn't going to touch any of her erogenous zones, until he was good and ready. She lay half-naked, his eyes still firmly fixed on her, touching her and kissing her all the time. Then he rolled her onto her stomach and began massaging her toes and running his fingers along the balls of her feet. She wriggled at his touch. He ran his tongue slowly along the back of her legs, just so that he could then blow them dry. He stopped suddenly at the buttocks. She quivered. He was teasing her mercilessly. She whispered his name and tried to turn over, but Thomas held her down. As he moistened the full length of her spine, he gently removed her panties. She wanted him to take her there and then, but Thomas feeling how wet she was, decided to hold it a moment longer. It turned him on. He eventually turned Max onto her back. He got up off the bed and undressed, without removing his eyes from her once. She lay there waiting, anticipating. This man wanted her to beg. His eyes seemed to penetrate right through her. His eyes surveyed her body. She wanted to pull him down towards her. This man was too much. She allowed her eyes to rest between his legs as she stretched out her arms. As the word "please!" escaped from her lips, Thomas knew this woman was his.

They made love for hours. In so many different positions, trying out new things all the time. Before long, Max was screaming, "Mercy!" This guy was the most. And when she was ready.... the two of them took off at the same time.

By the time they were finished, beads of sweat covered their bodies. He carried her to the bathroom so gently, so masterfully, that she was thinking, this man is addictive. How could she give him up? His seat was solid and he was broad shouldered. A perfectly formed shape of a man.

Thomas meanwhile had spared a thought for Beverly and his marriage. If only a marriage licence was like a Jamaican driver's licence which expired every two years, he thought to himself wishfully.

Max knew what she wanted from a man. She could attract whoever she wanted, so she went for the best. She only wanted the creme de la creme. Some girls would look and say, 'Well, what's she doing with that attitude? How can you only pick the cream of the crop?' Max's argument was, 'if you think you're the queen, then surely your partner should be the king.' What could she possibly want with the peasant? That don't make no sense. If you aim low, you'll get low. If you aim high and you get somebody who falls short, you're still making it. You're still coining it in. Some would say Max was selfish, self-centred, conceited, full of her own opinions. On the other hand, you could just as easily say she was single-minded, strong, determined. And that's what it's about, or else she'd be left at the starting post. The world is divided between those who think about doing something and those who do it. Max was one of those people who do it. Of course, like everybody else, she wanted love, children and marriage - eventually. If it could work that way. This was the 1990s however, when reality sometimes comes at a very high price.

As a rule, Max never allowed men to answer her phone. But she was on such a high after a great carnival, she couldn't be blamed for allowing herself to slip a little. She threw caution to the wind together with her oversized night shirt and stepped into the shower. The rush of hot water from the shower tap made her deaf to the world. Thomas, who had returned to a deep slumber in Max's comfortable bed shortly after carrying her to the bathroom, was awakened by the persistent ring of the telephone. He didn't know where he was at first. He was so sleepy, he thought he was at his own house and reached clumsily for the phone.

"Hello!" There was a momentary pause on the other end of the line, Then he heard Beverly's unmistakable voice.

"You bastard!" she yelled.

ELEVEN

Merlene had been expecting the knock on the door for a couple of weeks now and she was almost relieved when it finally came.

"So wha'pn Merle, you nah come to work no more?" Barrington asked as she opened the door.

"Look, Barrington," she began. "I've been meaning to phone you and explain everything, I've just had a lot of problems."

Barrington invited himself in, taking a swig from his can of brew as he did so.

Dressed in a cream coloured off the peg Burton suit and a full length black leather overcoat, Barrington was a refugee from another era. He would have been better placed in a 70's black exploitation film like Shaft or Superfly, than in downtown Brixton. But you didn't take the piss out of Barrington. He was one of the local dons whose business wavered along the thin line between legality and illegality.

Barrington made his way through to the living room, and looked around studying everything Merlene owned, in between swigs of brew. There was silence between them for a moment. Barrington took his time, and then began nodding his head slowly.

"So you nevah manners?" he asked. "Me come ah your yard an' you don't even offer me tea."

"Oh I'm sorry," Merlene said anxiously. "I thought you were drinking...." she pointed at the can. "I'll just go and make some tea."

She rushed to the kitchen to put the kettle on the boil. She had been expecting Barrington, but now that he was here in her house, and making himself very comfortable, she was nervous. She didn't know what he was capable of doing, but she had heard the stories. It was one thing to owe the guy money but it was a totally different thing to cross him. She hoped he didn't see it that way. The kettle filled with water, she turned and walked smack into Barrington, who had crept up behind her.

"I want all the money now!" he hissed threateningly.

In the early fifties, Jamaicans still believed the streets of England were paved with gold. People reasoned that with their colonies and the slave trade and all, the English must have had so much money, they didn't know what to do with it. So they paved their streets with gold. On arriving on these shores and finding nothing but squalor and concrete paving, the hordes of new immigrants walked around dazed, wondering where all the money was. Several Jamaicans and other Caribbean newcomers walked around for years asking any Englishmen they bumped into, "Where's all that money?"

For Barrington Holt however, the streets really were paved with gold. He was forced to make a hurried departure from Kingston in 1956 aged sixteen. A whore by the name of Pussy Blue had skanked him. She had lifted a wallet from the breast pocket of an American client in a crowded bar, but the Yank soon realised his cash was gone. In the panic that ensued, she shouted out that the yout' Barrington was the sticks man. She had seen everything. Barrington, who was just leaving the bar, had to make a hasty retreat as the Yank and every hustler in town chased him to get their hands on the loot. Kingstonians love a good yarn. By the end of the day, the story was that Barrington had lifted $50,000 from the Yank's wallet. Remember, this was 1956!

Barrington first decided to lay low in the country for a few weeks until things died down. But unfortunately, the story had reached the ears of Sergeant Eric 'Eradicator' Rodney of the Jamaican police force. Eradicator heard that it was $100,000 and had vowed to seek and recover the money for himself. Word got through to Barrington that he was on the Eradicator's hit list and the young hustler knew that his days in Kingston were numbered. That night he and a friend had stowed away on a banana boat to England or more precisely, Tiger Bay. On arrival, Barrington swore that no woman would ever skank him the way Pussy had done.

After only a short time in London, Barrington had acquainted himself with the small but blossoming, black underworld community. In 1957, Barrington was the first black man to bus' gun in a bank robbery in England. By the end of the fifties, Barrington and a posse of other Jamaican rudies were working for slum landlord Roger Goldstein, doing the strong arm bit for him any time his tenants were late with the rent. It meant violently evicting whole families from their homes around the Notting Hill area. These families were mainly black, but Barrington had no remorse about his job and carried it out like a professional.

By the early sixties, Barrington was a pimp, controlling half of the women working on the All Saints Road. But he was set up by one of his girls and the Metropolitan Police who planted drugs on him and accused him of being a dealer. Six years of nothing but pigswill is enough to make any man feel bitter. Barrington blamed his incarceration on the whore who was "dumb enough to play policeman's nark." He took a solemn oath while doing his time, that "any bitch who crossed this man again was one dead bitch." His half-brother Errol, Barrington's junior by twenty years, came over from Kingston in 1975. Together they had built an empire that included girlie clubs in Soho and running raves in Brixton, as well as their shady dealings.

"Me nuh leave your yard before I get every penny," Barrington said coldly.

"Look, easy man. I've got the money alright?!" Merlene found it distasteful discussing money with a one like Barrington, but she had made her bed and now she had to lie in it.

She walked back into the living room, Barrington following close behind. She walked to the back of the room and lifted up the carpet, over in the corner by the French windows. She pulled out an unmarked white envelope and handed it to Barrington. He opened it and pulled out a bundle of fifty pound notes held together by an elastic band. He looked at Merlene quizzically as he gently tossed the bundle up and down in his hand.

"This feels like five grand," he said.

"It's five thousand five hundred," Merlene replied. "That's all I owe after deducting the money from my commission at the club."

Barrington chuckled to himself and pulled out the contract from his breast pocket. He slowly unfolded the soiled sheet of paper and handed it to her.

"Read the small print," Barrington commanded. " You broke the terms of the agreement, so two hundred percent interest me ah deal wid."

Merlene held the contract shakily. She suddenly felt ill. She wished she had never borrowed the money but at the time, Barrington was the only person she was able to turn to. Andrea claimed Winston never left any money and Beverly never ever had any money anyway. The one person she could have borrowed the money from was Max, but she was in Jamaica. Barrington may have had a dodgy reputation, but faced with Fitzroy's blackmail Merlene conveniently forgot the stories she had heard about him being this and that and about the clubs and bars in Brixton which paid a 'donation' to him for 'security services provided.'

So Barrington had put up the bail. In return Merlene had

signed a contract to work at his club until the money was paid off. In effect, he had bought her for the duration. After the incident with the Japanese businessman however, Merlene had not returned to The Bowler Hat Club. She had been expecting Barrington to show up since then. Max had withdrawn a large sum of her savings from the bank after her sister told of her predicament. But, could Merlene really have been so desperate that she never realised she would have to pay an extortionate amount of money back?

"You're crazy, man! You don't expect me to pay two hundred percent interest for money I borrowed not even a year ago!" Merlene was foolish to dismiss the proposition out of hand. Barrington had been in this game longer than her.

"Okay," he said slowly. "I'm going to give you until twelve o'clock tomorrow to get the rest of the money. If you haven't, I'll be making one phone call to Brixton Town Hall about a certain number of students who don't exist." He smiled at Merlene, knowing that he had just played his trump card.

Again Merlene felt nauseous. It seemed like everybody in Brixton knew the skank she had pulled. It was just a matter of time before the police would find out.

Still spinning from the recent revelation, Beverly walked around Brixton in a daze for what seemed like hours. Somehow, she had managed to make it back to Brixton from Plaistow, but she had no memory of the journey. Even amidst the familiar surroundings of Brixton, she found it hard to distinguish dreams from reality. She had walked mechanically, up Brixton Hill, to the old windmill. Even though she had lived in Brixton all her life, she had never visited the windmill, just a stone's throw away from her home. She hadn't even known it existed, until a couple of years ago when a friend had asked her if she knew that the last working windmill in London was situated just half way up Brixton Hill.

Beverly hadn't come to sightsee, however.

When she first heard Thomas's voice on the phone, she thought she had mistakenly dialled her own number. When she realised she had dialled correctly, everything suddenly fell into place. She had been blind, but she could see clearly now. Thomas hardly knew Max. There was only one reason for him to be at her flat that early in the morning. As far as she knew they had only met once, at her wedding. The wedding? Beverly wondered whether her husband and her best friend had been getting off with each other since then, but decided it was inconceivable. They couldn't have. It must have been a coincidence that Thomas began to brutalise her on that night, she convinced herself.

She couldn't remember how she got there, but by early evening, Beverly was standing in front of Merlene's house, looking like a woman who needed answers to some questions.

Merlene was surprised to see her, but thought nothing more of it.

"Hi, Bev," she said cheerfully. "What a nice surprise! Come in. I've only just got back from work." Beverly entered Merlene's house, walking slowly and deliberately. "You already know, don't you?" she said.

Merlene paused for a moment, studying her friend closely. "Look, come through," she said eventually. "I'm in the kitchen."

Beverly followed her friend silently down the narrow hallway to the rear of the house. Once in the kitchen, Merlene resumed the preparation for the evening meal. The silence between them was deafening. Merlene could feel Beverly standing right behind her, though her friend said nothing and did nothing.

Merlene's heart pumped fast and furiously. The moment she had been dreading had finally arrived, but no amount of planning could have prepared her for this. Questions fired through her mind mercilessly. How was she going to play this? Could she say it was none of her concern? Should she admit that she knew about the situation, or deny it outright? She didn't know what Beverly knew, but her friend's question was so vague, it didn't mean anything.

"I've always looked at you as one good sister," Beverly broke the stalemate nervously, "and the rest of the crew, just like sisters. But I know Thomas is seeing Max. You see Merlene, what nobody seems to understand is that I'm the one who can't sleep. I can't eat, I can't think straight. So, answer me. It's true isn't it?"

Beverly's eyes had become moist. Try as hard as could, she couldn't hold back the tears and began to cry uncontrollably. Merlene wanted desperately to put an arm around her friend and comfort her, but her conscience wouldn't let her. There was nothing she could say. She had known for some time that Thomas was sleeping with Maxine. She didn't approve, but there wasn't a lot she could do about it.

"Beverly I can't help you. I wish there was something I could do. All I can say is do what you have to do. I wish there was some way I could wave everything away."

Beverly dried her eyes slowly.

"Merlene, I know you're Max's sister, but....there are so many....Max could have anybody. Why Thomas? I expected him to play away from home, but not with Max! Not with Max. I mean, that is just like....I can't even find the words to explain how I feel. One of my best friends? With my husband? It's sick! Merlene, it's sick, it stinks! How the fuck am I supposed to feel about it? Tell me! How am I supposed to feel about this?

"I tell you one thing, Merlene, she's not having him! I don't care what it takes. Y'know. She's not having him. I can't even begin to say what I feel about that girl. I just wanna....to me....your friend....You don't do that to a friend, it makes no sense. I don't deserve that. She can have the pick of any man? Why? Why did she have to do this?

"She already has her rich sugar daddy. What's the matter with the girl, she ain't satisfied? I'll fight her for him. I want him by my side, I need him by my side. I just....Merlene, you don't know how bad I feel, y'know. To wake up and look at this man who professes to be my husband...." she broke down sobbing again.

Guilt had got to Merlene and she comforted her friend with a gentle embrace. She realised that Beverly already knew, so there was no point in confirming or denying anything. At the same time, Max was her sister and blood is thicker than water. Beverly couldn't expect her to take sides against her own flesh and blood.

"All I can say is that you should speak with Max," Merlene advised. It was a problem for Max, Beverly and Thomas to resolve. She didn't want any part of it.

Beverly shrugged off Merlene's embracing arms and said coldly, "If you knew you should have said something earlier. This is somebody who I intend to spend the rest of my life with and you did not deem it fit enough to come and tell me what was going down. I look a bloody fool!"

She had tricked Merlene into confirming her suspicions, but the fact that Merlene hadn't said anything previously burned her.

Beverly departed. Max was the person in the forefront of Beverly's mind. She had to see her, speak to her and make her understand that Thomas was 'other people's property.' That Beverly could not allow her to have him.

Alone in the kitchen, Merlene wondered if she could have done anything to prevent Max's affair with Thomas, but remembered her similar situation with Winston. Nobody could have stopped her at the time. She was crazy about the guy, as simple as that. If Max had determined to have a thing with

Thomas and he was happy about it, there wasn't much anybody else could have done to stop it. They were two consenting adults, who knew what they were doing. They were prepared to take the risk and now that they were found out, they would have to pay the price, whatever it was.

Andrew reclined on Max's sofa. He looked troubled, not paying much attention to Max as she ironed a pair of jeans by her living room window.

Max felt uncomfortable. She knew that something was bothering him, and she had a good idea what it was. But she didn't want to bring the subject up. She threw a glance out the window unto the street. It was a clear, sunny day and people were out in force. From her first floor flat, you could get a good view of the traffic outside on Brixton Water Lane. She watched as the BMW posse cruised by slowly in brand new cars, their booming systems providing a roughneck ragga soundtrack that disturbed the neighbourhood. Max's windowpanes shook threateningly as Buju Banton's voice blasted out from below at 300 watts. It was the Saturday after the Notting Hill Carnival. Max was preparing to travel up to the Birmingham Carnival with Thomas. He had assured her that the Birmingham Carnival in Handsworth Park was really something special.

"It's different from Notting Hill," he told her. "You don't see any cops around at all, they just let people get on with enjoying themselves. People are a lot more relaxed. I'm tellin' you Max, it's wicked."

Max had to admit it sounded like fun and she was looking forward to going. He had promised to come by and pick her up that evening. Evening couldn't come soon enough for Max. But then Andrew showed up and insisted on parking himself on the sofa without saying much.

It was the first time he had come round in weeks. Since the disasterous visit to Scotland, their relationship had become strained, which suited her fine as she had found pleasure with Thomas.

Her relationship with Andrew was stale. You outgrow things, she reasoned. It happens.

She wanted to tell Andrew that she loved Thomas. She wanted the world to know. She was confused, and no longer felt she knew what that word 'love' meant any more. Nobody out there knows what's going on, she told herself.

"How ya feeling?" she asked Andrew eventually.

He snapped out of his silent meditation, rubbing his eyes.

"I'm just irie," he answered nonchalantly.

Merlene grunted. She hated it when Andrew tried to be hip and use words that were trendy. Irie, means you rule your internal, she thought to herself. From the worried look on his face, it looked like Andrew's internal did run t'ings.

"So you're going off to Birmingham with this guy....what's his name?"

"Thomas!" Max replied with a sigh. "And yes. I didn't know you were coming. You haven't called, you didn't let me know. I've got my life to lead as well, y'know."

"You've been seeing this guy recently, have you?" Andrew asked.

"Every now and then," Max answered, seeing no reason to avoid the truth. "Why, are you spying on me?"

Andrew knew the rules. She was there for him, but she wasn't tied to him with a ball and chain. What was she going to do if he didn't show up? She had urges too. And anyway, she didn't ask the same questions of him.

As far as Max was concerned, her relationship with Andrew was over in everything but name. She had decided however, to keep it going. The mortgage had to be paid on the flat. She couldn't do that without his help. What's more, he had the contacts she needed in the modelling world. But she wasn't going to hang around waiting on him to marry her anymore. Oh no, all that was over with. And she didn't care either, if he no longer shared her bed.

All this was not lost on Andrew. He had stayed away because he had been seeing Max long enough to pick up on her vibes. But he was dejected, because he didn't want it to end this way. In his heart, he knew it was over. They had lost whatever they had. The flame had fizzled out. He was hoping that Max would say the words to make their relationship null and void.

"Look, we have to talk seriously," Andrew began, jumping off the sofa and walking over to where Max was busy ironing. She could feel his warm breath on her neck. "Just tell me what's going on. If something is wrong I want to know. If you've found somebody else, then fine. It will hurt, but I'm a man. I can take it. I'll survive."Andrew placed his hands gently on her hips and kissed her tenderly on the nape of the neck.

Max stopped her ironing. Andrew wanted to compromise her and make her feel guilty, but she wasn't having any of it. She had thought about ending things after the disastrous trip to his family, but felt sorry for him. However, this time she was determined. Why should I feel guilty about this, she asked herself. It's ridiculous. Life was too short to feel guilty. You've got enough time only to do what you've got to do.

"Look, this is crazy. I really can't do this anymore," she said. "Our relationship isn't going anywhere. I haven't seen you for weeks, but I'm supposed to be here waiting when you show up! I'm beautiful and I'm bright, Andrew. I don't deserve this."

He looked at her sympathetically. "What do you want me to do?" he asked.

For a moment, she thought of telling him exactly what she wanted. She wanted him to open her up sexually, when they made love, as Thomas did. She wanted him to stop in the middle of a sex session, so they could take time to bathe each other in a hot bath, massaging each other with oil until they were both relaxed and ready to go again. She wanted him to flirt with her. She wanted to make love all night long, to find out how many times a night he could do it. She wanted them to share a spliff together before intercourse, because since discovering its joys with Thomas, she couldn't bring herself to have sex without a spliff again. She thought of all the things she could ask Andrew to do, but decided against it. He was dead stock

"Nothing," she answered finally. "Our relationship is going nowhere fast."

"So, you want us to stop seeing each other? I'm not angry. I knew it was going to end this way and now that it's happened, I'm upset, but I'm not angry. I'm just glad that one of us had the nerve to end it."

The entryphone buzzed.

"Who is it," Max answered speaking into the receiver.

There was a pause.

"It's me," Beverly replied.

Beverly wasn't expected. The sound of her voice threw Max off balance. She didn't know for sure why Beverly had come round, but the tone of her friend's voice was ominous. The hairs on the back of her neck stood up. She was anxious, but decided that if she played her cards right she could get Beverly out of the flat without getting a black eye, or losing some vital part of her body.

Her legs unsteady, Beverly walked slowly and deliberately up the stairs to Max's flat. She hadn't decided how to play things. She trembled slightly, knowing she was capable of doing something lethal.

Max met Beverly at the door. They stood there for a moment, simply staring at each other, neither knowing how to play the next move. Out of the corner of her eye, Beverly saw Andrew standing in the background.

"I don't want to talk to you," she warned him over Max's

shoulder. "Just get out!"

The beef was between herself and Max. If she was going to let rip, she didn't want anybody there.

Andrew hesitated, looking at Max as if to ask 'do you really want me to leave you in this room with this girl, when quite clearly she's upset?' With a nod of her head, Max signalled that it was alright. Andrew got his things together hurriedly. On his way out, he kissed Max lightly on her cheeks.

"If you need me, just call on the mobile," he said, obviously reluctant to abandon Max at a volatile moment. He didn't know for certain what the whole thing was about, but he guessed that it had something to do with the guy Max had been playing around with. He was old enough to see that Beverly's eyes spoke the murderous intentions of a wronged woman.

Beverly held the door open for him, waiting for him to leave. He frowned at her as he left. Luckily for him her eyes were superglued to Max, because in the state she was in she couldn't really business with no frown from anybody.

Beverly entered the flat, slamming the door shut behind her. Max thought it best to keep her mouth shut. She led Beverly into the living room.

Beverly looked at her coldly. She had forgotten the words she'd prepared. She couldn't remember any of it. If she opened her mouth there and then, nothing but expletives would come out.

They must have stood facing each other silently for a full minute before Beverly managed to utter the one word, "Why?"

"I don't know Beverly, what are you asking me?" Max answered innocently, hoping that there was still room to manoeuvre. There was no point in admitting to anything if Beverly didn't have any concrete evidence.

"You've not answered my question. I want to know why?" Beverly repeated forcefully.

"Look Beverly, I don't know what you're talking about. Why about what? How can you come to somebody's house, be rude to their guests and just say, 'why'?"

Beverly looked at Max in disgust.

"You're fuckries....There's no other word for it, you are fuckries. Don't tell me no shit about 'why'. I've known you from time, you've known me. You've known how I stay. I knew you before you start spread your legs for white man. So don't come with me and tell me you don't understand what I'm talking about. We talk the same language."

She drew closer to Max.

"I want to know how long Thomas has been fucking you?"

Max tried to speak, but no words came out.

Beverly continued.

"Yes Maxine, yes Miss High and Mighty, yes the kept woman....obviously your boops with all his money isn't fucking you good enough, so you feel it necessary to take the husband of one of your best friends! Out of all the men you could have taken, why my husband? Why shit on your own doorstep?"

Max said nothing. What could she say? Beverly, who usually refrained from profanities, was in no joking mood.

"I want you to keep your fucking hands off my man. Right?! As far as I'm concerned, you've taken our friendship and spat on it."

Max was a good five inches taller than Beverly. Beverly had to almost stand on tiptoe to look into Max's eyes. Despite her diminutive figure, however, there was no mistaking which of the two was the most threatening.

"Tell me something Maxine," Beverly continued. "When you lay down with Thomas, do you not see my face. Did he never accidently call my name instead of yours?"

Max sucked her teeth.

Undaunted, Beverly continued. She was beginning to warm up.

"You feel it necessary to take my man from my bed. To entice my man from his home, his family? I've got news for you, Maxine, Thomas is staying in my bed tonight, tomorrow, next week, next month - for the next twenty years until I have finished with him. The man belongs to me. "

Max sighed heavily.

Beverly realised she wasn't making her point forcefully enough. She wanted to cut the lecture and just thump Max again and again, until there was no strength left in her body. But she had to work herself up to it.

Max remained silent, hoping that would take the heat out of the situation.

"Can't you get a man of your own, Maxine?" Beverly challenged, pacing around the room with her hands on her hips. "Can't your slim figure, pretty clothes and flash car get you the man you want?"

Max had had enough. She felt she had to say something. She spoke slowly and deliberately to let Beverly know she wasn't running scared.

"I'm a grown woman and I can do what I like."

Beverly didn't need to be prompted. Max had thrown down the gauntlet and she was going to pick it up and slap her about the face with it. She walked over to Max slowly and took position. A moment later, a trickle of saliva trickled down Maxine's face. Max lifted up her hand as if to hit Beverly. Undaunted, Beverly moved up close and repeated the gesture, managing to secrete a lot more spit the second time. Before Max could respond, Beverly had slapped the taller woman down with the palm of her hand.

Max lay crumpled on the floor, with Beverly standing menacingly above her.

"People like you make me vomit, Maxine." A heartbeat later, Beverly sounded remorseful. "Poor Maxine," she began with overstated sympathy. "Poor little Maxine. Why don't you let me help you Maxine?"

She offered Maxine her hand. Max looked up from the floor, wondering what Beverly was scheming up now.

Beverly knelt down as if to lift Max up, but instead pushed her hand in Max's face, smearing the saliva all over.

Enough was enough. Max lashed out at Beverly, with a blow to the ear. The blow triggered Beverly's stored up emotions. She lost it completely and jumped on top of Max, kicking, punching and screaming relentlessly. She wanted to hurt her. All the anger and frustration she had stored up for Thomas was let loose on Max.

Max was the bigger and stronger woman however, and in a matter of moments, was able to restrain Beverly. She pushed the hysterical woman aside and got up.

"Get the fuck out of my flat," Max commanded threateningly. "There's no way you can fight me in here and you live. Right? Just take your arse out of here and go home to your Thomas."

Thomas was incensed when Max told him what had happened with Beverly.

"How did she find out?" Max asked.

"Me nuh know," Thomas lied. He hadn't mentioned Beverly's phone call while Max was in the shower. There was no point in mentioning it now, either. Not when they were on their way to a sweet weekend together. The motorway sign indicated that Birmingham was 100 miles away. Thomas smiled to himself, thinking he could make it in an hour. He depressed the throttle some more and the BMW responded eagerly, its speedometer twitching past the speed limit untethered.

Max reclined the passenger seat and lay back dreamily. She was excited about their first weekend together.

"I don't even want to think about Beverly for the next two days," she insisted.

"Don't worry about her," Thomas promised. "I've started sorting things out. She's going to be out of our lives permanently. Just give me a bit of time."

Max had no idea what Thomas was talking about. She didn't know anything about the obeah man and she didn't know about the cloves of garlic Thomas had been leaving around the house. Neither did she know that after weeks of waiting around for the chance, Thomas had finally found a lock of Beverly's hair on a comb she had left on the coffee table at home. It was a stroke of luck. He had gone home to get a few clothes for the weekend and there it was, lying there. He grabbed his chance immediately and drove out to the old man in Plaistow. The obeah man had reluctantly carried out a ritual with the lock of hair and assured Thomas that the woman would leave his life for ever. Max didn't know about any of this. She was only interested in a dirty weekend with Thomas.

It was already getting dark when the BMW cruised into the maze of motorways that criss-crossed Birmingham town centre. Thomas suggested that they check into the hotel and wait until the next morning to drive out to Handsworth for the carnival. That was okay with Max. It had been an eventful day. She couldn't think of anything better to cheer her up than a whole night of passion with Thomas.

Max was pleasantly surprised to see the hotel they were staying at. It was one of the grandest in Birmingham, just a stone's throw away from the Bullring. Thomas knew how to impress a woman. He had to entertain Max in the standard she was used to, and had borrowed £500 to impress his dream princess. The hotel suite alone was £150 a night, but it was worth every penny. There was a king size bed which you could sleep on (or make love on), widthways as easily as lengthways. There was a sunken Jacuzzi in the sumptuous bathroom and they had their own private balcony outside. The room was made for lovers.

Max threw her arms around Thomas's neck and kissed him impulsively, but deep and passionately.

"Bwoy, you really know how to turn a girl on!" she giggled, winking at him as she pulled him down onto the bed.

"Nah worry yourself, Max," he assured her. "Everyt'ing's going to be cool between us.

They rolled around on the bed, kissing and caressing. Thomas turned her on, the way only he knew how. His hand wandered in her jeans and he very gently caressed those spots

167

that drove her wild. He massaged her all over, thrilled to be stroking that body Max had developed through hard work - an hour's exercise a day - and a fat-free diet. Starvation couldn't get you a body like Max's. Hours of aerobics couldn't do it, either. Max's motto had always been 'an hour's sex a day, keeps the droopy breasts and droopy bum at bay.'

"Don't wait, Thomas," she whispered breathlessly."Give it to me now. Please Thomas, give it to me now."

She was as hot as she would ever be, with sweat oozing out of every pore in her body.

Thomas turned to sit on her, pulling down his trousers with one swift hand movement. It was then she noticed his droop.

"What's the matter, Thomas," she asked, gulping for air. "Aren't you ready yet?"

Thomas looked down at his briefs and realised that he evidently wasn't. Strange, he thought. He felt ready and willing, but he was far from able.

"Just a minute, just a minute," he said. "It'll come in a minute."

He took her hand and placed it in his briefs. Max didn't need any more prompting. She went straight to work, holding and caressing and pumping away. Thomas rolled over on his back and urged Max to go down on him. She obeyed dutifully. Now when it came to blow jobs, few women were as skilful as Max. But try as hard as she might, she just couldn't get it going on for Thomas.

For him, there was no better feeling than Max's tongue working its way around his manhood and scrotum. It was a sincere pleasure for him.

"Just keep going on," he whispered. "It's coming on, just a bit more. Just a bit more."

So it went on for the next two hours. Max could feel him stiffen momentarily and then lose it. What was happening?

Finally, they both collapsed on the bed from the effort.

Max lay on her back, exhausted, staring at the ceiling.

"What are you thinking?" Thomas asked nervously.

"I was just thinking about something I read recently, that everybody is bound to everybody else in this world, by a trail of just six people. Six degrees of separation between me and everyone else on this planet. Isn't that crazy? A trail of just six people connects me with the President of the United States, the Queen or the starving kids in Somalia. It's scary when you think about it."

Thomas didn't get her drift, but dreaded that it had something to do with his failure to perform.

"I don't know what's happening?" Thomas said apologetically.

"Don't worry about it," Max reassured him. "It happens like that sometimes for everybody. We'll try again in the morning."

She was too tired for anything now and promptly fell asleep.

Thomas on the other hand, stayed awake all night long, terrified that his worst nightmare had come true.

The same thing happened the next day. Max tried for hours to get him going, but finally gave up. Thomas couldn't believe it. His manhood had never let him down like this before. He could see on Max's face that she was disappointed. They were together in an expensive hotel for the weekend. It was like their dreams had come true. The one thing missing was sex. If he couldn't get it together, he knew he would lose this woman. For a moment, he thought about the obeah man. He had instructed the old man that he wanted Beverly out of his life. Nothing untoward had happened to Beverly. Instead, it looked like Max would be out of his life.For the whole of their long weekend together Thomas tried to make love to Max. Time and time again his manhood let him down. For Max it was the ultimate insult and she began to think that the love affair with Thomas had been a dreadful mistake. One moment she had been madly in love with Thomas, now she felt indifferent. She began to question whether she had ever really been in love with her best friend's husband.

By the time they began to journey back to London, Max had decided that she had to try and get Andrew back. Thomas was no good to her now. Her best hope was to secure her financial future.

TWELVE

Barrington ordered his driver to stop off at Tasty Patties on Acre Lane. There was nowhere to park outside however, so the Mercedes stopped abruptly in the middle of the road, double parked. The burly driver jumped out cursing the angry motorist behind, as he held the back door open for his boss. Barrington stepped out with a big smile on his face. The sun was shining, business was good and he had just received the news that a local Chamber of Commerce had nominated him as their Man of the Year for 'services to the community.' He was definitely in a good mood. As he filled his lungs with a sharp blast of South London air, he considered himself invincible. 'Brixton is mine,' he assured himself and made his way into the restaurant.

Tasty Patties was an important stop on Barrington's daily runnings, because he loved his chicken and his goat well curried, and nobody cooked a better portion than Tasty.

Merlene rushed around the house in a state of panic. She didn't have much time to play with. Barrington could arrive at any moment. The photos and ornaments were unceremoniously swept off the mantlepiece and into a plastic shopping bag. There was little room for sentimentality. She stopped in front of the fireplace where until last night her stereo system rack occupied pride of place, and pondered on the events of the last year and how quickly she had lost everything she had worked hard to build up. The stereo system, like the television and video had been sold at a ridiculously low price. All her jewellery and other valuables had gone the same way. It was either that or ask Max for more money, something Merlene wanted to avoid.

It was the middle of the month. Though Merlene was reluctant to forego her next pay check, she couldn't afford to wait until the end of the month to get paid, so she had spent the last few days selling her belongings.

"Here's my rucksack like you told me mum," Marlon said on entering the living room.

"Great!" Merlene replied. "Look, go upstairs and pack just the important things you're going to need with you."

"Are you going to tell me what's going on?" Marlon asked solemnly.

"I told you already," Merlene insisted. "We're just going on holiday for a while, that's all. Now, you know we're in a hurry, so go upstairs and bring anything you need for a short trip. Okay?"

Merlene kissed her son reassuringly on the forehead, but his fears were far from allayed.

"So how comes we're going so soon? You never told me anything about this. You've never mentioned it before."

Merlene sighed. "Marlon, I'll answer all your questions once we're out of here, I promise. But if we don't leave very quickly, we'll be in trouble. Do y'hear me? So pack as much as you need into your rucksack."

Marlon turned to go upstairs, still unconvinced, but aware that his mother meant business.

It was a risky move, but one Merlene had to make. If she stayed in Brixton, she would have both Barrington and Fitzroy blackmailing her. She wasn't prepared to live with that forever.

"Let me know as soon as you're ready so I can call a cab!" she called up the stairs to her son. Fumbling for matches in her pocket, she lit a cigarette and took a soothing drag as she peered anxiously out the living room window.

Max turned down Queensway, walking in a daze and looking for a taxi. The words of the doctor kept echoing in her thoughts: "Miss Livingstone, I'm pleased to inform you that you are about to become a mother!"

To her surprise she had learned that she was pregnant, though she couldn't figure out how it could have happened. She took precautious with both Andrew and Thomas. Yet, here she was pregnant. She had gone up West to the clinic, because her regular-like-clockwork period, was two weeks overdue and she had begun to feel peculiar. Now the doctor had confirmed her worst fear she didn't know what to do. She didn't know whether to call Andrew or call Thomas. For crissakes, she didn't even know whether the baby would come out black or coffee-coloured. What was she going to do?

Max climbed into the cab and mechanically gave instructions to be driven to Brixton. She sat back, unable to make sense of her pregnancy. Her mind wandered off and for a moment, she began thinking about what she would call the baby. She knew that she would definitely go ahead and have the baby. There was no question about that. She wondered whether either Andrew or Thomas would offer to take care of the baby. She couldn't see Thomas offering to support the baby financially. In a way, she hoped it was Andrew's baby. At least that way she could rely on maintenance.

"I'm telling you man, somebody put some obeah on me!" Thomas was exasperated. He had tried for an hour to convince the doctor that the loss of his virility had nothing to do with the male menopause, but the man wasn't having any of it. 'Ah dat dem call 'specialist'', Thomas thought to himself. The guy just didn't have a clue.

"I can assure you that it's quite a common complaint," the doctor repeated. "It's probably psycho-sematic. It's not as bad as you think. Really, I wouldn't worry about it. It could have been worse. Why, just the other day a Jamaican gentleman came in here, with far more reason to be distressed than you. His penis had actually broken in two during intercourse. A painful experience I can assure you."

If the doctor had meant to ease Thomas's mind, he was doing a bad job of it. Thomas could think of nothing but the loss of his manhood. Which woman would want him now?

Barrington walked down a half block and entered the bookies to check what ah gwan. Ailey of course was in there along with the other small-time hustlers who virtually lived in the smoky betting shop. He spotted Barrington straight away.

"Yes boss!" the youth called out.

Barrington nodded casually in response. He didn't have anything against the youth, but knew well that such an eager greeting from Ailey was usually met by a request.

"Beggin' you a fifty pence, boss."

Barrington sighed. He had heard it all before.

"You too beggy-beggy, y'know Ailey. Ev'rytime I see you it's the same thing 'beggin' you dis, boss, beggin you dat. Cho!"

"Respeck boss," the youth said humbly, "but this time you bound to get the money back." Ailey waved the tipster's page of the daily paper in front of Barrington. "Dangerous Liaisons," in the two-thirty at Kempton Park."

Barrington glanced at the paper disintrestedly.

"Don't budda with that, Ailey," he started, "The las' time you guaranteed a winner, the horse run like it only have t'ree leg!"

"It run like it kicked the bucket, y'mean," Horsemouth chipped in. "Boy, if I only had t'ree leg I woulda win the race meself!"

Barrington and Horsemouth enjoyed the joke, while Ailey shifted uneasily from one foot to the other. He only had a couple of minutes wait before Barrington relented and tossed him a fifty pence coin. Barrington didn't really have time for chit chat.

He had far more important things to do, like paying Merlene a visit and collecting the outstanding money.

"I bet you, twenty pounds dat the third person to walk through that door is a woman," Horsemouth challenged, facing Barrington with a mischievous glint in his eye.

Barrington smiled. The bet didn't surprise him. He had known Horsemouth long enough to know that the man would bet on anything.

"Okay," Barrington agreed, to humour Horsemouth more than anything. "A'right!"

The two men shook hands on the deal.

Both men fixed their gazes in the direction of the door, as the punters sauntered in and out. A scruffy elderly man came through first, followed closely by his shabbily dressed partner. Both men tensed up in anxious anticipation as they waited for the third person to cross the threshold. Horsemouth more anxious than Barrington. Twenty pounds was a lot to lose for a man who lived by his wits alone. For Barrington however, the money was insignificant. He was a betting man that regarded losing as an occupational hazard. You win some, you lose some. The bet was the thing. You cast your die and you lived by it. The law of the jungle, but Barrington would lay his life on it.

"Yes!" Horsemouth exclaimed in victorious jubilation as a drunken woman crashed through the doors with a midday Tennants in her hand. "Yes! See my gyaal deh?!"

Merlene paced back and forth, too restless to sit down while Marlon got his things ready. An echo of tension filled the whole house. Constantly her eyes swept out through the living room window, where she watched the garden path, dreading that any moment the doorbell would ring....waiting and panicking, like a woman expecting a time bomb to explode. There was a terrifying feeling in her mind, that Barrington would arrive at any moment and her plan would be exposed. What would she do then? He wouldn't take her attempt to escape lying down. His reputation went before him, and if he realised that she was trying to abscond from her 'debt'....Merlene knew she had every reason to fear what his response would be.

"Mum, I'm ready!" Marlon called out as he made his way downstairs.

Relieved, Merlene rushed out to meet him in the hallway. She hugged her son and told him everything was going to be just fine.

"We're going to Jamaica to visit grandma," Merlene explained as she rushed over to the phone and called a minicab. "You'll love it."

No sooner had she put down the phone and relaxed, than the droning buzz of the front door exploded throughout the house.

"What you man have?"

"Three aces, now," Jeremiah answered, confident that he held a winning hand.

Lucky Chester stared down at Jeremiah's hat trick of aces thoughtfully. They were both veterans of the informal poker sessions in the back room at the bookies. They both knew how to lengthen the reflective moment that every gambler is allowed before calling his shot.

Realising that he had stepped through the door at a crucial stage in the game, Barrington observed the unwritten rule of silence, allowing Lucky to savour every second of the delay.

"Come now man!" The suspense was too much for Jeremiah and he lost his cool. He was already down £80. If he lost this hand, it would bring his losses to £95. "Play your cards man!"

Unruffled, Lucky slapped his cards down slowly but purposefully on the table.

"I man have four jacks, rasta....Jack of hearts! Jack of clubs! Jack of diamonds! Jack of spades!"

Jeremiah stared at the upturned cards in disbelief. No matter how much he wanted them to disappear, they remained as confirmation of the losing hand he had been dealt. Losing four games in a row was too much of a coincidence to contemplate. He knew he had been hustled, but he didn't know how. Lucky seemed to know every card in the pack.

"But Lucky, where you find yourself with so much jacks man?!" the losing man shouted as if his life depended on it. "You ah steal I. You ah teef man! Me nah come back again, y'hear? No rasta. Me nah come back ina it again!"

The back room was a private member's club for hardcore gamblers. Not satisfied by the tepid thrill of a legal flutter, some of the old timers had convinced the manager to let them use the store cupboard at the rear of the shop as a 'coffee room.' The manager was cool about it as long as it was just 'members only.' It didn't do any harm to business and apart from anything, the regular money that this handful of old timers spent on legal gambling, was the bread and butter of his trade.

After placing his legal bets, Barrington had sauntered over to the back room to see if he could get in a game of seven card stud.

174

But he could see that Lucky and Jeremiah were about to drag him into their argument so he left. He didn't have time to discuss who was or was not cheating. It was time to go and collect the money from Merlene.

He hailed up the few members of the Brixton Punters' Association standing in the doorway as he left the shop, and stepped out into the fresh air. His driver was waiting patiently in the car for him. The powerfully-built man with the funki dreds lifted his huge bulk out of the driver's seat to open the door for Barrington.

"You ready to go, boss?" he asked in a deep, booming voice.

"Yeah drive over to that daughter's yard. We still have some business to finish."

The big man grinned slowly. This was Corbin, Barrington's driver/minder. An ex-con who now worked full-time for Barrington. He had proved himself a good man to have covering your back. Corbin was a solid heavyweight. Only a hustler with scant regard for his personal safety would attempt to take him on. That had been one of Barrington's considerations when he employed him.

Merlene's heart sank, as she dropped to her hands and knees in terror. She motioned to Marlon to hide behind a door and to keep quiet. The startled boy watched as his mother made her way to the living room on all fours to peer through the window.

It was only Max. relieved, Merlene jumped up and opened the door for her sister.

"Max....oh, I'm so glad it's only you," Merlene said as she embraced her sister.

"What's up, sis. You look like a wreck!" Max replied, taken aback by the obvious distress on Merlene's face.

"Oh come in. Come in quickly. I can't stand on the door chatting," Merlene said, casting a furtive glance up and down the street to make sure there was no sign of Barrington's Mercedes.

Max stepped in the house, stepping over a pile of clothes in the hallway.

"What's going on, Merle?" she asked anxiously. "My goodness, look at this mess! What's going on?"

Merlene looked at her sister thoughtfully. She knew that her sister would try and help her out if she explained everything. But she didn't want that. She had already borrowed enough money from Max. No, this was her problem and she had to sort it out by herself.

"Well, you know after you gave me that money," she began

slowly and deliberately, "I paid Barrington, but he's claiming that I still owe him money...."

Max remained silently digesting everything her sister said. Merlene told her about Barrington's threats and how she had come to the conclusion that Barrington and Fitzroy would always be able to blackmail her if she remained in Brixton, and how she had decided to take Marlon and run off to Jamaica until things cooled down.

Merlene paused when she came to the end of her story, wondering whether she had the guts to fill Max in fully. Merlene finally decided that she couldn't keep her secret from her sister any longer.

"I was having an affair with Winston!" she blurted.

"Never!" Max exclaimed. "Does Andrea know this?"

"No, I haven't said anything. I doubt if she suspects anything. But that's how come I got myself in this mess in the first place. Me and Winston tried to pull a skank...."

Before she could continue, there was a repeated honk from a car horn outside. The taxi had arrived.

"Look, sis, I've got to go before Barrington gets here. I'll call as soon as I get to mum's. I'll write you a letter and explain everything. I promise."

The two sisters embraced hurriedly.

"Take care of yourself, sis," Max advised. "And Marlon, promise your Auntie Max that you're going to be a good boy and look after your mum!"

Marlon nodded his head sulkily. Max grabbed the boy and gave him a hug.

"Don't worry Marl, I'll come over and see you both as soon as I can."

They said their goodbyes and Max helped them out with their luggage."

"We're going to Gatwick Airport," Merlene shouted at the cab driver. "As fast as you can, we've got a plane to catch."

The cab pulled away and sped off. Max stood on the pavement for a moment, waving at its passengers until they were only a speck in the distance. She turned and walked back to her Beetle parked a few houses down the street. What a day it had been, she thought to herself. She stroked her stomach with a hand to see if she could feel anything and then remembered that she had totally forgot to mention the reason for stopping by to her sister.

Barrington's Mercedes pulled up outside Merlene's house. Corbin got out and dutifully opened the rear passenger door for his boss. Barrington stepped out and walked up to the house, motioning to Corbin to wait in the car.

Barrington knocked on the door but nobody answered. Straight away he smelled a rat. He had given her strict instructions to be in at noon and he didn't believe that she had the bottle to test him. He tried to peer in through the windows, but had his vision obscured by the net curtains. He bent down and looked through the letterbox. Again he saw nothing. He walked around the side of the house and niftily jumped a wall that a younger man would have found difficult, landing in Merlene's back garden.

In this type of situation, everything is done on the spur of the moment. It wasn't that Barrington was an expert housebreaker, simply that he wasn't prepared to allow anything to stand between him and money. He found a window and simply broke it, gaining entry into the house.

Once inside the empty house, Barrington walked slowly and purposefully around, the scene before him confirming his suspicion. It was evident that the bird had flown in a hurry. There wasn't a soul in sight. Clothes and other belongings lay strewn everywhere. Barrington rushed upstairs. On entering Merlene's bedroom, he cast a cursory glance at the clothes piled several feet deep on the floor. But there was no sign of Merlene or her son.

Barrington walked back downstairs into the kitchen. The refrigerator door stood open, its contents recently raided.

The anger boiled within him. In his rage, he grabbed the refrigerator by its open door and dragged it towards him, sending it crashing to the ground. He then turned his fury unto the plates, which lay stacked neatly in a cupboard and sent the whole of them crashing to the ground with a deafening smash.

He looked quickly through the house for anything he could sell, but soon discovered that there was nothing but useless trinkets remaining.

"Did you take care of business?" Corbin asked innocently, when his boss emerged through Merlene's front door.

"She tek me for a fool," he growled, trying to control his agitation. "Giving me the runaround. No, man! Me nah take dat from any 'ooman. When I get her. I'll knock all her blasted teeth out!"

"You just missed them," a shaky voice squeaked from a first floor window of the house next door.

Barrington spun around to see a little old lady peering down on him.

"What did you say?" he asked her.

"Merlene and that son of hers, they left about five minutes ago.

In a cab," the old lady repeated.

"Do you hap'n to know where they were going?" Barrington asked anxiously. "I'm a friend of theirs."

"It don't matter to me who you are," the old lady said. "They've gone to the airport. S'pose they're off on holiday."

"Airport?" Barrington looked genuinely worried. "Do you know which one?"

"Yeah I heard them tell the cab driver when he come," the old lady informed him. "Gatwick it was. Gatwick Airport."

Barrington jumped into the front passenger seat of the Mercedes "Just head for Gatwick Airport," he instructed Corbin who responded immediately by shifting the car into gear and roaring away.

The chase covered twenty miles as the Mercedes raced through the crowded streets of south London, the speedometer flicking past seventy miles per hour at times, screeching around corners, weaving between cars and ignoring traffic lights while scattering pedestrians with a blaring horn. They missed disaster several times by a matter of inches.

Corbin hunched over the wheel with ice cool concentration.

Barrington remained silent while gently caressing a half empty can of Heineken. He rolled the events over in his mind. He could come to no other conclusion than that she was trying to skank him in which case she would have to pay. Barrington didn't like being skanked.

En route to the airport, Merlene sat in the back of the minicab relaxed and happy to have left all her troubles back in Brixton. She didn't know what she would do in Jamaica and how long she would be there, the main thing was that she would be away from Fitzroy, away from Barrington and all the other worries. She had never intended to take Barrington's exorbitant demands lying down. She knew also that he wouldn't take her flight lightly. Crossing Barrington, was like skating on very thin but she had no choice.

An unexpected storm had sent rain pouring down as Thomas drove slowly along Peckham High Street contemplating his situation. He had tried to call Max over and over again but she was avoiding him. After umpteen phone calls, he got the message. Max had dumped him, there was little he could do about that. But, he resolved, if she breathed a word about his condition and it got around, she wouldn't live too see the next year. He would make sure of that.

His mobile phone suddenly sounded its shrill alarm.

"Ah who dat?!" he answered.

"Thomas, this is Beverly. All your belongings are in black plastic bags outside the house."

Beverly had replaced the receiver before Thomas could respond.

"The bitch!" he cried aloud. It didn't sound like a false alarm, this was serious. He managed a nifty u-turn on the narrow street and headed back to Brixton at breakneck speed.

By the time he arrived Thomas' belongings were piled neatly around the dustbins in Beverly's front garden, the rain pouring down on them. He was furious, yet despite his anger, he counted himself lucky that it wasn't a Thursday when the dustbin men came. He meant to go in and give Beverly what for, but discovered he had been locked out. His key no longer matched the front door keyhole. This incensed Thomas some more, and he began to pound furiously on the door with both fists.

"Beverly, open up! Beverly?!" he commanded through the letter box but to no avail.

Soaked to the skin, he finally gave up and decided to at least save his belongings from the rain. As he picked up the first bag, he noticed the wet Post It still clinging on to it. The message was still legible despite the rain: I don't want you to set your foot back in my house. He frowned as he read the note, then swung round as he heard the front door creek open. He couldn't believe it. Beverly was standing there as bold as anything, sneering down at him with her hand resting tauntingly on her hip.

"I'm going to kill you," he threatened as he started up the garden path.

Beverly responded immediately producing her other arm from behind her back and pointed viciously at her husband. Thomas stopped dead in his tracks his eyes fixed on the bread knife in his wife's hand.

"Read the note," Beverly said coldly, "I don't want you to set your foot back in my house."

For a few moments, neither of them said anything, each occupied with their own thoughts. Thomas decided that the best approach was to play for time, he just couldn't be sure of what Beverly was capable of.

"Look, I'm sorry, I made a mistake," he began, taking a few cautious steps towards her. "I did you wrong...."

Beverly looked at him pitifully. Sorry was all he could say. After all the hell he had given her, after all the suffering words still didn't come easily.

"Don't test me," she warned, jabbing the knife in his direction. "Just don't test me!"

Thomas eyes' darted from Beverly to the knife and back to Beverly again. It was obvious she meant business. Thomas backed off hesitantly, he couldn't afford to test her. He casually straightened his coat, keeping his eyes on the knife and slowly began to pick up his belongings.

"Well alright," he began with a sinister threat in his voice. "Why not put down the knife and we'll find out how tough you are?"

Beverly didn't bother responding so Thomas continued.

"Me gone for now. But nah worry yourself, anywhere you go I'll be right there behind you, until one day, you're going to get what you asked for."

With rain water dripping in his eyes, Thomas dumped his belongings in the back seat of his car and sped off furiously.

Driving conditions had been made hazardous by the downpour but that didn't worry Corbin, they had driven down the motorway at 100 miles an hour. He steered the Mercedes expertly around the roundabout on the approach road to the airport, without slowing down. Barrington sat beside him stony faced.

He was thinking about Pussy Blue and how she skanked him back in Kingston all those years ago. And he was thinking about the whore who had juggled things so that the police could frame him. It burned him to think that these women had played him in a man's game and won. And now Merlene. 'I won't be responsible for my actions when I catch up with her,' Barrington convinced himself. He could feel the anger rising in his chest, reaching out to take a vicelike grip on his throat. His jaws locked so tightly that his teeth ached.

"There she is!" he screamed as he saw Merlene and Thomas jump out of a car up ahead.

Corbin's eyes darted around the airport terminal, but it was too late, Merlene and her son had already scurried into the building. "Where?" he asked finally.

"There, over there!" Barrington yelled frantically, pointing to the spot from which Merlene had now departed.

Corbin raced in the direction his boss was pointing. Barrington leapt from the car before it had stopped rolling and sprinted determinedly after Merlene. For an old man, Barrington was still had a healthy body, which manifested itself in the pursuit of money.

Inside the crowded departure lounge, Barrington had to stop a moment, to get his bearings. It suddenly occurred to him that he didn't know where Merlene was heading. He thought about it for a moment while looking on the departure and arrivals monitor for any clues. Then suddenly the calm voice of a woman came over the tannoy system.

"This is the last call for passengers on British Airways flight BA 765 to Miami."

Without pausing for thought, he rushed around looking for the British Airways desk. Most travellers to the Caribbean travel through Miami. It was just a long shot, but it was somewhere to start.

A letter from Andrew awaited Max when she got home later that afternoon dripping with rain. The neatly typed letter was just his style. She opened it casually. The letter came straight to the point, their relationship was no longer working. He offered to pay the mortgage for the next month, but explained that he wanted her out after that, so that he could sell the flat.

Max sat down slowly, taking it all in. She wasn't expecting this. It was typical of Andrew to end their relationship in a letter. He always liked to avoid confrontation. It took a while for the full impact of her situation to sink in, but when it did, Max couldn't contain herself. She broke down sobbing. She had lost her friend, her lover and her financial security and she was strapped on her own with a baby. Everything she had planned for her future was now lost.

Thomas drove to the address he had been given by the estate agent. The house was a four-storey Victorian building in the no-man's land between Stockwell and Clapham North. A sign in a downstairs window announcing "Rooms To Let" reassured him that he had come to the right place. Thomas had managed to get a front room on the third floor.

The landlord met him at the front door, and led him up a flight of unevenly carpeted stairs to the dingy room with a faded rug on the bare floor, a rickety bed and a wicker armchair.

"Home is what you make it," the landlord insisted with a broad grin. He collected the two month's rent and departed.

Alone, Thomas peered through the greyish shroud that served as a lace curtain, to the cars that cranked noisily past on the main road outside. It was hard to believe that he had fallen so swiftly from grace. He winced as he looked around the dingy room, its stained wallpaper in a huge flowered design, unrelieved by anything but a pin-up calender tacked to one wall.

Thomas giggled to himself nervously. The thought crossed his mind that Max and Beverly had somehow got together with the obeah man to do this to him. He had lost his wife, his lover, his home and something was wrong with his virility. How can anybody have so much bad luck? Maybe they were all in this together and were now laughing at him.

"Yes sir, Miss Livingstone has checked in. You've just missed her, she should be on her way to the departure lounge."

Barrington barely waited for the check in attendant to finish what she was saying, before he resumed his chase at breakneck speed along the terminal towards the departure lounge. The speed at which he was going he probably couldn't have stopped even if he had seen the trolley piled high with suitcases.

Barrington hit the vehicle full on and sent cases flying anywhere. He himself landed sprawled out on the floor, a painful exercise for an old man, even one as fit as Barrington.

"I'm a'right!" he cried out, dismissing a helping hand and climbing to his feet unaided. He resumed his chase. He hadn't got very far however, when he felt a sharp tugging on his jacket. Barrington spun around to see the chubby, sweaty face of the traveller he had just collided with.

"What about my camera?" the man insisted in a yankee drawl while hanging onto Barrington's jacket as if his life depended on it.

"What the hell..." Barrington began ready to thump the man, but deciding against it at the sight of a policeman coming towards him. "What you ah talk 'bout?" Barrington hissed angrily.

"My camera," the traveller repeated, waving a damaged camcorder in Barrington's face. "You crashed into me. You weren't looking where you were going and you sent me flying. So what are you going to do about it.

By the time Barrington had managed to placate the American with a fifty pound note, he had lost a few valuable minutes. He raced on undaunted towards the departure lounge. And then he saw her standing at the front of a queue at passport control. Barrington rushed forward past other passengers waiting obediently at the queue. He would get her now.

"Passport and boarding card please," came the passport officer's voice as an authoritative hand halted Barrington's progress. "Merlene!" Barrington called as she walked through the passage into the departure lounge. Merlene turned momentarily but continued walking through, ushering Marlon ahead of her.

Beverly popped open a bottle of champagne and quickly poured the bubbling liquid into their glasses. Andrea didn't feel like celebrating too tough, but Beverly had insisted.

"Here's to you and to the Ebony Hair Salon," Beverly announced merrily, clinking glasses with her friend. "May she sail through the recession and come out a gold mine at the other end."

Andrea wondered whether Beverly had forgotten the significance of the date. It was exactly a year since Winston died. It seemed inappropriate to be toasting each other's good health and good fortune today of all days.

Beverly had become a regular visitor to Andrea's salon during the last month. She would arrive religiously at two in the afternoon, every day, to have her hair done. Andrea was now Beverly's most intimate friend, and they enjoyed their afternoons together, more for the gossip than the beautification. Andrea was only too glad of the company.

"Guess what...? I got a letter from Merlene!" Andrea announced enthusiastically as they emptied their glasses. "She's in Jamaica! Can you believe it!? All this time, we're here wondering what's happened to her and the bitch has gone to Jamaica without telling anyone!"

Beverly merely grunted. "So, what did she have to say for herself?" she asked. "Why did she disappear? She must have explained something."

"It's a strange letter. I'm telling you, Bev. I couldn't make head or tail out of it. She seemed....well, you read it."

Andrea pulled the neatly folded pages of the letter from her pocket and handed it to Beverly, who slipped on her reading glasses and read aloud:

Dear Andrea,
I hope that this letter finds you in good health, and that things are looking up for you generally. You have no idea how my life has been hell the past year. No one knows the pain I have felt and suffered. Until recently, I was smoking cigarettes by the pack and drinking spirits heavily. I couldn't face anybody. I was ashamed of certain things I had done, and I didn't know how even you, my own friend, would take it when everything was revealed. I couldn't take another day under those conditions so I've decided to be with my friends and

family out here until things cool down for me back in London.

Here, life is hard but easier than London (I haven't got a penny in my pocket, but I feel like a millionaire). True, Kingston's hot, and that's no joke thing. But out here in the countryside, I live amongst people who greet you in the morning with "God bless you child!" I live amongst people like that. No fussing or cussing or fighting, just plain good and decent people.

It's taken me all this time to realise how low I had sunk. In London, I was lying and cheating and stealing, all kinds of rubbish. Not any more.

Out here, people know the true meaning of love, Andrea. Love is caring, sharing, crying, laughing - all those things and more. Real love will blow your mind, just you wait and see. True devotion, honesty, fidelity, gratitude....I never really understood that love was all those things, Andrea. And please be honest with yourself, neither did you! None of us loved wisely, Andrea, we loved too much. I've had to lose those closest to my heart to realise. I once thought I had love but when I check it now, I was blind to the light of the world. I just couldn't or wouldn't understand the signs. Andrea, friends may tell you bad about me, but please, judge me as you knew me.

Max arrived here yesterday. She's pregnant and depressed. I just hope she'll be alright. None of us is perfect, but we should stop blaming each other for what we have done wrong. Max was wrong sleeping with Thomas, but I've done wrong things as well, which I have to take responsibility for. But no woman is an island, Andrea. No woman should have to stand alone.

Marlon found it strange out here at first and missed his friends. But he has made some new friends and is settling in well at his new school.

At last I have found peace in my life. I'll stay out here for a while. I made my mum a solemn promise to try my best to take care of Max.

Andrea, I've had to learn the hard way that a good friend is better than pocket money. Even though we're far apart, there's a place for you in my heart. Always.

Love

Merlene.

"Well Jeezus!" Beverly exclaimed. It was the longest letter she had ever read. "So Merlene turned poet now! What is she saying? I don't understand any of it."

"Innit?!" Andrea agreed. "It's like she's trying to say something, but she doesn't get to the point. It's like we're supposed to unravel some kind of message from what she wrote. She mus' t'ink we deh 'pon Mastermind or sump'n!"

"Songs of Praise more like! So Merlene turned poet and she turned Christian - all in one go. Can you believe it!"

Beverly knew well that Merlene's letter was a cry for help. But she didn't have much sympathy for her or her sister. Not since the way they had treated her when she was at her lowest ebb. Max had betrayed her, and Merlene had turned her back on her when she most needed her. Beverly didn't know what trouble Merlene had got herself into and didn't care. As for Max, Beverly's conclusion was that the deceiving whore had been given a taste of divine retribution. 'Pregnant,' she thought, 'I bet the bitch don't even know who the father is!'

"She's out of order!" Beverly exclaimed. "I'm telling you! Talking 'bout how Max is depressed. Bettah she sits down and thinks about how I feel after what her sister did to me! If your works are evil, God will cut you down! Don't take it from me. Ah de Bible seh so."

Andrea didn't want to get into any slanging match. She knew how Beverly felt about Max's infidelity with her husband. Nothing Andrea had to say would ever erase the pain her friend felt. The Four Musketeers could never be again. Beverly had vowed that she would never find it in her heart to forgive Max her indiscretions. Andrea suspected also that Beverly held Merlene guilty to some extent. "Merlene is her sister's keeper," Beverly had insisted several times, and Andrea had to agree that Merlene had always held her younger sister by a tight leash, and that Max's behaviour followed Merlene's example. If Max was capable of sleeping with her best friend's husband, then wasn't Merlene capable of the same thing? Beverly certainly did have a point there.

"I just think that you should let bygones be bygones," Andrea offered. "We were all best friends before. You can't just throw all that away. Friends do things bad to each other sometimes. Oh Beverly, at least try and forgive them. Anyway Max and Merlene have come out worst of all."

"That's easy for you to say, Andrea. You don't know what it feels like to discover that your husband is sleeping with your best friend. I don't give a toss about Thomas. I can accept that he was a bad choice of husband, but I'm the one who has got to live with the shame of having my friend, someone who I ought to know and trust well, sleeping with my husband. I hate Max, Andrea. That's not going to change, and Merlene happens to be her sister, so I'm not exactly over the moon about her either!"

Andrea could see that Beverly wasn't going to shift her position. She couldn't argue with her. Whenever someone throws in the argument, 'how would you know unless you experienced it'

there's nothing much you can say. To be honest, Andrea didn't
know how she would have reacted. She would have hoped she
had enough generosity for her friend, that she would have
forgiven her eventually. But then it's easier to say that when it
hasn't really happened to you. As far as Andrea was concerned,
it wasn't all Max's fault. Max didn't exactly rape Thomas, did
she? She didn't drag him into her bed. He went there of his own
free will, knowing full well what the consequences were. As far
as Andrea was concerned, Thomas was Beverly's responsibility.
She should have had him on a short leash. But the mood Beverly
was in, Andrea didn't have the bottle to say it to her face.

"Nut'n nah hap'n y'know, Beverly?! You must understand
everyt'ing......Not a t'ing hap'n. Whatever you see, it was there
before! Thomas was bad from before, but you married him. Max
was that way before, but she was your best friend. An' before
you found out what was happening between them in bed, you
were able to live sweet wit' the two ah them! You've got to dash
way those bad vibes and try to live positive and be nice. 'Cause,
you see me? No gyaal nah badder than me! I could box down
anybody who mess wit' my man! You understand? But you have
to love reality y'know, Bev! If my friend and my husband ah go
sleep with one another, me should know from time! Me should
see dem intentions ina dem *heye*. Me know which friends you
can look 'pon an' see if dem is a real friend, more than girls who
just ah hustle it. Yeah, me know dem! Don't get me wrong Bev.
I'm not saying we mus' remain friends. Personally, I can survive
without Max and Merlene as friends. Me was all alone, by
myself long before me meet any friend."

"We were four girls," Beverly answered after a long pause.
"We were four girls who went through some real hardships in
the old days. But we stuck together through joy and pain,
through pregnancy, through births, marriage and even death.
Now two girls leave. Well that's alright. Whoever moves with us
is the posse. If four of us formed the posse, and the four of us
can't work together, then it's better not to waste time. Thinking
about the things we've been through just gets me vexed. I don't
care if Max don't come back. She made her own decision.
Nobody wants to talk about what really happened - Max stole
my husband. I'm her best friend. That's not supposed to happen.
And up to now, I don't know the reason! Friendship is supposed
to come first before all other considerations! Love doesn't come
first, friendship comes first, I don't care what the situation.
When I begged Merlene to speak to Max, she seriously dissed
me. I can't forget that. 'Cause I'm a woman who suffers same
way. No man, protect me from my friends, now that I know all

my enemies."

Andrea didn't know what to do. Beverly was her only true friend now. They had all lost out. She had lost Winston, Beverly had lost Thomas and Max had lost Andrew. Andrea showed Beverly a photograph in one of the national papers. The picture showed a smiling, handsome man and his fiancee. The man was Andrew, who had become an Earl on the recent death of his father. He had announced his engagement to a wealthy heiress. It had been covered by most of the press. The papers described Andrew as one of the most eligible bachelors in the country. No mention of the black woman he had been seeing for the last three years.

"Well, if you ask me," the still bitter Beverly offered, "that's where all her troubles began. From she was with that white man, she just lost her mind. She needs to know her culture, the way she just put up herself with the white man and started acting stush when she find out seh him have 'nuff money! You know how much she love jewellery, Andrea. Max was always shine eye. Her eye was bigger than her belly. She deserved what she got. You can't be greedy, Andrea. You must learn to be satisfied.

"No, I found out what Max is, the hard way and I've made up my mind that I can get along without her. I may have to work seven days a week just for my pickney to have some place to sleep an' eat. But still, I would rather live poor and clean. Look at Max now. She's lost her money and she's lost her friends. It's like her whole life is finished. But I'll never forget what she did."

Andrea's mind had wandered off. She had resigned herself to the situation. There was no point in thinking that the four of them would one day be friends again. Nobody could tell Beverly sorry, 'cause sorry couldn't satisfy her. She had come to her verdict. She was both judge and jury and had found Max guilty without a trial. She hated Max with a passion. If only Beverly would accept that anybody could have done what Max did. Because no matter what you say otherwise, morality goes out the window when it comes to love. Max wanted to have her cake and eat it. But that's how the youth of today were carrying on a way. An' it noh funny. You never stop to think, 'who is getting hurt?' Andrea couldn't swear to God that she wouldn't deceive a friend. They had all played O.P.P. when they were younger. But nowadays those things seemed dumb. Some women will come hold you 'bout dem man. They should know puss, dog and stray cat keep good company. If there was one thing Andrea's discovery of Winston's infidelity had taught her, it was that, when the rice nuh swell, man's belly nah go full. You give a man too much free time, he's going to look elsewhere. Andrea counted herself lucky that she and Spence had a good thing going. He had turned out real sweet and couldn't get enough of her. Everyday was an Andrea day as far as Spence was concerned, to be spent with the woman he loved. Andrea was experienced enough to know that this was the real thing and she had accepted his proposal.However much she trusted Spence however, Andrea made sure that every move he made, she was right beside him. Whether he was going up town or down town, whether going up country or going to foreign, she would tell him to bring her. She had learned from Beverly's mistake.

"What make your face so long?" Beverly asked after a while. The words shook Andrea out of her day dream.

"Oh, I was just thinking that everything you do in life you're in a struggle...."

In actual fact, Andrea was floating away on a natural high thinking about how lucky she was having someone to go to bed and wake up with; a true love to go through good times and bad times with, to share the laughs with, while sparing each other the tears. Love was truly a mystery.

"....Me work so hard," Andrea continued, "that sweat 'pon my shoe and people ask me, how your shoe so wet up? And yet it's hard making ends meet, because recession deh 'pon my back like trials and crosses. Well, I tried a t'ing to lif' up myself an' I find seh it nuh easy. It's tough trying to turn things around to make the salon profitable. I think I might just close it down. I can't make enough money on the hairdressing, so really I would have preferred to expand the business as one of those all in all health centres, y'know? That's the new trend that people are going for, a complete health centre, where they can come in and do keep fit, and where you also offer beauty care and manicures as well as hairdressing. I asked the bank for a loan, but dem tek too long fe come, so me gone!"

"How much money do you need exactly?" Beverly asked casually.

"Why, are you offering to give me the money?" Andrea teased.

"You never know," Beverly answered coyly. "Seriously, how much do you need?"

"Probably about twenty grand, but if I put up ten grand myself, the bank will definitely match that with another ten."

"Ten thousand pounds? I think I can manage that. What do you think Andrea, do you fancy taking on a partner?"

"You're not serious, are you?" Andrea looked hard at her friend to confirm her suspicions, but Beverly was in earnest. "So where you get ten thousand pounds from?"

"Oh, I've had a little money of my own stashed away for some time now, y'know, for a rainy day. There's lots of things about me you don't know. So what you saying, Andrea? My investment is your chance for business to come back strong. You nuh hear me, man? Partners, always together?"

Andrea thought long and hard before answering. She didn't mean any disrespect, but the salon was her baby. She had set it up on her own, because she didn't really want to depend on any other individual. A partner would mean that things may have to change or be rearranged. Supposing they couldn't agree and fell out with each other? She remembered how they had fallen out over Winston as teenagers. How Beverly claimed that Winston was her man and had blown her top when she discovered that Andrea was sleeping with him. It was all a misunderstanding but Beverly had cursed her for it. "You bitch, Andrea," she had screamed. "I hope you get seven years of bad luck for this."

At first, Andrea thought Beverly was simply blowing a lot of hot air. Andrea's life began to fall apart little by little, however. When Winston discovered that the baby she had carried would have been a boy child, his attitude changed. He began staying out all night and coming home smelling of perfume. Her dream prince quickly turned sour.Ever superstitious, Andrea suspected then that Beverly's curse was coming to fulfilment. She resigned herself to quietly suffering her seven years of bad luck. Seven years that came to an end when Winston died. But Andrea still watched her step around Beverly, afraid to incur her friend's wrath a second time.

But then again, what choice did she have? High interest rates were killing her business. Beverly's offer was her only real hope if she didn't want to go out of business. The death of another black business. Jamaicans get the blame for everything that happens. All over the world, people say Jamaicans have the most cocaine, and have the most gun, and kill people recklessly. True, when they can't take the strain of day to day living, certain ghetto youts will turn to crime, but more time Jamaican yout' want to make their name with legal shots, and the only way to do it is to get together. Rarely will anyone but your own sistren and bredrin help you to success. Andrea and Beverly were so versatile, that they could turn their hand to anything. Together, they could be an explosive team. Andrea decided to accept Beverly's offer and go into business with her friend.

"Maybe we won't find it easy," Beverly offered, "but we can still work sum'pn out."

"I'll call a solicitors up tomorrow, and get them to draw up some papers!"

"Good!" Beverly shouted as she took her leave. "I won't have my hair done today in that case, I'll come back tomorrow when I'm part of the business. It's free then, I hope."

"Oh, of course!"

The two women laughed.

"By the way," Beverly remembered, reaching into her handbag. "You left your comb at my house when you came 'round the day before Carnival remember? I've been meaning to get it back to you, but I keep forgetting."

Andrea took the comb. She had looked for it all over, but couldn't remember where she left it. The last time she remembered using it was when Max came in to get her hair done on the Friday before Carnival.

Andrea stood in the entrance to the salon, watching her friend climb into her gleaming new, baby blue BMW. Beverly was a strange one, Andrea thought. She could have sworn that her friend didn't have much money, but she had gone out and bought herself a brand new luxury car recently, and here she was offering to put ten thousand pounds into the salon! Well, what a turn up for the books!

What a way Beverly could lie. Sure, she had the ten thousand pounds. And sure, she was going to invest the money in the salon. But it wasn't out of any love for Andrea. Beverly checked in her rear view mirror as she pulled away. She could see Andrea waving her goodbye. If only the bitch realised what she had up her sleeve. Beverly hated Andrea as much as she hated Max. Unable to forget how Andrea had ruthlessly robbed her of Winston, the first boy she ever loved back in their schooldays, Beverly had always held a grudge against her friend.

"Good things come to those who wait," she chuckled to herself. "Time soon ripe for me to show my strength and fling my might. And when it drops, Andrea's going to feel it. She won't know what hit her."

Unlike the rest of the posse, Beverly as a teenager was innocent and lacked confidence with boys. After many false starts, she met Winston. He was a couple of years older and only interested in getting his end away as many times as he could before his next birthday. Beverly had lost her virginity to him. It was sacred to her at the time, and she felt that he belonged to her. But he soon turned his attentions to her friend Andrea, who was only too willing to oblige. It resulted in the two girl's relationship being strained for months, until Merlene with a little help from Max, managed to get the two women to call a truce, or so they thought. Andrea claimed it was a misunderstanding, an unfortunate mix up; she didn't know that Beverly was interested in the boy. As far as Beverly was concerned, Andrea had used her, tricked her and then robbed her. Though Beverly agreed to kiss and make up, she knew she would never forgive the Andrea she had once adored. She was vexed. She knew that one day she was going to come out on top. She would pay Andrea back, if it took her forever. And like a stalking lion, she had spent the next seven years waiting for an opportunity to pounce on her.

She took her time and wooed Winston back to her. She knew that one day he would keep his promise and run off to the Caribbean with her. So they had embarked on a secret relationship which she had nurtured over the years. By the end of his life Winston loved her more than anything in the world.

She had taken a chance with the money, but as she thought about it now, she decided it was divine retribution, if the money from Andrea's boyfriend was the same money used to bring about her downfall.

Not wanting to drive around with £34,000 in his car, Winston had deposited the money round at Beverly's late on the afternoon of his crash, after banking the cheques Merlene had given him into several false accounts. Winston hadn't told Beverly he was seeing Merlene, or that the £34,000 came from her office. Beverly was the love of his life that was all he was interested in. They would run off to the Caribbean together and build a home on a little plot of land near a beach. For Beverly, to elope with the man Andrea had stolen from her after all these years was something akin to divine retribution.

Winston thought he was in control of the situation, but in fact Andrea made him fall in love with her, by whispering those sweet nothings that tickle a man's ear, and by making love to him like he had never been made love to before. In reality she cared little for Winston but she enjoyed thinking about the hurt her affair would cause to Andrea. She was surprised when Winston showed up with £34,000 in cash.

After Winston's death, Beverly sat on the money, not knowing what to do with it. She didn't know where it came from, but she didn't exactly intend to return it anonymously to a police station. There aren't many women who would. It's not everyday that you see £34,000 in one lump sum. If she hadn't taken the chance, she would have had nobody but herself to blame, when later on in life her kids came up to her and said, 'Bwoy wha'pn mek you nevah do it?'

Keep your friends close, but your enemies closer.

Beverly smiled happily to herself as she eased herself into the driver's seat. As she put her foot on the accelerator, she told herself, 'from hereon in, it's my show.'

First there was YARDIE....
 Now soon come the sequel....
  A Victor Headley original

The @*$!*@***

Voted *Best Book Of 1992,* Yardie topped the bestseller charts for months. Now the novel everyone's been waiting for....The book's so hot we can't even reveal the title. Whatever happened to 'D.' the original don? Has his empire come to an end? If so who's the new don of dons?

Coming soon....

COP KILLER

"A young nigga on the warpath,
  and when he's finished there's
   going to be a bloodbath of cops dying...."
 After his mother is shot by the police, he swears vengeance on the officers concerned. In the orgy of violence that follows there's only one question remaining.... Can they stop him before he takes them out ?